Remington Firearms:

The Golden Age of Collecting

by Robert W.D. Ball

Published by

 **krause
publications**

700 E. State Street • Iola, WI 54990-0001

Please call or write for our free catalog of firearms/knives publications. Our toll-free
number to place an order or obtain a free catalog is 800-258-0929 or please use our
regular business telephone 715-445-2214 for editorial comment
and further information.

Library of Congress Catalog Number: 95-79727
ISBN: 0-87341-360-1
Printed in the United States of America

Acknowledgements

The Richard A. Bourne Co., Inc., Hyannis, Mass. for their helpfulness and generosity in allowing me access to their photo files and catalogs over the years. The majority of the pictures used in this book are from the catalog compiled for the Karl Moldenhauer collection auction. Thanks, my dear friends!

The Museum of Connecticut History, Capitol Avenue, Hartford, Conn. The joy of sharing knowledge has no better practitioner than Dave Corrigan, museum curator, who is always willing to go that extra mile to find the previously undiscovered treasure in the warehouse area. I owe you more than just another coffee, my friend.

Leon Wier, Jr., Gary Philips, Slim Kohler and Roy Marcot, to name a few, all members of the Remington Society of America; these great guys have shared information, expressed tremendous enthusiasm, and willingly made themselves available for me to bother with questions at any hour of the day or night. Their help in keeping me well informed over Remington minutiae is greatly appreciated, and I am doubly grateful to have made new friends as a result.

Kevin Cornell, curator of the Remington Arms Company Museum; thanks to Kevin, I've been able to access the historical B&W photos that help bring the growth years of the Remington operation alive for the reader. Kevin's enthusiasm for the project has helped me during the dry spells, of which there were many!

Henry Wichmann and Lothar Frank, my two "Old Comrades" who have patiently listened to me whine about the hours on the computer, the broken back from shooting pictures, and all the rest that goes into pulling a book together. They were there with their years of experience and knowledge when I was stumped, and more times than not, they had the right answer.

H.J. Swinney, curator of the Rochester Museum and Science Center, Rochester, New York, for his most scholarly advice and assistance in making sure that the facts offered in this book are as correct as history knows it.

Last, but never least, I have the honor of having the best reviewer and editor of first copy the world has ever seen in my dear wife Joanne. I have cringed when she has wielded her red pen to correct my copy, but at least I know that it'll read one heck of a lot better than when it first came off the computer. Thanks, Honey. I can't do without you in many more ways than one.

Contents:

REMINGTON FIREARMS

REMINGTON LONG GUNS

The original Remington Forge, birthplace of Remington Arms.

6

REMINGTON, THE COMPANY

It is not my intent to make this a book of facts, figures, and dates concerning the early development and growth of the manufacturing entity known as the Remington Arms Company; my concern is with the firearms produced during what collectors refer to as the Golden Age of Collecting Remington Firearms. It is also my belief that this book may well introduce a new generation of collectors to the Remington story, and for that, a review of the Remington path through history is required. This is a story of two separate companies, Remington and Union Metallic Cartridge Company, the latter founded long after Remington, but their fortunes were closely intertwined until they were joined in one great industrial complex.

In 1799, Eliphalet Remington II, a member of a well-to-do family and called "Lite" by his family and friends, moved from Suffield, Connecticut, to a town called Litchfield in Herkimer County, of upper New York state. He lived on a rather large holding, presumed to be approximately 300 acres, which had been cleared and developed under the direction of his father, Eliphalet Remington. Besides farming, part of the family business was a forge that did a thriving trade within the local farming community. The Remingtons produced wrought iron bar stock from scrap cast iron and pig iron for sale to blacksmiths; they also produced agricultural instruments such as crowbars, plowshares, harrow teeth, etc. In 1816, needful of a new rifle, the story goes that "Lite" Remington was convinced that with his smithy experience he could forge the barrel himself, and forge it he did. After painstaking efforts, he had a beautifully hand-forged barrel, which was later reamed and rifled. It is assumed that all the metal mountings, not including the lock, which may have been an import from England, were hand cast of brass for Remington, while the stock was hand carved from fine grain walnut. It is now presumed by some authorities that this first rifle was finished and assembled by Riley Rogers of Utica, New York.

When used at shooting matches, the excellence of Remington's rifle was universally admired, and people were quick to press him to forge a barrel for them also. By the time of the opening of the Erie Canal in 1822, guns with barrels produced by Remington were beginning to be found throughout upper New York state and beyond. Making gun barrels soon became the main function of the Remington forge, although the Remingtons continued their line of agricultural tools at the same time. The business grew, and with it the variety of gun barrels produced. By the end of the 1820s, any barrel desired, be it long or short, rifle or fowler was being supplied: plain iron at $3.00; steel at $6.00; and Stubbs damascus twist barrels at $7.50. With annual production of approximately 300 barrels (some records indicate much higher production figures), quality was never sacrificed, and each barrel continued to be subjected to what was then excellent quality control.

With the advent of the Erie Canal, all indications were that by early 1825 the Remingtons were prepared for expansion, yet they hesitated for another three years. By 1827, decisions were being made as to the most suitable location for the business, and sometime in the spring of 1828, a deed was drawn up for the purchase of at least one hundred acres of land, stretching from the south bank of the Mohawk River, across the Erie Canal, and up the rise later known as Armory Hill. The present day Remington complex in Ilion, New York, stands proudly today on the land purchased in 1828. With the deed signed, preparations for a new stone triphammer forge building were immediately put into effect, along with a new house to accompany it. Tragically, in June of 1828, while hauling wood for the new house, Eliphalet Remington, father of Lite, was accidently killed by a runaway wagon.

When winter cut off the water-driven power to the forge, Remington put his workers to the task of assembling and completing stock items from the parts produced during the open power season. In 1832, the capacity of the business was doubled with the erection of the first regular factory building, situated up the hill from the forge. The mill raceways ran under this building, turning its wheel, and then continuing downhill to power the forge below.

A good illustration of working conditions in the Ilion plant, showing final finishing and fitting. Note that the majority of men on the floor are wearing white shirts, ties, and vests, long the proud uniform for professional workmen of this era.

During this same period, in a search for new business, Remington began his sales trips around the state, leaving the operation of the plant in the hands of A.C. Seamans, the shop foreman. In 1839, in partnership with Ben Harrington, a smelting plant was erected to make pig iron that would later be made into wrought iron. Agricultural tools and mill parts were also produced, and a saw mill was built. It was in this year that two sons, Philo and Samuel, entered the business with their father. Philo was noted for developing the method by which gun barrels are inspected and straightened to this day, as well as for facing the trip hammers with steel, making for far more accurate workmanship than was previously possible.

In 1840, the Remingtons succeeded in designing a drill that, with painstaking care, could drill a small-caliber hole four feet long through a round bar of steel, thus revolutionizing the gun barrel industry by producing an unwelded barrel of solid steel. Tragedy seemed to plague the family, however, and in 1840, in an accident eerily similar to that which claimed his father, Remington's wife, Abigail, was killed by a runaway carriage, the effects of which he carried to his grave.

In 1844 the John Griffiths Company of Cincinnati, Ohio, holder of a contract for 5,000 Harpers Ferry rifles, fell behind in its deliveries to the government. Urged by the government, Remington purchased the contract from Griffiths and was immediately rewarded with an order for an additional 5,000 rifles. As quickly as he could, Remington began construction on the building known as Armory No. 1, which remained in use until 1915. In addition to floor space, Remington needed more machinery than the Remington and Harrington plant could supply, and edging machines for gunstocks were purchased and installed.

On a trip to Massachusetts to the N.P. Ames Company plant in Chicopee, Remington purchased the entire gun-making portion of the Ames operation, including machinery, contracts, guns and parts, and most importantly of all, the services of William Jenks, the inventor of a new breech-loading carbine that Remington felt could be made into the best breechloader of the day. Improvements were made to the design, and the guns delivered to the Navy in 1847 were the first unwelded steel barreled ones used by the armed forces. Initially designed as percussion, all guns made by Remington were equipped with the Maynard tape priming system. Those weapons supplied to the Navy were quite spectacular in appearance, with all brass fittings and a tinned barrel. A cavalry model was also produced at the same time, but this was unfortunately declined by the Ordnance Department. The name of Jenks is relatively unknown outside the field of collectors; however, his contribution to the development of modern firearms through the introduction of the first really successful breechloader, other than the Hall's patent breechloading rifle, was immensely important.

Government contracts were all well and good, but the main concern of the Remington operation was the production of rifle barrels and some sporting guns, and, during the 1850s, the plant produced a myriad of pistols designed for civilian use. In addition to some complete rifles, the Remingtons continued to supply barrels to gunsmiths, who then completed the gun. The company imported shotguns from abroad, and advertised them as imported. In 1852 Philo and Samuel became full partners and the firm changed its name to E. Remington & Sons. Business and cash flow were excellent, with much money being reinvested in the form of physical plant expansion; two new, large buildings were erected and steam engines were installed to supplement the seasonal water power. In addition to plant expansion, in 1856 the Remingtons built a large foundry across the Canal, enabling them to manufacture machinery for the Armory.

The Remington plant was operated on the contract system, whereby the contractor was given floor space within the factory, as well as the required machinery and tools. The contractor's obligation was to produce a specified number of parts, or in the case of assembly contracts, a certain number of guns within a specified period of time. Labor contracting was solely the responsibility of the contractor; as long as the terms of the contract were lived up to, and the work met rigorous quality standards, the contractor was left in peace. This meant the Remingtons became mediators between contractor and workman, who trusted their sense of justice implicitly. This successful contract system was continued during the time the Remingtons were in control of the business. That it worked is evident by the fact that there was never a strike against them and, during troubled financial times of the Philo and Samuel Remington stewardship, the contractors and workmen alike came forward with money to keep the business solvent.

Going back briefly to 1847, at that time Eliphalet Remington was looking for good gunsmiths to bring into his expanding operation. He found Fordyce Beals working for the descendents of Eli Whitney and hired him to be superintendent of manufacture. The fact that he had just patented a pistol did not hurt his job opportunity! In trying to circumvent Colt's lock on the revolver market, Remington and his team reworked the first patent Beals revolver, which was a poor second to the Colt, but in 1856, brought out the Remington-Beals First Model Pocket Revolver series. This was a superb pistol, equal to, if not better than, the Colts then in use. Beals later developed a revolving rifle working on the same principle as his revolver.

The Old Armory on the hill, Ilion, New York, 1862.

While Beals was busy with his line, Remington added Joseph Rider to his ever-growing stable of inventor-master gunsmiths, a stroke of genius, since Rider was to be the co-inventor of the Remington Rolling-Block rifle, the most famous weapon ever produced by the company. Also in 1859, Rider was responsible for creating the first double-action revolver ever made.

William Elliott joined the team of inventors in 1861, and it was due to his invention of the Double Derringer in 1864 that Victorian virtue was upheld; popular with men and women alike, this derringer was produced up to 1936. Elliott's first contribution was the Remington-Elliott Pepperbox Derringer, while, next to the Double Derringer, his most popular invention was the Remington-Elliott Zig-Zag Derringer. William Moore, another young genius to join the Remingtons, came up with a first when he invented a cylinder that swung out on a crane for loading! Inspired by

these young bloods, John Thomas, the Armory's master mechanic turned inventor, developed in 1858 the most unusual weapon of all, the Remington Rifle Cane, popular with gentlemen who took to the idea of combining elegance with self-protection.

With the approaching advent of the Civil War, Lite Remington was summoned to Washington by Secretary of War Cameron. Now it was not a question of selling, but a question of how many orders the plant at Ilion could fulfill and how fast. Remington accepted the challenge and received orders totaling many millions of dollars. In fact, orders from the Army and the Navy eventually totaled $29,196,820.01. To satisfy this commitment, an enormous amount of work had to be done, and done fast! Two large new buildings were erected, the power plant was tripled in size, and a vast network of power-transmission shafts and belts was installed. At its peak, the plant was producing 200 pis-

E. Remington & Sons broadside, showing the Armory at Ilion, 1870.

A long view showing the gunracks on wheels, with each workman at his own work station.

tols and 1,000 rifles per day. In addition to gun production, thousands of bayonets were also drop-forged. A cartridge department was established and a total of 9,759,750 cartridges were delivered to the services. The hope that there would be an early end to the war was dashed by the Battle of Bull Run and the nation grimly buckled down to a long, hard road to eventual victory, fraught with much sacrifice. It seemed to all involved that it was impossible for anyone to work as hard as Eliphalet Remington had in the past, but if anything, he strove even harder. Few his age, which was close to 70, could stand the continual strain, and during the first week of August 1861, Lite's health broke completely, and he died on the 12th.

Management of the company now rested with the three sons. Philo had inherited the mechanical skills and organizing abilities of his father. Samuel served as the visionary and salesman, and Eliphalet III, the financial man of the operation, was thankfully able to get the accounts in order, for, like many of his day, Lite had carried the business in his head. The brothers

continued to search for and hire new brainpower for the business, persuading Leonard M. Geiger to join the company. As a result, Geiger's breech-loading mechanism became the basis for the Remington Rolling Block Rifle. Soon demand outstripped capacity, and when an order was received for 20,000 Geiger carbines from the Ordnance Department, it was necessary to contract it out to the Savage Arms Company of Middletown, Connecticut, under license and produced on Remington-made and leased machinery.

The combined talents of the brothers were the heart and soul of the Remington operation. However, with the death of Samuel, who was the sales-minded member of the trio, the winning combination was broken and the Remington industrial empire began the long, slow, slide into disaster. That the company was saved from financial ruin was due to the efforts of another pioneering industrialist, Marcellus Hartley. Because the Remington Arms Company was held in the family, with only one major change in the course of a century, there existed a strong individuality that stamped

12

itself on the character of the company. Eliphalet Remington would be perfectly at home in today's boardroom because of this quality that still permeates the firm. Fortunately for all concerned, Marcellus Hartley was infused with the same characteristics as Eliphalet Remington.

The circumstances leading to Hartley's leadership of the Remington Arms Company began in 1867 when the Remington brothers "bet the farm" on what was to become known worldwide as the Remington Rolling Block Rifle...foolproof, easy to operate, and immensely strong. The first order for Rolling Block rifles was placed in 1866, and by 1872 1,500 guns were being produced daily. Financially, however, the picture was far from bright, since cash flow had to be diverted from one operation to another to satisfy creditors. In those years, the country was literally awash in surplus guns, not good ones, to be sure, but guns nevertheless. Sam Remington went off to Europe to increase sales, and increase them he did, with contracts from the French as well as the Turks. In that area of New York state, the decade between 1870 and 1880 can well be called the "Decade of Prosperity." The town of Ilion prospered, the boom commencing with the construction of new buildings and an enlargement of the Armory. By the end of the 1870s, there were nearly 15 acres of floor space dedicated to

manufacturing in the Remington complex. Searching for diversity, the brothers plunged into the fields of electricity, typewriters, sewing machines, fire engines, and bridge building, as well as agricultural inventions ad infinitum. In an effort to pay off the creditors through all this empire building, misfortune and bad judgment plagued the Remingtons. In 1886, Philo Remington was forced to sell the Remington Typewriter business for a mere $186,000.

Even while they continued to slip headlong into bankruptcy, the Remington Arms Company turned out a superior product; no matter how desperate their plight, money was not stinted on the best of materials or workmanship. Young, inventive men continued to be hired, and among them was James P. Lee, one of the most brilliant. Formerly employed by Winchester, he came to Remington in 1877 where he was given a workshop and all the technical assistance necessary to transform his ideas into reality. The result was the Remington-Lee Bolt Action Magazine Rifle. Manufacture began in 1880 under a royalty arrangement with Lee; however, further work was necessary to insure safety in the design, which Lee did, thus making it one of the safest rifles in the world. In 1886, with the company entering receivership, rights to the gun reverted to Lee. From this gun came the famous Lee-Enfield of British fame. For five more years, the

Artist's rendition of the Remington plant at Ilion, circa 1875.

Street front view of the Main Street operation, including the drop forge (That really must have caused some local headaches!) in Ilion, New York, circa 1875.

company was able to continue operations, but then Samuel died in 1882. With the loss of Samuel, the brothers were doomed to failure. From 1882 to 1886, human nature being what it is, Philo and Eliphalet III tried to hold on to all they had, instead of giving up and retreating to a position from which they could survive and build anew. As a result, the company went into receivership from 1886 until March of 1888, when the company was purchased by Marcellus Hartley and Thomas G. Bennett. Rather than an end, however, this proved to be a new beginning.

Hartley's background was auspicious in its own right. In 1847, Hartley went to work for Francis Tomes and Sons, dealers in fine guns and sporting equipment, and, in 1854, along with two friends, J. Tutsen Schuyler and Malcolm Graham, established his own business. Thus was formed the firm of Schuler, Hartley and Graham. Hartley later bought out his two partners, founded the Union Metallic Cartridge Company, and saved the original Remington Arms Company from dissolution. Despite his youth,

Hartley traveled to England and successfully negotiated contracts with the premier English gun makers, and, due to its firm financial foundation, the young company weathered the bank failures of 1857. It was during these formative years that a strong business friendship developed between Remington and Hartley.

Throughout the Civil War Hartley was charged by President Lincoln to go abroad for the specific purpose of purchasing foreign arms from under the noses of the Southern arms agents. His success was so widespread by 1863, he virtually controlled the arms output of Europe, thus depriving the South of desperately needed firearms. In 1865, casting about for some new venture to which he could apply himself, Hartley remembered an old, hand-made brass cartridge he had found years before on a trip through the West. Another glance and a new business venture began to form in his head. He and his partners bought out two small Connecticut cartridge companies, including all their equipment and patents. In 1867, these two companies were moved to Bridgeport, Connecticut, and incorpo-

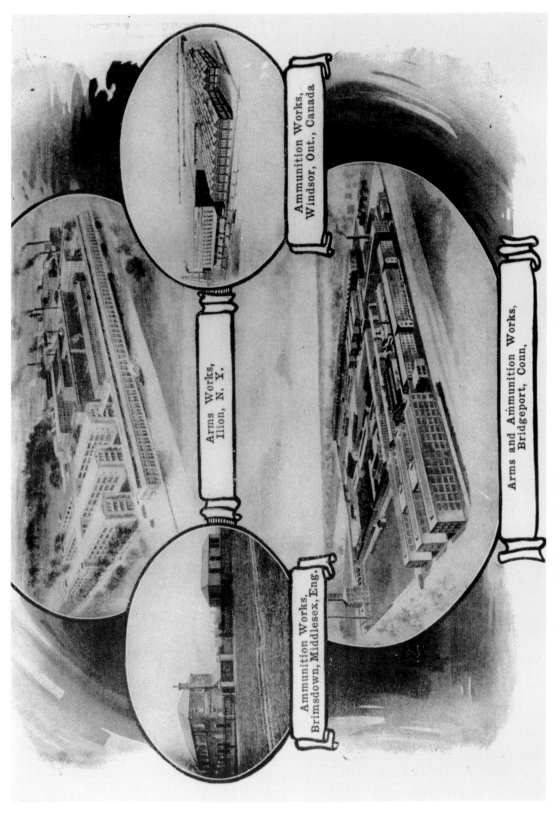

A montage, showing (clockwise from the top) the Arms Works at Ilion, New York; the Ammunition Works in Windsor, Ontario, Canada; the Arms and Ammunition Works in Bridgeport, Connecticut; and the Ammunition Works at Brimsdown, Middlesex, England, all part of the Remington Arms Company - Union Metallic Cartridge Company corporate works.

rated as the Union Metallic Cartridge Company. Their first stroke of luck was in hiring a mechanical genius by the name of A.C. Hobbs, who, in the twenty years he served as manufacturing manager, personally invented, built, and installed all of the machinery that took cartridge making out of the handwork phase and into an all-machine process. Another lucky break came when an Armenian gentleman evidenced interest in the purchase of some sizable lots of cartridges and asked for a tour of the plant. Humoring him, the partners complied, after which he identified himself as an agent of the Turkish government and gave them a contract for 10 million rounds of ammunition!

The third most important factor in the continued success of UMC was the arrival of Colonel Hiram Berdan. Berdan was a mining engineer and an inventor who held the patents on a new type of cartridge. When he presented it to Hartley and his partners, they real-ized that they held in their hands the answer to the search for the perfect cartridge. This was the first practical centerfire cartridge, and it was made by UMC in Bridgeport. Due to the inventive genius of Hobbs, UMC was able to begin production within several months after the ink was dry on the contract with Berdan, thus placing the company in the fore-front of the cartridge-making industry. The cartridge was an instant success, and orders flooded in from foreign governments, primarily Russia. In 1868, General Gorloff of the Russian Army was sent to Bridgeport to oversee the production of Russian cartridges, and his extremely high quality standards, set in the two years he was overseeing the operation, prevailed throughout the life of the company. During the Franco-Prussian War, the company received an order from the French for 18 million cartridges, with the order being deliv-ered via balloon from beseiged Paris!

A famous Remington picture of three generations of the Howard family hard at work on the Model 17 shotgun. The picture, taken in 1912, illustrates the span from 1869 to 1912 in the working life of the Howards at the Remington factory.

An artistic rendition of the Ilion plant in 1915.

17

An overview of the Ilion plant, showing the close proximity of the housing to the factory buildings, circa 1916.

Unlike gunmakers who are tied to making certain types of firearms, UMC, unshackled, made cartridges for all types of guns. By 1900, the company was able to produce 15,000 different loads, from BB caps to 10-gauge shotgun shells. Credit for this goes to Hobbs and a 54 year employee of the company, William Morgan Thomas, known as "U.M.C." Thomas. It is likely that no other person contributed so much knowledge and ability to the improvement of ammunition as did Thomas.

Due to the worldwide resources of UMC, it proved most advantageous to merge the Remington Sales Department with that of UMC, resulting in expert marketing of both companies. The future and the fates of Remington and UMC were now completely interwoven. Smokeless powder was invented, and every army in the world demanded it, thus making all existing weapons of this time immediately obsolete. The Spanish-American War came and quickly passed, with the Remington plant called upon to supply rifles, while UMC produced cartridges for the Army and shell casings for the Navy.

Never sick a day in his life, Marcellus Hartley visited his doctor on January 8, 1902, after a slight bout of indigestion. Being pronounced "fit as a dollar," Hartley returned to his office and died that afternoon. Marcy Dodge, grandson of Marcellus Hartley, was suddenly thrust onto center stage at the tender age of twenty, while still attending courses at Columbia. With the backing of the rest of the family, Dodge was elected president of M. Hartley and Company on his twenty-first birthday. Ably assisted by George W. Jenkins, president of Remington, and William J. Bruff, president of UMC, Dodge quickly learned the intricacies of the empire he had inherited. One of Dodge's major moves was to acquire the services of the Browning brothers, who had already established a contract with Fabrique Nationale in Belgium, while retaining the United States rights and those of all countries outside of Europe for themselves. Thanks to the services of the Brownings, the first autoloading shotgun in America was produced at the Ilion plant in 1905, with the autoloading rifle coming off the assembly line in 1906. With a head start like this, no other American manufacturer was ever able to catch up to Remington in the field of autoloaders.

Young blood was needed at UMC, and a group of youthful engineers headed by Harry H. Pinney was hired. Under Pinney, the factory was thoroughly redesigned and updated, especially with regard to safety features, since Bridgeport had suffered more than its share of explosions rumbling through the city over the years. It was at this time that Dodge, having learned the business well, decided that his sales force and impact on the market would be greater if the names of

18

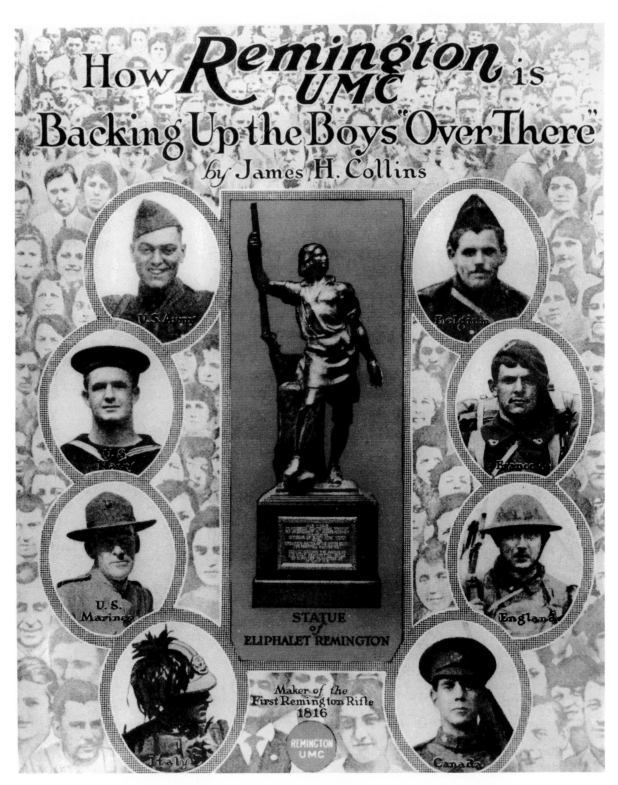

A montage done by the Remington Arms Company, illustrating their part in helping our troops and our allies during World War I.

the two companies, Remington and UMC, were combined. The outcome was a mouthful, with the resulting company named Remington Arms - Union Metallic Cartridge Company. It was in 1912 that Dodge became president and sole owner of the Remington Arms - UMC Company, with all stock held within the Dodge family.

Small wars in Europe were seen to be leading to the bigger conflagration. Nevertheless, the Greco-Turkish War and the First and Second Balkan Wars were all brush fires not to be ignored. With the assassination of the Archduke Franz Ferdinand, circumstances rapidly escalated, and the nations of Europe found themselves at war. Remington was offered more huge contracts by the Allies than it could ever fulfill under the limited capacity of its plant facilities, but Dodge felt a moral obligation to do all humanly possible. Rifles were made for the French, the British, and the Rus-

sians. Millions were invested in plant facilities and production tools, but the cash was not flowing fast enough to satisfy the creditors. A creditor's committee was formed, installing Harry S. Kimball as president of Remington Arms. Business improved during early 1917, with production at an all-time high, but disaster was only a heartbeat away. Just at the moment when success in overcoming the company's financial problems seemed imminent, the Russian Revolution erupted into chaos...contracts were repudiated, and the Communist leaders had no money to pay for what was already delivered. The effect on Remington can be compared to running into a brick wall at full throttle; the plants were idled and thousands were thrown out of work. Only after America declared war on Germany on April 2, 1917, were there any signs of relief. The U.S. government bought the bulk of the Russian rifles on hand, reducing Remington's debt from millions to several hundred thousands of dollars. Many

One of the drafting departments at the plant in Ilion, circa 1930.

20

An aerial view of the Ilion facilities taken during the early 1950s.

Taken during the early 1980s, this aerial view gives an appreciation of the sheer size of the Remington Arms Company facilities.

of these rifles eventually ended up in the hands of the White Russian troops who were fighting the Communists. Others were used to train U.S. troops in this country, with the balance later sold as surplus through the Director of Civilian Marksmenship and the NRA during the 1920s and 1930s. An interesting bit of history is the fact that the 339th Infantry Regiment from Detroit was sent to North Russia and equipped with these rifles during the American intervention in Russia after World War I.

The war enabled Remington to provide American troops with the Model 1917 Enfield, converted to .30-06 from the British contract previously fulfilled. The Russian rifle factory in Bridgeport was converted to produce Browning heavy machine guns and barrels for automatic rifles, as well as Colt Model 1911 .45 pistols, Very pistols and bayonets.

With the armistice of November 11, 1918, no one was looking forward to the peacetime production of sporting weapons and ammunition more than Remington. It was determined that the war-time factories had a production capacity that far exceeded any possible peacetime use, so first priority was given to trimming the physical plant to more manageable proportions. This involved the disposal of three plants, which still left more manufacturing facilities than were needed. Other ventures were explored; however, sporting arms and ammunition remained the foundation of the business. In 1926 Remington developed and perfected "Kleanbore" ammunition, the non-corrosive and nonerosive round fired by the first primer made in the United States without a corrosive element. With the advent of the Great Depression, Remington's sales fell through the floor, and in the spring of 1933, E.I. du Pont de Nemours & Company acquired the controlling interest of Remington common stock. Keeping Remington a separate entity, the new board elected C.K. Davis General Manager of Remington Arms. Under the leadership of Davis, Remington's fortunes were completely turned around, leading the company to some of its greatest achievements. Acquired were the Chamberlin Trap and Target Company, followed by the Peters Cartridge Company and the Parker Gun Company of Meriden, Connecticut.

Due to the strict neutrality laws in effect, the outbreak of World War II made virtually no difference in the day-to-day operations of Remington; however, this was to quickly change. When President Roosevelt went before Congress to request defense rearmament, C.K. Davis promptly put all actual and future Remington production at the service of the government, accepting no contracts other than those approved by the War Department. At Remington, the Springfield Model 1903 was redesigned to produce the Model 1903 A-3, as well as the sniper's model, the A-4. The production of ammunition far outstripped the manufacture of rifles, with Remington accepting the challenge and responsibility for setting up ammunition plants and production facilities across the United States. The most amazing fact is that all of these tasks were completed and plants were operational prior to Pearl Harbor! During World War II, Remington was responsible for the manufacture of 1,084,000 rifles and more than 16,000,000,000 rounds of ammunition, all used by the government.

After the war, Remington activated a reconversion and modernization program to keep pace with peacetime needs, producing better guns and ammunition for the sportsman by means of the most modern methods available. The Korean War found Remington readjusting its priorities to handle the ammunition needs of the time. From the end of the Korean War up to today, the Remington Arms Company focus has been on the sportsmen of the world and their weapons, constantly endeavoring to improve its products and broaden its markets. It was in 1980 that DuPont purchased all outstanding shares of stock, assuming total and complete ownership of the Remington Arms Company. On November 31, 1993, the company was sold to the Remington Arms Acquisition Group, with the company being managed by Clayton, Dubilier and Rice, a New York City investment firm.

And this is the point at which we leave this venerable firm, still a major factor in the market, proudly bearing a name that stands for quality, inventiveness, and an historical record of service and ingenuity exceeded by none.

REMINGTON HANDGUNS

REMINGTON-BEALS FIRST MODEL POCKET REVOLVERS

First Model, First Issue

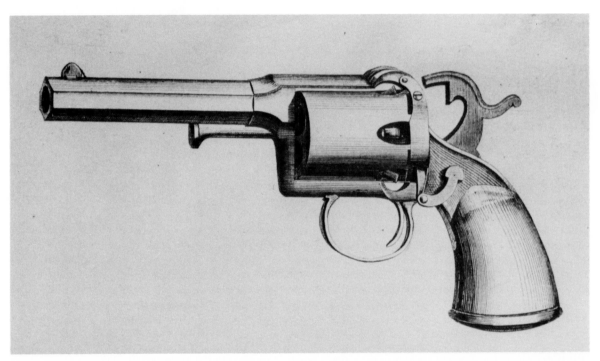

Original engraver's proof for advertisment and loading instruction sheet for the Beals First Model Pocket Revolver.

REMINGTON-BEALS FIRST MODEL POCKET REVOLVER

Produced for only two years, the total quantity of Remington-Beals First Model Pocket Revolvers is estimated at approximately 5,000. Percussion .31 caliber five-shot round cylinder with 3" barrel. Grips of gutta-percha with smooth finish. Blued overall finish with casehardened hammer and silver-plated brass triggerguard. The distinguishing feature is the outside pawl, located on the left side of the frame, serving to advance the cylinder when the hammer is cocked.

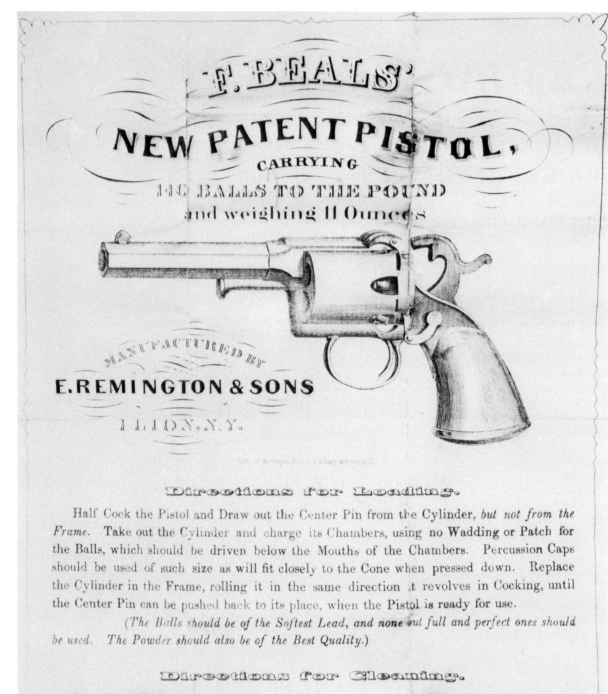

F. BEALS'
NEW PATENT PISTOL,
CARRYING
140 BALLS TO THE POUND
and weighing 11 Ounces

MANUFACTURED BY
E. REMINGTON & SONS
ILION, N.Y.

Directions for Loading.

Half Cock the Pistol and Draw out the Center Pin from the Cylinder, *but not from the Frame.* Take out the Cylinder and charge its Chambers, using no Wadding or Patch for the Balls, which should be driven below the Mouths of the Chambers. Percussion Caps should be used of such size as will fit closely to the Cone when pressed down. Replace the Cylinder in the Frame, rolling it in the same direction it revolves in Cocking, until the Center Pin can be pushed back to its place, when the Pistol is ready for use.

(*The Balls should be of the Softest Lead, and none but full and perfect ones should be used. The Powder should also be of the Best Quality.*)

Directions for Cleaning.

Take the Cylinder from the Frame, wash it in warm water, dry it thoroughly, Oil and replace it in the Frame; also, Oil the Pin upon which the Cylinder revolves.

NOTE.—If at any time the Pin should be withdrawn entirely from the Frame, it can be replaced by turning back the Small Screw on the underside of the Frame, forward of the Guard.

Rare original loading instruction sheet for the First Model Beals Pocket Revolver, 7.38" by 9.63". It is generally accepted that there are only two copies in existence.

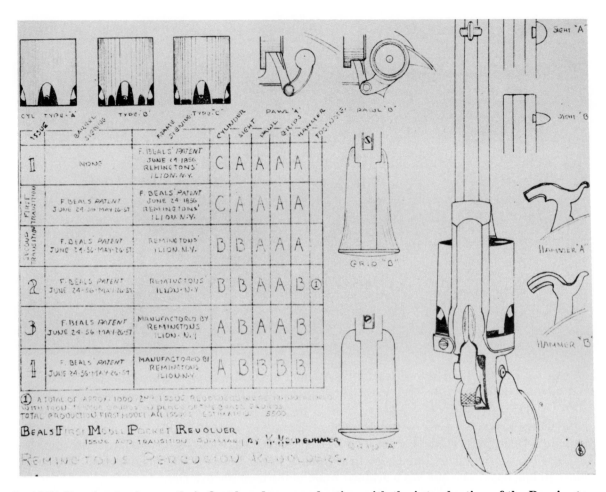

ISSUE	BARREL SIGNING	FRAME SIGNING	CYLINDER	SIGHT	PAWL	GRIPS	HAMMER	FOOTNOTE
I	NONE	F. BEALS' PATENT JUNE 24 1856 REMINGTONS' ILION. N.Y.	C	A	A	A	A	
FIRST TRANSITION	F. BEALS PATENT JUNE 24-56 MAY 26-57	F. BEALS' PATENT JUNE 24 1856 REMINGTONS' ILION. N.Y.	C	A	A	A	A	
SECOND TRANSITION	F. BEALS PATENT JUNE 24-56-MAY 26-57	REMINGTONS' ILION. N.Y.	B	B	A	A	A	
2	F. BEALS PATENT JUNE 24-56 MAY 26-57	REMINGTONS' ILION·N·Y	B	B	A	A	B	①
3	F. BEALS PATENT JUNE 24 56 MAY 26-57	MANUFACTORED BY REMINGTONS ILION·N·Y	A	B	A	A	B	
IIII	F. BEALS PATENT JUNE 24 56-MAY 26-57	MANUFACTORED BY REMINGTONS ILION·N·Y	A	B	B	B	B	

① A TOTAL OF APPROX. 1000 2ND ISSUE REVOLVERS WERE NUMBERED WITH 1000, 2ND ISSUE IN PLACE OF THE BRASS BACKED. TOTAL PRODUCTION FIRST MODEL ALL ISSUES ESTIMATED 5500.

BEALS FIRST MODEL POCKET REVOLVER
ISSUE AND TRANSITION SUMMARY BY V. MOLDENHAUER

REMINGTONS PERCUSION REVOLVERS

In 1857, Remington began their first handgun production with the introduction of the Remington-Beals Pocket Revolver series. As part of his research, Mr. Moldenhauer developed this illustrated chart for the identification of the basic First Model Beals Pocket Revolver.

Remington-Beals First Model Pocket Revolver, serial #150. View of the right side of the pistol; this pistol is in very fine condition, but lacks the front sight. The overall blue has thinned and turned blotchy with age, and the color has turned at the top of the stocks, possibly due to acidic action from the gutta-percha stocks.
(Museum of Connecticut History)

Left side view of the Remington-Beals First Model Pocket Revolver, serial #150, showing the cylinder advancing pawl on the left frame to good advantage. *(Museum of Connecticut History)*

This grouping of pistols, top to bottom and left to right, is as follows: (next page)
Remington-Beals First Model Pocket Revolver, serial #31, shown in the original cardboard carton (8.0" x 4.0" x 1.50") containing the brass mold, brass bullet starter/loading rod, and 3.55" embossed bag flask. The box has a grained wood pattern on the exterior.

Remington-Beals First model Pocket Revolver First Issue, serial #54. The spring is mounted on the left side of the frame, the left side of the barrel is stamped "W. 19," while the top strap bears the usual company markings.

Remington-Beals First Model Pocket Revolver, First Transition, serial #270.

Remington-Beals First Model Pocket Revolver, Second Transition, serial #1065, complete in the original box (7.0" x 4.25" x 1.50"), with brass bullet mold, spare cylinder, brass loading rod with attachable steel cleaning rod fitting, as well as 4.0" embossed powder flask.

Remington-Beals First Model Pocket Revolver, Second Issue, serial #33. This is an extremely rare variation, with an iron triggerguard.

Remington-Beals First Model Pocket Revolver, Second Issue, serial #176, complete in the original cardboard box (6.75" x 4.0" x 1.50") with simulated wood pattern exterior, complete with an extremely rare original combination nipple wrench and screwdriver, brass bullet mold, loading tool with attachable steel cleaning rod fitting, plus 3.75" embossed powder flask.

Remington-Beals First Model Pocket Revolver, Second Issue, serial #342.

Remington-Beals First Model Pocket Revolver, Second Issue, serial #456.

26

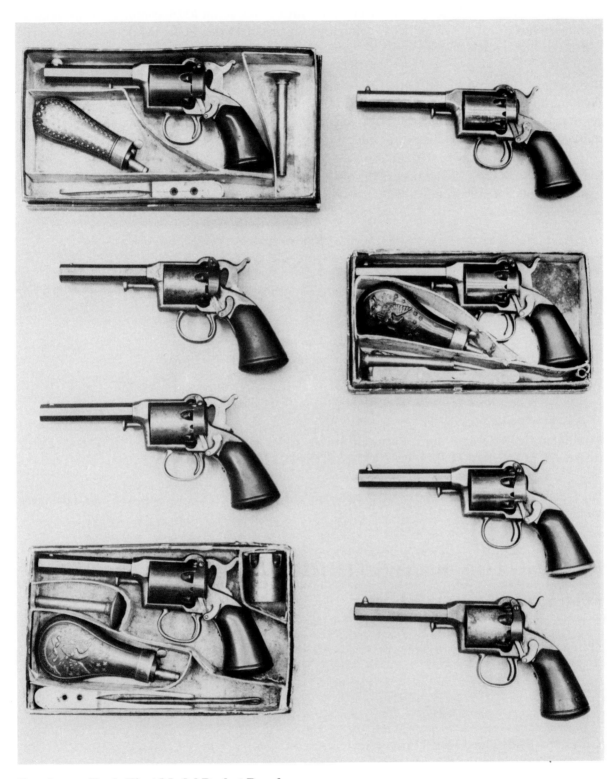

Remington-Beals First Model Pocket Revolvers.

Remington-Beals First Model Pocket Revolver, Third Issue, serial #515, complete in the original cardboard box (6.75" x 3.75" x 1.50") containing the original brass bullet mold, brass loading rod with steel cleaning attachment, and 3.87" embossed powder flask.

Remington-Beals First Model Pocket Revolver, Third Issue, serial #705, complete in the original cardboard box with simulated wood grain exterior. This pistol has the correct German silver triggerguard. Accessories include the brass mold, brass loading tool with attachable steel cleaning component, plus a 3.87" embossed powder flask.

Remington-Beals First Model Pocket Revolver, Fourth Issue, serial #171, complete in the original cardboard box with brass bullet mold, brass loading tool with cleaning rod attachment, and 3.75" embossed bag flask.

REMINGTON-BEALS SECOND MODEL POCKET REVOLVERS

An improved version of the First Model; differences in the Second Model were a squared butt with grips of checkered hardened rubber, spur type trigger, and outside disc pawl on the left frame.

Remington-Beals Second Model Pocket Revolver, circa 1858-1860; total estimated production 1,000 pieces. Serial #907 is known.

Right hand column: (next page)

Remington-Beals Second Model Pocket Revolver, serial #684, barrel marked "BEALS PATENT 1856 & 57, MANUFACTURED BY REMINGTONS, ILION, N.Y."

The frame, barrel, hammer and pawl of a Second Model Beals Pocket Revolver, showing the basic configuration.

REMINGTON-BEALS THIRD MODEL POCKET REVOLVERS

Remington-Beals Third Model Pocket Revolver, circa 1859-1860; total production estimated at 1,000 pieces. Percussion .31 caliber five-shot round cylinder (cylinder is 1.63" as compared with 1.13" on the Second Model), 4" barrel, spur-type trigger. Larger than its predecessors, this is the only Beals pocket revolver fitted with a rammer type loading lever; the lever must be lowered before the center pin can be removed.

Right hand column: (next page)

Remington-Beals Third Model Pocket Revolver, serial #36.

Remington-Beals Third Model Pocket Revolver, serial #49, fitted with the rare original floral-etched cylinder. This weapon is shown here in the original black cardboard box, with simulated waterstained exterior (8.38" x 4.38" x 1.50"), brass bullet mold and 3.83" embossed powder flask.

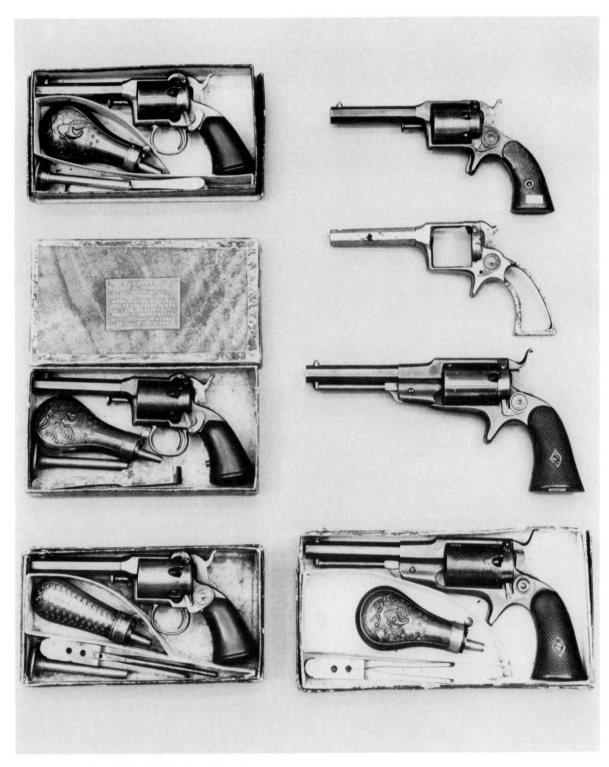

Remington-Beals Model Pocket Revolvers.

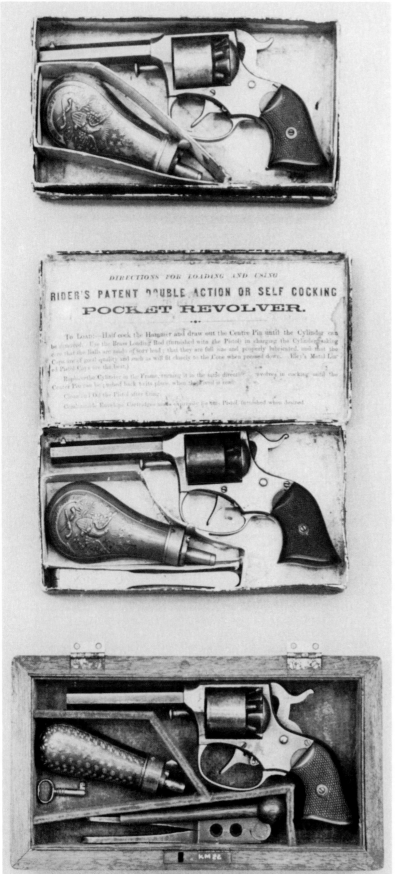

From top to bottom:

Boxed Remington-Rider Percussion Revolver, serial #77. Fitted with cone front sight. The original black cardboard box measures 7.0" x 3.75" x 1.25", with a partition holding a 4.0" embossed powder flask.

Remington-Rider Percussion Revolver, serial #821, in the original cardboard carton (7.0" x 3.75" x 1.25") with printed instructions glued to the lid; box contains a brass bullet mold and 4.0" embossed powder flask.

Remington-Rider Percussion Revolver, serial #2575, in the original walnut case (8.25" x 4.50" x 2.0") lined with red velvet; accessories include a wooden loading rod, two-cavity iron bullet mold and a 3.50" embossed powder flask. Also shown is the original case key.

REMINGTON-RIDER POCKET REVOLVERS

Remington-Rider Pocket Revolver, circa 1860-1888, with total production estimated at 20,000. Weapons were apparently numbered in batches, making serial numbers extremely misleading. The scarcity of percussion versions of this pistol leads one to believe that most pistols were produced in the cartridge configuration. Percussion .31 caliber, five-shot mushroom shaped cylinder, with 3" octagon barrel. Large oval shaped brass triggerguard, checkered hard rubber grips. Standard finishes were either blued, blued with nickel plated frame, or full nickel plated.

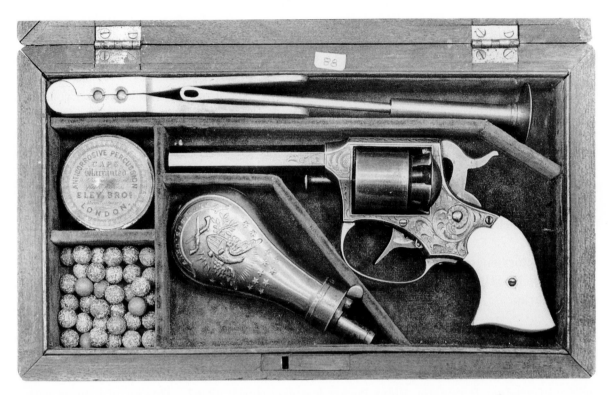

Remington-Rider Percussion Revolver, serial #6382, an extremely rare factory-engraved version. Scroll engraved about the barrel address on the top flat; small amount of scroll engraving on the left and right barrel flats, with the frame, backstrap, butt and triggerguard profusely engraved. The weapon is fitted with the original ivory grips. The original walnut case (9.50" x 5.25" x 2.0") is lined with green velvet and includes a brass bullet mold, brass loading rod with steel cleaning attachment, Eley Bros. cap tin, and a 4.0" embossed powder flask. Note the compartment filled with oxidized lead balls.

REMINGTON CONVERSIONS

On November 28, 1865, Joseph Rider was granted U.S. Patent 51269 for the conversion of a front-loading percussion cylinder to a breech loader, with the patent being assigned to Rider and E. Remington and Sons. The basis for granting the patent was primarily the bevel cut on the rear of the cylinder at a point where it intersected the chamber, so arranged that when a cartridge was inserted into the chamber, the head of the cartridge would extend beyond the lower diameter of the bevel, allowing a hook-shaped extractor to engage the cartridge head and pull the empty cartridge from the chamber. In a factory conversion to metallic cartridge, the factory installed a newly-made cylinder with removable cover at rear merely inserted, instead of the percussion cylinder; there was a slight modification to the hammer to allow the interchangeable use of either a cartridge cylinder or a percussion cylinder. Later production showed no capping cut-out on the recoil shield, indicating that they were produced as original cartridge pistols. Some pistols were also produced with shorter barrels.

From top to bottom, left to right: (next page)

Converted Remington-Rider Pocket Revolver, serial #48. Fully factory engraved overall and fitted with original ivory grips. The engraved pattern covers the three side flats on each side of the barrel with extensive scroll engraving covering the frame, backstrap, triggerguard and cylinder. Case-hardened hammer with blued cylinder pin and trigger.

Converted Remington-Rider Pocket Revolver, serial #19. Retained in the Moldenhauer collection along with the pistol above as a pair, there were many extremely minor differences in the engraved pattern, i.e., the triggerguard on this pistol is not engraved, to differentiate between them.

Converted Remington-Rider Pocket Revolver, serial #7867. All steel parts with blued finish, apparently most unusual in a converted Rider pocket revolver, as most of those produced appear to have been nickel plated.

Original factory-engraved Converted Remington-Rider Pocket Revolver, serial #9006. Engraved on the three barrel side flats, with profuse scroll engraving on the frame, triggerguard, cylinder, and backstrap.

Original Cartridge Remington-Rider Pocket Revolver, serial #29. Fitted with a 2.375" octagon barrel and factory original ivory grips.

Original Cartridge Remington-Rider Pocket Revolver, serial #2262. This pistol is fitted with a 2.0" barrel marked "REMINGTONS ILION N.Y."

Original Cartridge Remington-Rider Pocket Revolver, serial #2548. Fitted with a 3.0" barrel marked "MANUFACTURED BY REMINGTON'S, ILION, N.Y./RIDER'S PT. AUG. 17, 1858, MAY 3, 1859."

Converted Remington-Rider Pocket Revolvers.

33

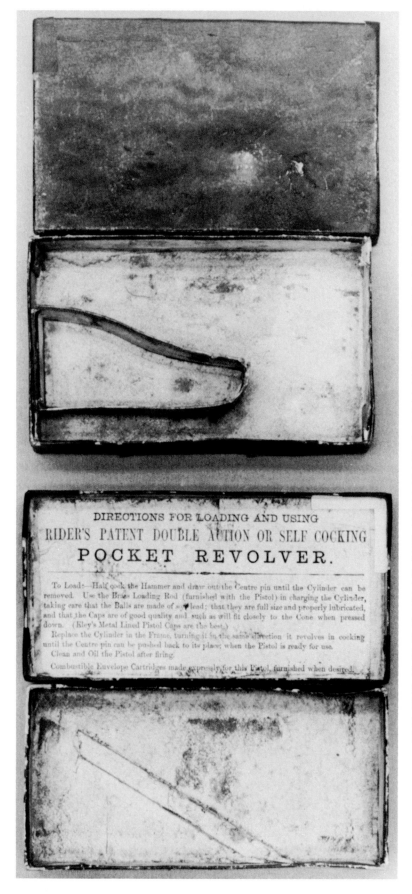

Two wonderful original boxes for Remington-Rider Pocket Revolvers; from top to bottom:

Original cardboard box for a Remington-Rider Double-Action .31 caliber revolver. The box is 7.13" x 4.25" x 1.25". There is a cardboard partition within the box for a powder flask; black exterior with a swirled waterstained pattern.

Original cardboard box for a Remington-Rider Pocket Revolver. Measures 7.50" x 3.75" x 1.25". Black exterior with simulated waterstained pattern, the interior of the lid of the box with the original instruction sheet, "Directions for Loading and Using Rider's Patent Double Action or Self Cocking Pocket Revolver." The box is originally fitted with a single diagonal partition that created a 5.25" x 3.25" triangular compartment. The shape of this compartment led Mr. Moldenhauer to believe that this box was for a conversion, despite the label in the lid giving directions for loading a percussion revolver. Supporting his contention is the fact that the box is smaller than the standard one normally used. There is also a small label at the bottom of the box, "Double Action Pocket Revolver."

REMINGTON-BEALS ARMY MODEL REVOLVERS

Beals Army Model Revolvers, c. 1860-1862, with total quantity manufactured estimated at 2,000-3,000. Percussion, .44 caliber, six-shot round cylinder, with an 8.0" octagon barrel with barrel threads concealed by the frame. Early production specimens had a single projecting ear on the head of the cylinder pin. Walnut grips, blued finish with case-hardened hammer and loading lever. Serial numbers located under the barrel and on side of grip frame. Barrel markings: "BEALS PATENT SEPT 14, 1858/MANUFACTURED BY REMINGTON'S ILION, NEW YORK."

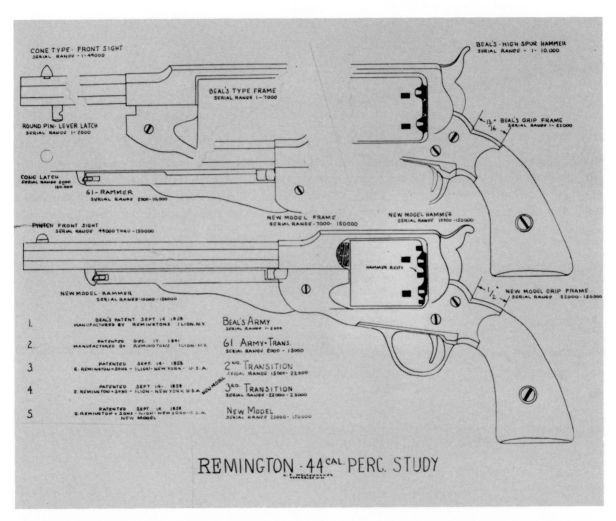

As an aid to Mr. Moldenhauer's research and collecting, he developed the following illustrated chart as a simple method of identifying the many features of the various models of the Army revolvers and their numerous transitions.

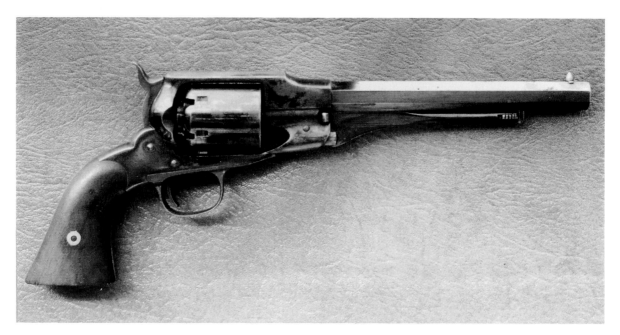

Remington-Beals Army Revolver, serial #765. This pistol is in excellent original condition, with the overall blued finish showing a loss of approximately five percent, with the balance of the finish thinning and turning blotchy with age. The pistol shows little, if any, hard useage, with all markings crisp and sharp. The stocks are in very good condition, with little surface marring. *(Museum of Connecticut History)*

Remington-Beals Army Revolver, serial #765, showing the left view. *(Museum of Connecticut History)*

Remington-Beals Army Revolver, serial #91, showing the engraving on the butt.

From top to bottom: (next page)

Remington-Beals Army Revolver, serial #91, with the original inscription, "Dan Steele, Ilion, N.Y." on the butt. This inscription is of interest due to the fact that Ilion was originally named Steele's Creek. It is reputed that Dan Steele carried this weapon during the Civil War.

Remington-Beals Army Revolver, serial #421. Note that the cone front sight is a replacement, the tip of the hammer has been broken off, and that the top strap has been filed down, with a file cut made perpendicular to the strap.

Remington-Beals Army Revolver, serial #623. Note the sharp, crisp condition of all edges and angles, as well as the condition of the walnut grips.

Remington-Beals Army Revolver, serial #1729. This specimen is martially marked with sub-inspection marks struck on the left side of the front of the frame, left side of barrel, and front of the triggerguard and cylinder, with the inspector's cartouche on both grips.

REMINGTON-BEALS NAVY REVOLVER

Remington-Beals Navy Model Revolvers were produced c. 1860-1862, with the total quantity of approximately 15,000. They were almost identical to the Army Model, but made to a slightly smaller scale. Percussion, .36 caliber, six-shot round cylinder, 7.50" octagon barrel, with the barrel threads concealed by the frame. Walnut grips, blued finish with case-hardened hammer; serial numbers started with number 1 on up, and the serial range duplicates into the Model 1861 Navy Revolver production. Barrel markings: "BEALS PATENT SEPT. 14, 1858/MANUFACTURED BY REMINGTON ILION, NEW YORK."

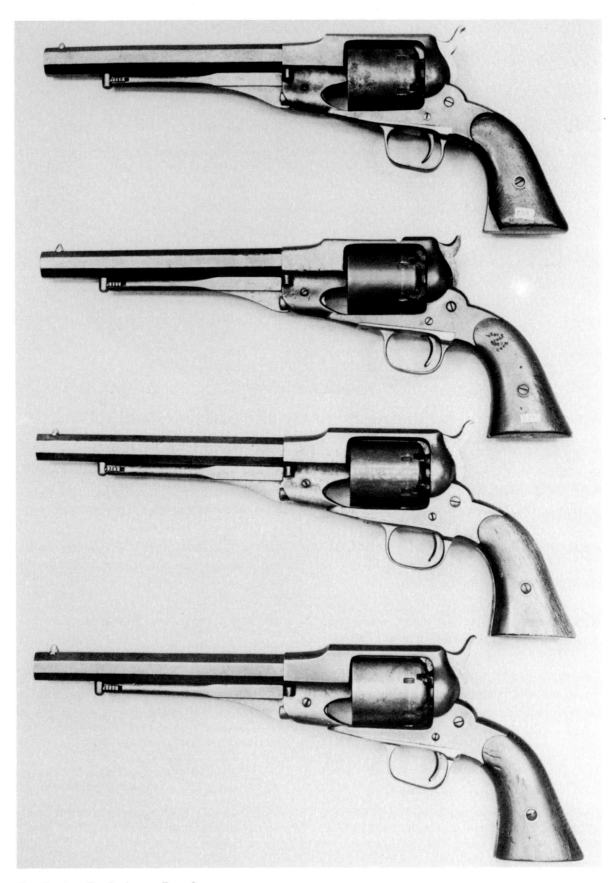

Remington-Beals Army Revolvers.

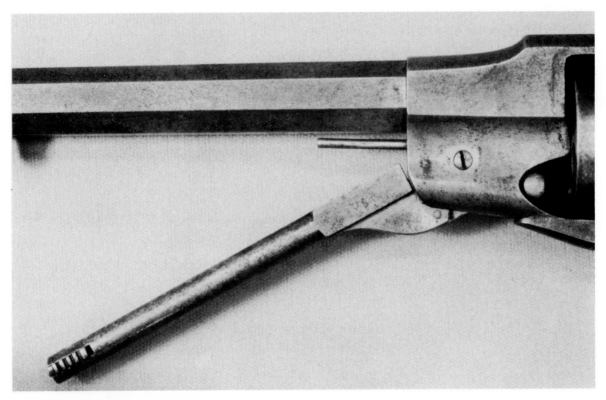

Detailed view of Remington-Beals Navy Revolver, serial #63.

From top to bottom: (next page)

Remington-Beals Navy Revolver, serial #52, fitted with the early loading lever, but not channeled with the small integral rod extension forward from the cylinder pin as is usually found on very early production revolvers.

Remington-Beals Navy Revolver, serial #63, fitted with the extremely rare cylinder pin with the small integral rod extension (approximately 1.50" long) forward from the cylinder pin, and seating into a slot in the rammer lever. The purpose of this extension rod was to prevent the entire cylinder pin from being lost when withdrawn to remove the cylinder. The cylinder pin could be withdrawn by lifting it up and back; otherwise it would hit on the loading lever catch. This problem was overcome by flattening a portion of the cylinder pin so that it could not be removed without first removing the screw securing the attachment of the loading lever. Other guns noted with this rare cylinder pin are numbered 1, 5, 6, 21, 45, and 51.

Remington-Beals Navy Revolver, serial #398, a rare factory-engraved specimen with scroll engraving on the flat portions of the barrel lug, on the top strap, and on each side of the frame, with a simple line engraved along the edges of the frame and down the backstrap; the cylinder is etched with foliate decoration. Fitted with high quality walnut grips. This is considered to be one of five known factory-engraved specimens.

Remington-Beals Navy Revolver, serial #4305. This weapon is factory engraved similarly to the piece above, except that the cylinder engraving covers the full length of the cylinder, including the area between the nipples, and there is a small amount of scroll engraving on the backstrap. The walnut grips appear to be a lesser grade than those on the previous pistol.

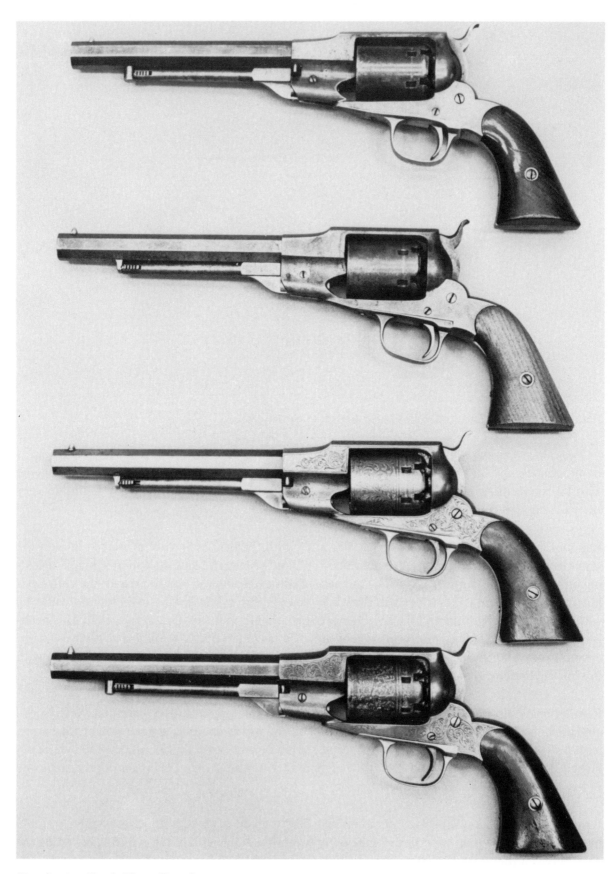

Remington-Beals Navy Revolvers.

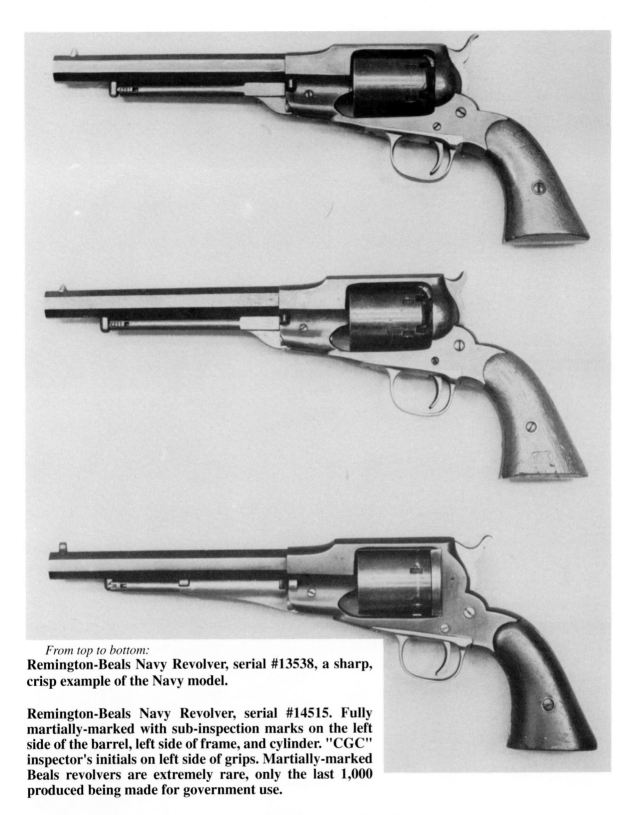

From top to bottom:

Remington-Beals Navy Revolver, serial #13538, a sharp, crisp example of the Navy model.

Remington-Beals Navy Revolver, serial #14515. Fully martially-marked with sub-inspection marks on the left side of the barrel, left side of frame, and cylinder. "CGC" inspector's initials on left side of grips. Martially-marked Beals revolvers are extremely rare, only the last 1,000 produced being made for government use.

Remington-Beals Navy Revolver, serial #14786, conversion #900. The pistol was originally a martially-marked specimen with correct sub-inspection markings on barrel and frame, the conversion done via a new cylinder having a recoil shield with loading gate fitted into the frame at the rear of the cylinder; mounted with an ejector rod on the right side of the frame, the head of the rod fitting into a specially cut slot in the original percussion loading lever.

41

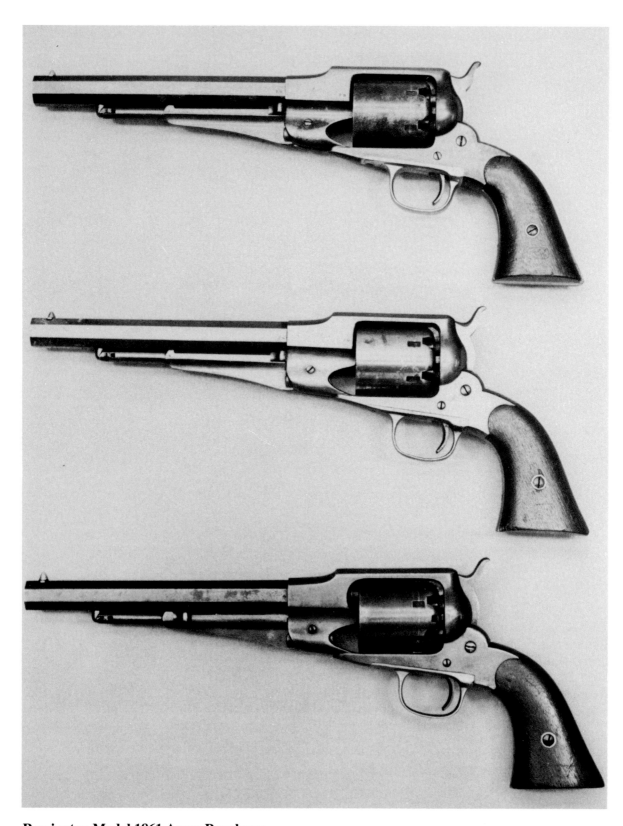

Remington Model 1861 Army Revolvers.

REMINGTON MODEL 1861 ARMY REVOLVER, A.K.A. "OLD MODEL ARMY"

1862-1863. Total quantity produced estimated between 9,000-12,000; in the opinion of Mr. Moldenhauer, the entire production was purchased by the United States government, since he uncovered only two specimens that were not martially-marked, and which he considered "lunch box specials." Apparently, the Model 1861 Army revolvers were not acceptable for military service. Many were returned to the factory, where the rammer channel was blocked by a filister screw so that the rammer had to be dropped in order to remove the cylinder pin and cylinder. As manufactured, the cylinder pin could slide forward for removing the cylinder with the loading lever in locked position. Safety notches between the nipples appeared on the later versions of this model and in 1863 the feature resulted in Remington being granted an increase in the cost of the weapon.

Manufactured in percussion, .44 caliber, six-shot round cylinder, 8.0" octagon barrel, with threads visible at the breech end of the barrel. Walnut grips, blued finish with case-hardened hammer, serial numbering commenced at the end of the Beals Army production with numbering continuing to approximately 19,000. Barrel marked "PATENTED DEC. 17, 1861/MANUFACTURED BY REMINGTON, ILION, N.Y.

From top to bottom: (previous page)

Remington Model 1861 Army Revolver, serial #5551. Fully martially marked with sub-inspection marks on the left side of the barrel and frame, triggerguard, loading lever, and cylinder; "CGC" inspector's stamp on left grip.

Remington Model 1861 Army Revolver, serial #6012. Fully martially marked with sub-inspection marks on the left side of the barrel and frame, triggerguard, loading lever, and cylinder; inspector's stamp on left grip. This particular specimen has had all of the original blue finish carefully removed except in the most protected areas.

Remington Model 1861 Army Revolver, serial #7398. Fitted with the later New Model style frame and fully martially marked; the inspector's cartouche on this piece is especially light on the left grip.

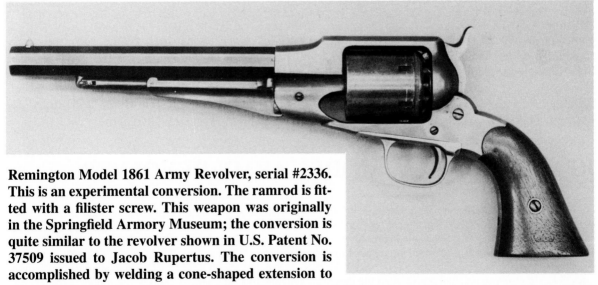

Remington Model 1861 Army Revolver, serial #2336. This is an experimental conversion. The ramrod is fitted with a filister screw. This weapon was originally in the Springfield Armory Museum; the conversion is quite similar to the revolver shown in U.S. Patent No. 37509 issued to Jacob Rupertus. The conversion is accomplished by welding a cone-shaped extension to the hammer, cutting off the rear of the cylinder, and adding a removable rear plate drilled with 12 holes. This accommodates the hammer, with six holes to fire the cartridges and six holes as safety notches. Remingtons with this type of conversion cylinder are known and recognized in Rider double-action Pocket and Belt Models, Police, and New Model pocket single-action belt revolvers. This is the only known .44 caliber conversion of this type. As can be seen in the photo, the extremely fine left grip retains the inspector's cartouche.

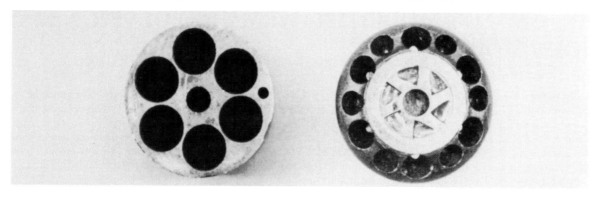

Detail of the cylinder conversion previously shown.

From top to bottom: (next page)
Remington Model 1861 Army Revolver, serial #2372; a factory conversion to .44 centerfire, the rammer fitted with filister screw and the conversion done with a new full-length cylinder having a thin plate fitted into a specially milled section at the rear of the frame. Original nickel plate finish with fine grips.

REMINGTON MODEL 1861 NAVY REVOLVER, A.K.A. "OLD MODEL NAVY."

1862, with total quantity produced estimated at 7,000-9,000, all purchased by the U.S. Government. This weapon is substantially similar to the Model 1861 Army Model, but slightly smaller. Percussion, .36 caliber, six-shot round cylinder, 7.38" octagon barrel with the threads visible at the breech end. Walnut stocks, blued finish with case-hardened hammer; the serial numbering commenced at the end of the Beals Navy production. Barrels are marked "PATENTED DEC. 17, 1861/MANUFACTURED BY REMINGTON'S ILION, N.Y." As with the 1861 Army Model pistol, there is a channel cut along the top of the loading lever that acts as a means of identification. A few specimens have been observed with naval anchor markings on the top of the barrel, which would bring a collector's premium.

Remington Model 1861 Navy Revolver, serial #15792. Early Beals-type frame fully martially marked with the usual sub-inspection marks and inspector's cartouche on the left grip. A crisp, original specimen with excellent oil-finished grips.

Remington Model 1861 Navy Revolver, serial #17059. Later New Model style frame, fully martially marked. This is an extremely well-kept weapon, sharp and crisp, with well-oiled grips.

REMINGTON NEW MODEL ARMY REVOLVER.

1863-1875, with total estimated production of 132,000. Percussion, .44 caliber, six-shot round cylinder, 8.0" octagon barrel; threads visible at breech end, safety notches on cylinder shoulders between the nipples. Walnut stocks, blued finish with case-hardened hammer. Screw-in type steel front sight. Serial numbers continued from the Model 1861 Army revolver commencing approximately in the 15,000 range. Barrel markings: "PATENTED SEPT. 14, 1858/REMINGTON & SONS, ILION, NEW YORK, U.S.A./NEW MODEL." This was the last of Remington's .44 caliber revolvers, and represented the greatest challenge to Colt's Model 1860 Army model revolver.

Remington New Model Army Revolver Transition Model, serial #14328. But for the barrel, which has the 1861 stamping and cone front sight, this is otherwise a complete, martially marked New Model Army revolver. Apparently these weapons were assembled from parts on hand during the Civil War, while the known serial number range would indicate that approximately 5,000 transitional models were made during this period.

44

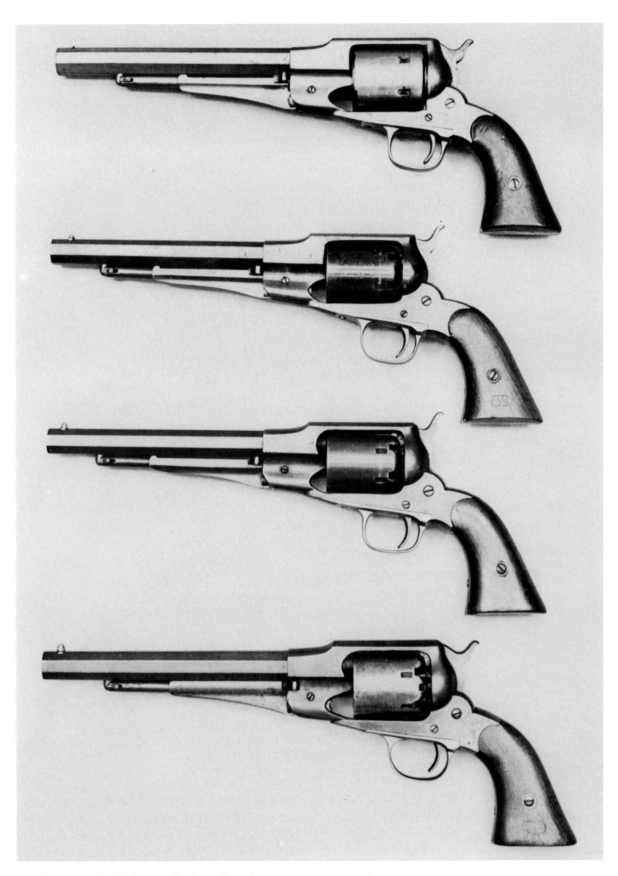

Remington Model Army & Navy Revolvers.

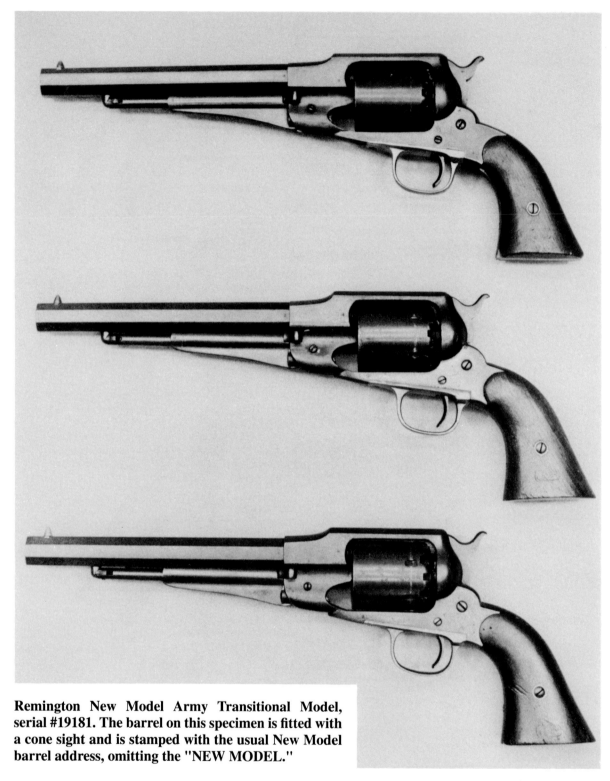

Remington New Model Army Transitional Model, serial #19181. The barrel on this specimen is fitted with a cone sight and is stamped with the usual New Model barrel address, omitting the "NEW MODEL."

Remington New Model Army Revolver, serial #22455. Fitted with the cone front sight; shows the usual barrel address, but with "NEW MODEL" at the rear of the address rather than beneath it.

Remington New Model Army Revolver, serial #28255. This revolver, fitted with the cone front sight, is in excellent condition, having obviously seen little use. Note the condition of the oil finished stocks.

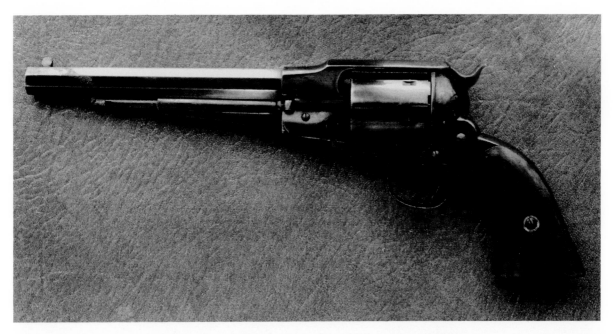

Left side view of Remington New Model Army Revolver, serial #70508. *(Museum of Connecticut History)*

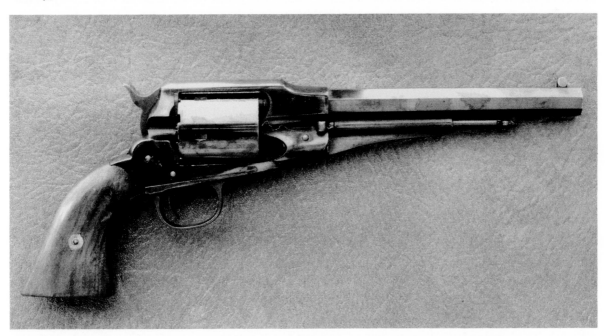

Remington New Model Army Revolver, serial #70508. Shown from the right, this revolver is in excellent condition, retaining at least 90+ percent of the original bright blue finish; the finish is splotchy with age and is thinning, but all markings are crisp and clear. The oil finished stocks are in prime condition. *(Museum of Connecticut History)*

Cased Remington New Model Army Revolver, serial #19. This is one of a series of special presentation revolvers with their own serial number range, the pistol being finished in a glossy bright blue with a silver-plated triggerguard and original carved ivory grips. The right grip is raised carved with an American eagle clutching three American flags, the American shield and olive branches. The left grip is carved with the official seal of the State of Missouri. These pistols were apparently made by Remington for the various states of the Union for presentation during the Civil War. Several other like pistols are known with differing state seals and all with low serial numbers. The pistol and accessories are housed in the original Remington walnut case (15.0" x 7.0' x 2.50") lined with red velvet. The following accessories are included: a tin of caps labeled "F. Joyce & Co., London, England," a brass-handled Remington cleaning rod, a steel two cavity mold, two packets of skin cartridges, and a 6.50" powder flask embossed on each side with a pattern of hunting dogs and pheasants.

Top photo: (next page)
Cased Remington New Model Army Revolver, serial #29. Another in the series of special presentation pistols with their own serial range. This particular specimen is fully factory engraved with etched loading lever and cylinder, while the frame, rear of barrel, bottom of triggerguard, and back strap are all scroll engraved. The etched pattern on the cylinder shows two mounted soldiers, one firing while in pursuit, with the one being chased looking over his shoulder at his attacker. The loading lever is etched in an unusual finish scroll pattern. The hammer is case-hardened, the trigger, cylinder, cylinder pin, and loading lever done in a glossy blue; the barrel, triggerguard and frame are heavily silver-plated. Further fitted with the original plain ivory grips. Housed in its original Remington walnut case,(15.0" x 6.75" x 2.50") with the following accessories: two-cavity iron mold with sprue cutter; a packet of skin cartridges; a tin of percussion caps labeled "R.D. Walker's Central Fire Waterproof Caps No. 57"; and a 6.75" powder flask embossed on both sides with a panel of two pheasants and a panel of a hunting dog. The original key is also supplied. This particular piece is in superb condition and a prize for any collector.

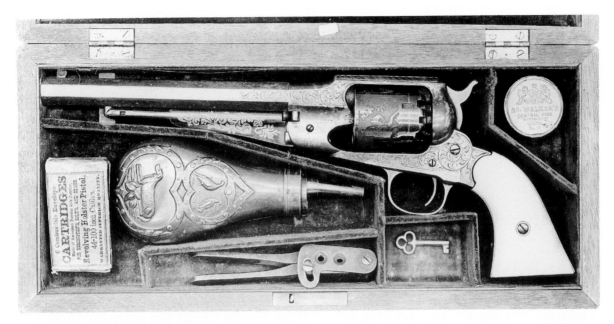

Cased Remington New Model Army Revolver.

Cased Remington New Model Army Revolver, serial #42323. Very profuse original scroll engraved overall, appearing to be the work of the famous engraver L.D. Nimschke. The frame, triggerguard, and barrel are silver plated; the hammer, cylinder and loading lever are gold plated, while the trigger is blue. A most unusual feature is the large, serial numbered oval plate screwed to the bottom of the butt in order to secure the original ivory grips without the use of screws, thus avoiding disfiguring screw holes. This also allows the grips to be slightly longer than usual. Housed in the original factory walnut case (15,0" x 6.75" x 2.375") lined with purple velvet and containing the following accessories: a packet of skin cartridges; the correct two-cavity mold; and a 6.75" copper powder flask embossed on each side with a scene of two pheasants and a dog. This weapon is in spectacular mint condition.

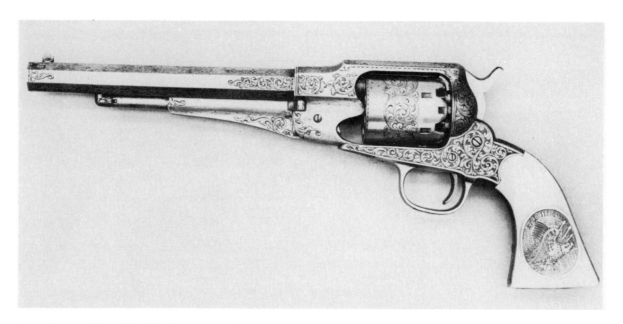

Remington New Model Army Revolver, serial #42326. Special factory full engraved deluxe version with heavy scroll engraving overall and fitted with the special oval screwed onto the butt for mounting the screwless original ivory grips--the right grip plain, while the left grip is carved in a raised oval showing an American eagle with three flags clutching an American shield and olive branches. The hammer, cylinder and loading lever are in their original gold finish, while the barrel, frame and triggerguard are silver-plated. This particular weapon is complete and original throughout and in sharp, crisp condition.

Detail picture of the special oval grip-retaining plate that screws onto the butt of the previous weapon.

Top photo: (next page)

Remington New Model Army Revolver, serial #59038. Note that the barrel is stamped "NJ" in large letters on the left side, indicating purchase and issue by the New Jersey State Militia. The weapon is clearly in excellent condition.

Remington New Model Army Revolver, serial #67389. This particular pistol, which is in very fine original condition, has some rare and unusual markings on the barrel in addition to those usually found. The lower right flat of the barrel is marked "CAST STEEL." Mr. Moldenhauer, in all his years of collecting Remingtons, had neither heard of, nor found another pistol so marked.

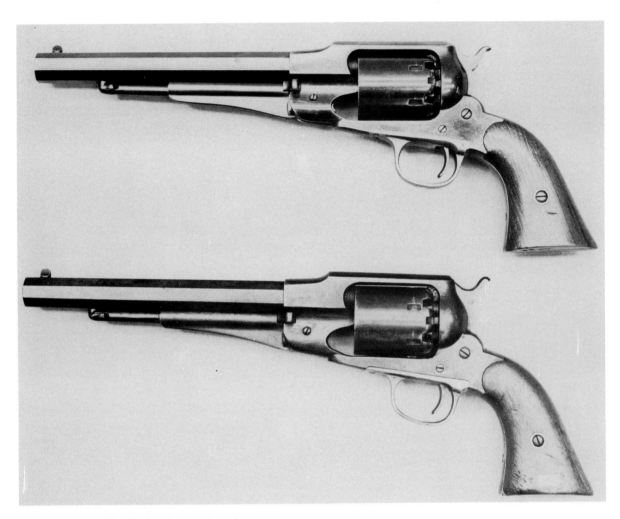

Remington New Model Army Revolvers.

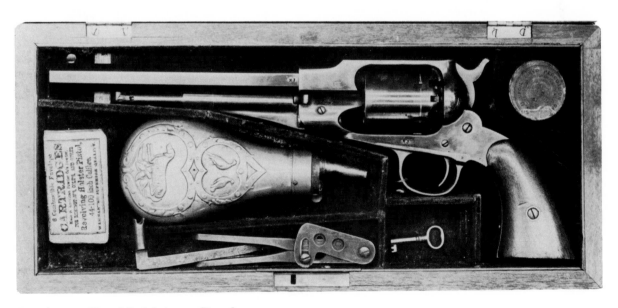

Remington New Model Army Revolver.

Bottom photo: (previous page)

Cased Remington New Model Army Revolver, serial #71672. In excellent original condition, this pistol is stamped "NJ" on the left barrel flat as well as on the left side of the frame. The original walnut case (15.0" x 6.63" x 2.25") is lined with green velvet and contains the following accessories: cap tin; correct two-cavity iron mold with sprue cutter; nipple wrench/screw driver combination tool; a mint packet of skin cartridges; and a 6.50" powder flask embossed on both sides with two panel scenes, one with two pheasants, the other with a reclining dog.

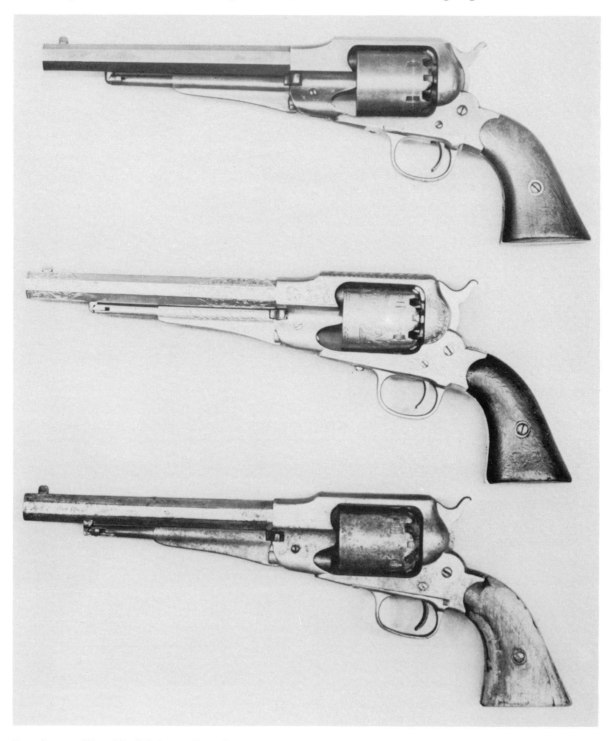

Remington New Model Army Revolvers.

From top to bottom: (previous page)

Remington New Model Army Revolver, serial #94235. This extremely crisp pistol was the start of Mr. Moldenhauer's Remington collection and was used as a shooter until 1960. Note the excellent oil finished walnut grips with a clear, sharp script "GP" inspector's mark.

Remington New Model Army Revolver, serial #102436. This gun was pitted overall, but had an excellent bore when purchased by Mr. Moldenhauer in 1960. It was polished, scroll engraved by Mr. Moldenhauer and then nickel-plated for use as his personal shooting weapon.

Remington New Model Army Revolver, serial #136584. This pistol is marked on the right barrel flat and cylinder with the initials "RM" over a sunburst indicating Mexican Government ownership. The pistol is further marked on the left and right shoulders of the triggerguard with the initials "R" and "M". This is one of only two such examples that were known to Mr. Moldenhauer.

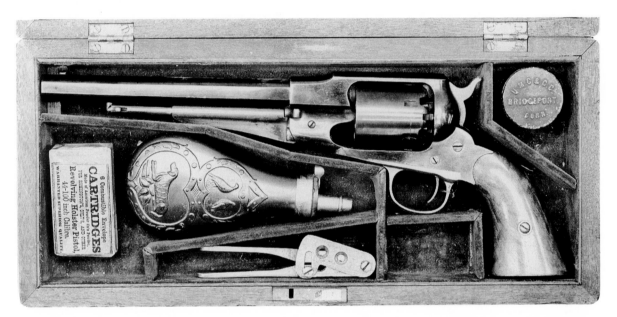

Remington New Model Army Revolver, serial #144304. Shown in its original case (15.0" x 6.75" x 2.25"), it is the civilian model of the New Model Army Revolver but without inspector's marks. The triggerguard is silver-plated, and you will note that the grips are of a higher grade of varnished walnut. The case contains the following accessories: the correct bright-finished two-cavity mold; "UMC Co., Bridgeport Conn" cap tin; packet of skin cartridges; and a 6.0" long late production powder flask, possibly of zinc rather than brass, embossed on both sides with panel scenes of pheasants and reclining dogs.

Top and bottom: (next page)

Remington New Model Army Revolver, serial #34071. Note that this pistol has been non-factory converted to .44 caliber centerfire by having had a spacer forged into the frame at the rear of the cylinder. Such conversions were not unusual.

Remington New Model Army Revolver, serial #84257. Note that this was conversion #842 to .44 caliber centerfire. The pistol was fitted with a loading gate by Frank L. Osgood, the inside of the left grip retaining an old paper label stating: "Remodeled by Frank L. Osgood, Bangor, Maine, May 28, 1903." According to Mr. Moldenhauer, there was only one other so-altered New Model Army in existence.

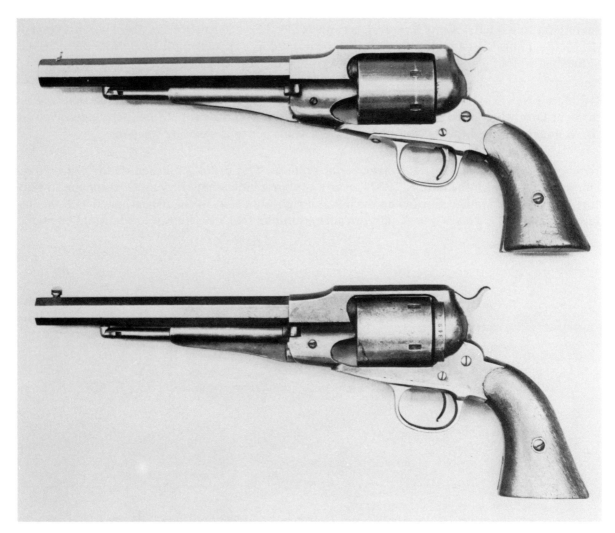

Remington New Model Army Revolvers.

Top and bottom: (previous page)
Remington New Model Army Revolver, serial #91870. This pistol has the experimental J. Rider's patent #51269 cartridge conversion. The pistol is not marked on the barrel and apparently never was, as the finish appears to be completely original. The back of the cylinder is beveled, the theory being that the loading gate would also operate as an extractor. It was Mr. Moldenhauer's belief that this pistol was originally in the Springfield Armory collection.

Remington New Model Army Revolver, serial #195592. This pistol was factory converted to .44 caliber centerfire. The left top strap is fitted with a thin shield that fits down to ride on the edge of the cylinder, the purpose being unknown. A rear sight has been added to the front of the frame. The walnut grips bear a slightly faded "OWA" inspector's mark.

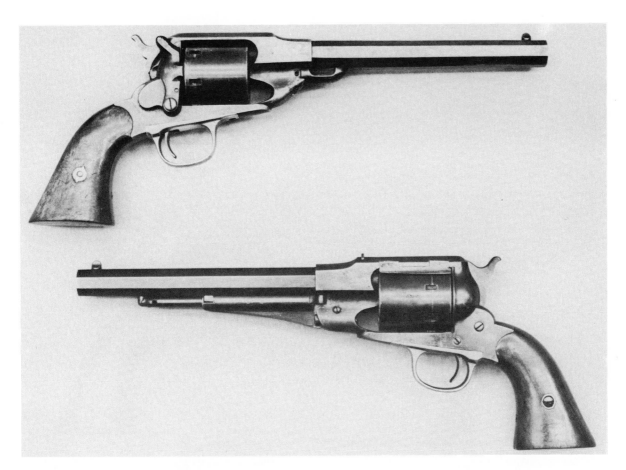

Remington New Model Army Revolvers.

From top to bottom: (next page)

Remington New Model Army Revolver, serial #120601. This pistol is fitted with a simple factory-style conversion to .44 caliber centerfire, fitted with a new cylinder and a small plate added to the frame at the back of the cylinder. Interestingly, three of the six cylinder stops have been slightly milled through into each chamber. The grips show faint inspector's marks, while the left grip has been heavily marked on the side with the number "427."

Remington New Model Army Revolver, serial #123308. This pistol illustrates a factory conversion to .44 caliber centerfire with an extractor added to the right side of the frame, slotted into the original percussion loading lever. The pistol was nickel plated at the time of the conversion.

Remington New Model Army Revolver, serial #136591. This pistol was converted to cartridge using the Rollin White patents, the cylinder marked "Patented April 3d 1855," conversion number 3553. There is a spare percussion cylinder, the rim being numbered "25" and "751." As can be seen, the pistol is in excellent condition with approximately 80 percent of the original finish remaining.

Remington New Model Army Revolver, serial #137455. This pistol was conversion number 1509 to .44 caliber centerfire, and is fitted with an ejector rod. The gun is complete with two cylinders, both marked "Patented April 3d 1855." The right grip frame is marked with a large letter "G," the letter "V," and the date "1879." This gun was converted under an agreement with Smith and Wesson between 1868 and 1869. It was Mr. Moldenhauer's belief that the pistol was nickel plated at the time of the conversion. This weapon and the spare cylinder are in immaculate condition, with sharp markings overall.

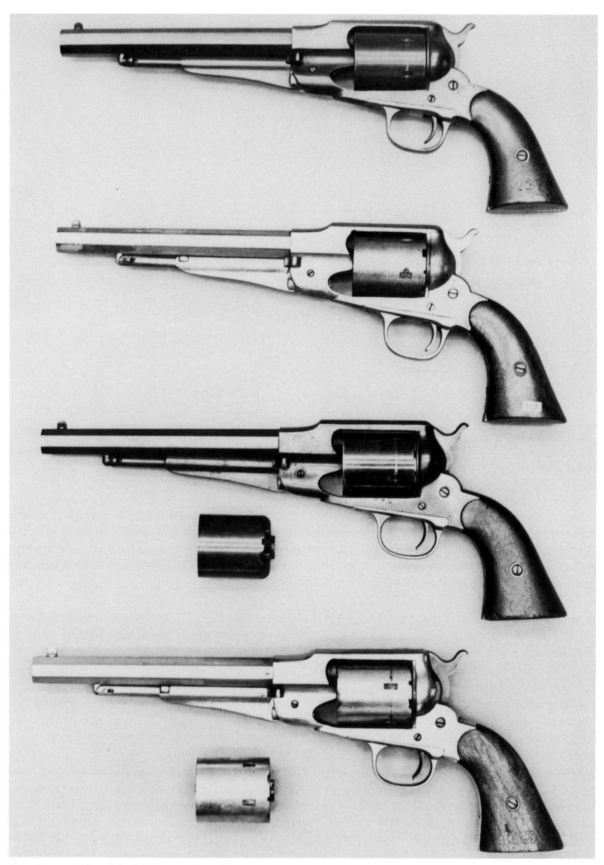

Remington New Model Army Revolvers.

REMINGTON NEW MODEL NAVY REVOLVER

The Remington New Model Navy Revolver was made c. 1863-1875, with the total quantity approaching 22,000; the pistol is almost identical to the New Model Army Revolver, but smaller in size. Percussion, .36 caliber, with a six-shot round cylinder. The octagon barrel is 7.375" long with threads visible at the breech end; there are safety notches on the cylinder shoulders between the nipples. Oiled walnut grips and a blued finish with a case-hardened hammer.

Serial numbers commence at approximately 23,000, continuing from the Model 1861 Navy Revolver. Barrel markings are: "PATENTED SEPT. 14, 1858/E. REMINGTON & SONS, ILION, NEW YORK, U.S.A./NEW MODEL."

Cased Remington New Model Navy Revolver, serial #98. This silver-plated pistol, which is in very fine condition, is a full factory engraved specimen with light engraving on the barrel and full scroll engraving on the frame, triggerguard, backstrap and butt plate; the cylinder is heavily etched with a chase scene featuring two men, one pursuing the other through heavily wooded foliage. The pistol is fitted with the original ivory grips. The original red velvet lined walnut case (14.75" x 6.75" x 2.25") comes with the following accessories: a tin of "100 Waterproof Percussion Caps For Central-Fire Breech-Loading Cases/Eley Bros., Ld., London"; a correct iron two-cavity mold with sprue cutter; a brass-handled cleaning rod; two packages of .36 caliber skin cartridges; and a 6.0" lacquered brass powder flask embossed on both sides with pheasants and a reclining dog.

From top to bottom: (next page)

Remington New Model Navy Revolver, serial #26461. This superb example shows practically no use, retaining over 95 percent of its original blue finish, and at least 98 percent of the finish on the silver-plated triggerguard. Note the beautifully varnished walnut stocks. This pistol was purportedly carried during the Civil War by Hamilton Mum.

Remington New Model Navy Revolver, serial #24724. This pistol was converted to .38 caliber centerfire with the extractor mechanism on the the right side of the frame, and is fitted with a loading gate. The top of the barrel is stamped with a Navy anchor.

Remington New Model Navy Revolver, serial #41920. This specimen has been converted to .38 caliber rimfire, conversion number 646. The pistol has been fitted with an ejector rod and loading gate on the right side of the frame. Note the fine oil-finished stocks.

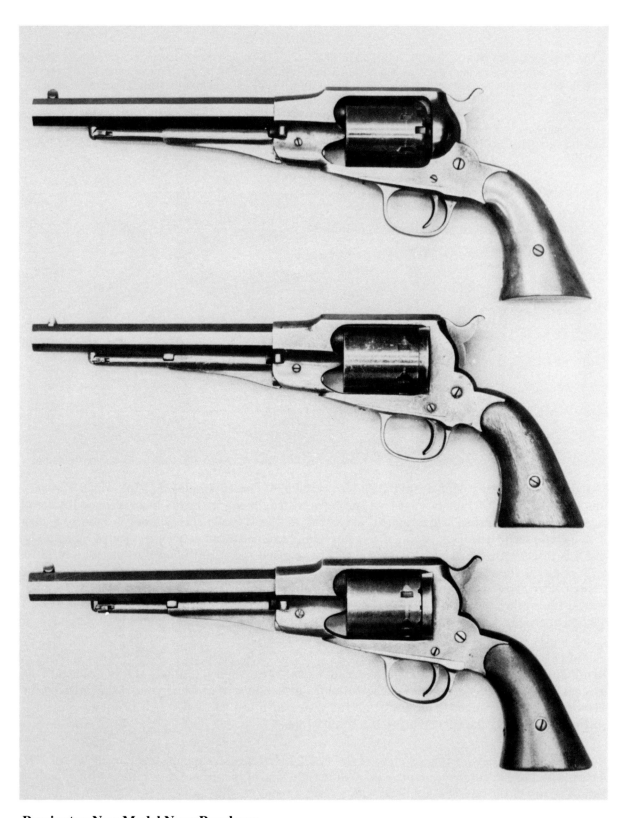

Remington New Model Navy Revolvers.

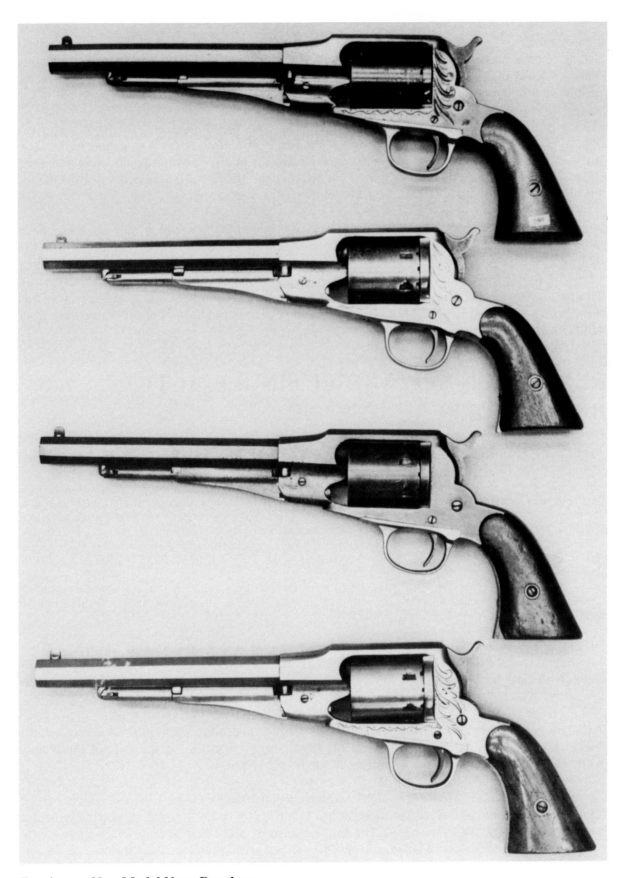

Remington New Model Navy Revolvers.

From top to bottom: (previous page)

Remington New Model Navy Revolver, serial #42807. This pistol is representative of the standard factory conversion, and also shows light factory engraving at the bottom and rear of the frame. While basically unused, this pistol does show the effects of careless storage, the finish turning an age-brown and the case-hardening turning dull.

Remington New Model Navy Revolver, serial #43084. This pistol illustrates the factory conversion, with original sparse factory engraving at the rear and bottom of the frame done at the time of the conversion. Of interest is the fact that the barrel is marked with both the 1858 and 1863 patent dates. The 1863 date is seen on the Police Model and the New Model Pocket Revolvers, but it is highly unusual to find it on the New Model Navy Revolver.

Remington New Model Navy Revolver, serial #43507. In excellent condition, this pistol has been factory converted to .38 rimfire; as with the preceding pistol, it also has the barrel marked with the 1858 and 1863 dates.

Remington New Model Navy Revolver, serial #48028. In near mint condition, this revolver has been factory converted to .38 caliber centerfire, while the rear and bottom of the frame have been lightly engraved at the same time.

REMINGTON NEW MODEL SINGLE-ACTION BELT REVOLVER

The Remington New Model Single Action Belt Revolver was made in percussion from 1863 to c. 1873; subsequent to 1873, the cartridge version was produced. Total production is estimated at 2,500-3,000.

As made in percussion, it is in .36 caliber with a six-shot round cylinder incorporating safety notches on the cylinder shoulders between the nipples; the octagon barrel is 6.50" in length with threads visible at the breech end. The pistol was blued overall with a case-hardened hammer, while some specimens were produced nickel-plated overall, or with a nickel-plated frame with the balance being blued. The stocks are walnut.

This revolver was serial numbered with the Remington-Rider New Model Double Action revolver. Barrel markings read: "PATENTED SEPT 14, 1858/E. REMINGTON & SONS, ILION, NEW YORK U.S.A./NEW MODEL."

It is actually a smaller version of the New Model Navy revolver, and a quick means of identification can be made by the screws that enter the frame from the right side (all previous models entered from the left) and the short barrel length.

From top to bottom: (next page)

Remington New Model S.A. Belt Revolver, serial #1718. This specimen is in complete original condition, with clear barrel markings, fine condition walnut stocks and, as the picture shows, a light age patina overall.

Remington New Model S.A. Belt Revolver, serial #3077. This pistol, while in good overall condition with a deep age patina, does show some light, scattered pitting at the rear of the frame. Notice that the bottom left of the walnut stock has been bruised.

Cased Remington New Model S.A. Belt Revolver, serial #7982. Fitted with the original ivory stocks. Cased in a purple velvet lined walnut box (13.0" x 7.0" x 2.0"), which inspection indicates is not of the same period as the pistol. The case is equipped with the following: correct two-cavity iron mold with sprue cutter; a blued conversion cylinder, serial number 304; a number of .38 caliber rimfire cartridges, as well as some lead bullets; a 4.50" brass powder flask embossed with a flaming lyre pattern on both sides.

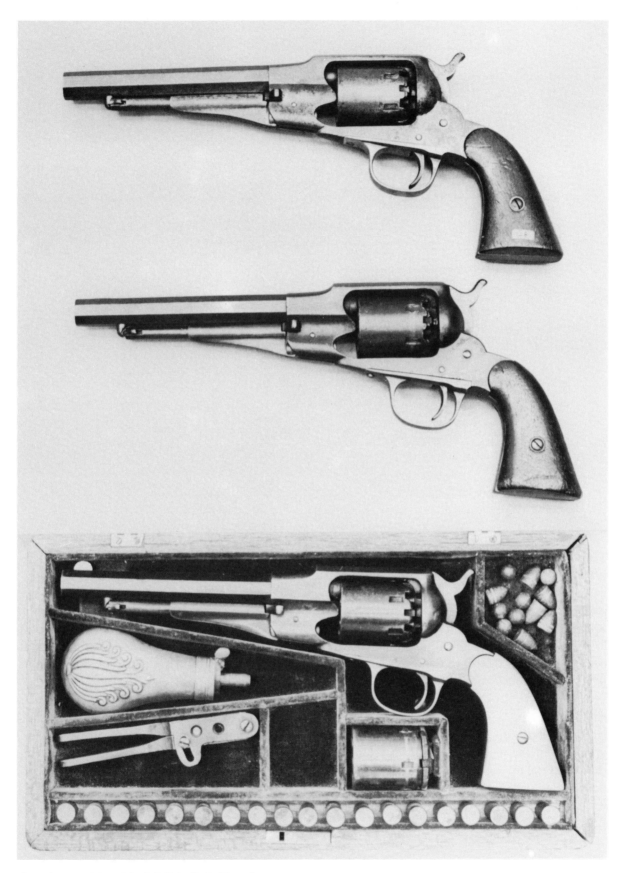

Remington New Model S.A. Belt Revolvers.

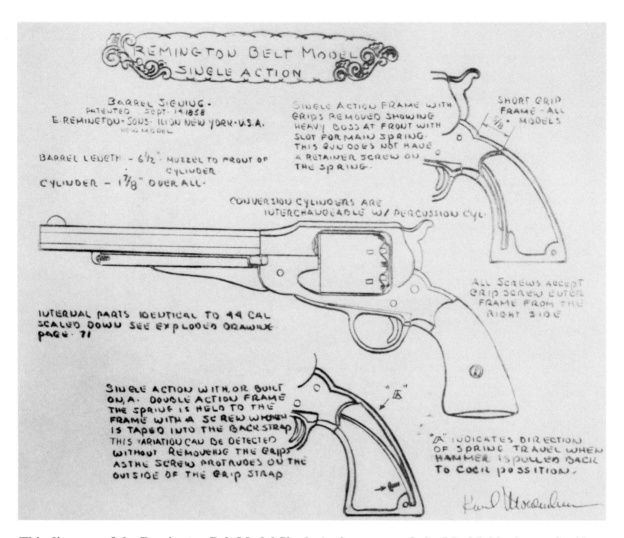

This diagram of the Remington Belt Model Single Action was made by Mr. Moldenhauer for identification purposes and illustrates various features peculiar to this model pistol.

From top to bottom: (next page)

Remington New Model S.A. Belt Revolver, serial #8985. As can be seen in the picture, this pistol is in fine condition, with finish having faded with age; the grips appear to be in excellent condition. Note the number "230" on the lower left side of the frame, which would appear to be some sort of property number.

Remington New Model S.A. Belt Revolver, serial #7663. This pistol was converted to .38 caliber rimfire and probably nickel-plated at the time of the conversion. The heavily varnished stocks are apparent in the picture. Considering the hard usage that most weapons endure, it is surprising that nickel-plate survives as well as it does.

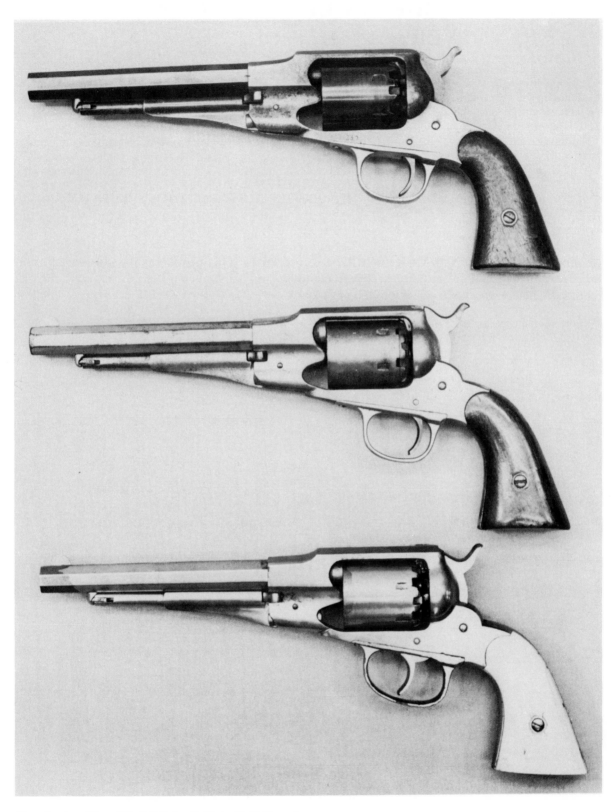

Remington New Model S.A. & D.A. Belt Revolvers.

REMINGTON-RIDER DOUBLE ACTION NEW MODEL BELT REVOLVERS

The Double Action New Model Belt Revolver was produced c. 1863-1873 in percussion, with subsequent production in metallic cartridge, with the total quantity produced estimated at 5,000. Made in percussion in .36 caliber with a round six-shot cylinder with safety notches on the cylinder shoulders between the nipples. The barrel is 6.50" long with threads visible at the breech end.

The finish is blue with a case-hardened hammer, with some specimens overall nickel plated, or with nickeled frame and the balance blued. The stocks are walnut.

Presumedly serial numbered along with the New Model S.A. Belt Revolver. Early specimens have the following barrel markings: "PATENTED SEPT. 14, 1858/E. REMINGTON & SONS, ILION, NEW YORK, U.S.A./NEW MODEL," while later examples were marked: "MANUFACTURED BY REMINGTON'S, ILION, N.Y./RIDER'S PT. AUG. 17, 1858, MAY 3 1859."

Bottom: (previous page)
Remington-Rider D.A. New Model Belt Revolver, serial #4. This pistol was possibly serial numbered within a special presentation series. In complete and original condition throughout, the pistol has the nicely age-mellowed original ivory stocks.

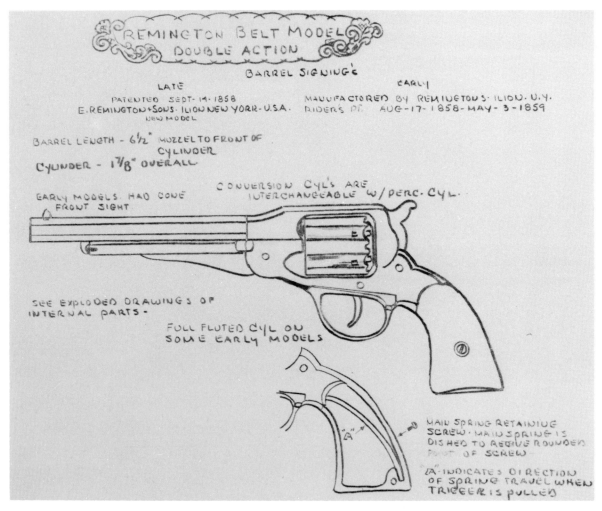

Diagram done by Mr. Moldenhauer of individual as well as overall features of the Double Action New Model Belt Revolver. Diagrams such as these incorporate years of research and collecting on a single page, and offer valuable information to the seasoned collector as well as the novice.

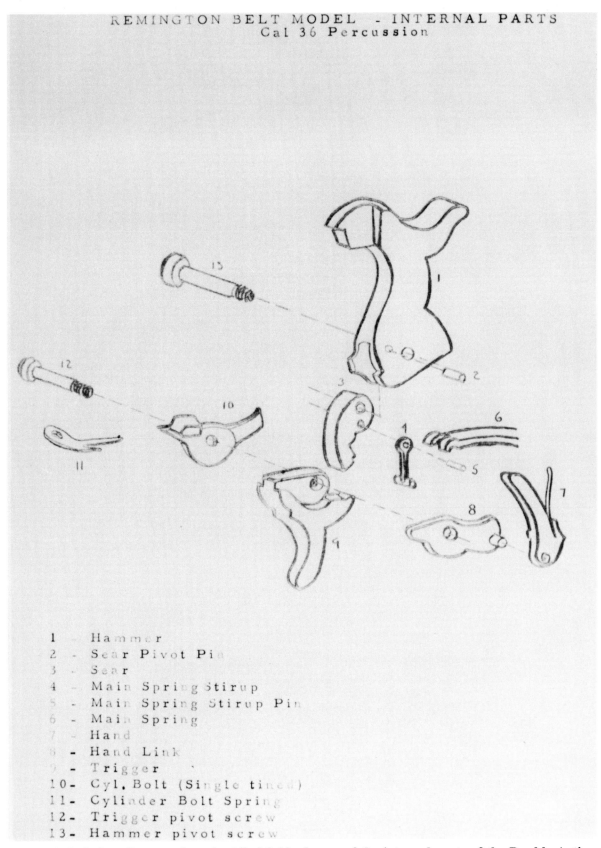

1 - Hammer
2 - Sear Pivot Pin
3 - Sear
4 - Main Spring Stirup
5 - Main Spring Stirup Pin
6 - Main Spring
7 - Hand
8 - Hand Link
9 - Trigger
10- Cyl. Bolt (Single tined)
11- Cylinder Bolt Spring
12- Trigger pivot screw
13- Hammer pivot screw

An exploded view diagram done by Mr. Moldenhauer of the internal parts of the Double Action New Model Belt Revolver.

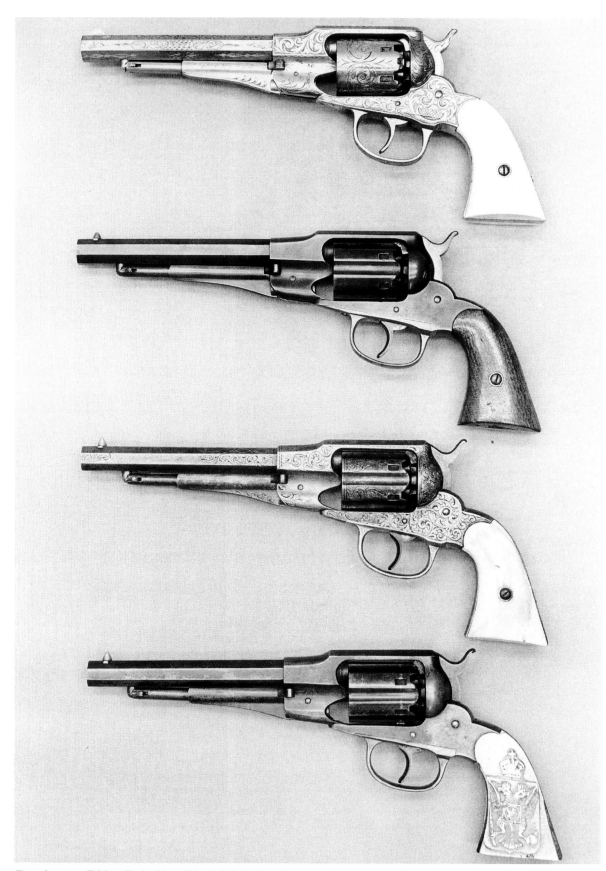

Remington-Rider D.A. New Model Belt Revolvers.

66

From top to bottom: (previous page)

Remington-Rider D.A. New Model Belt Revolver, serial #117. According to Mr. Moldenhauer's notes, this almost mint weapon was believed to be a special serial numbered series. Factory engraved with scroll coverage over the entire revolver, including the entire barrel and the rear of the loading lever; complete and extensive engraving on the cylinder and the triggerguard, as well as the frame, including the backstrap, triggerguard, and butt. The piece is fitted with the original ivory stocks.

Remington-Rider D.A. New Model Belt Revolver, serial #181. Complete and original throughout without any traces of pitting, this revolver comes with its original fluted cylinder. The barrel address is: "MANUFACTURED BY REMINGTON'S, ILION, N.Y./RIDER'S PT. AUG.17, 1858, MAY 9,1859." Note the excellent brass triggerguard and varnished stocks.

Remington-Rider D.A. New Model Belt Revolver, serial #191.
This gun was originally silver plated, but little of the plating remains. In complete and original condition with the rare fluted cylinder, the pistol was completely factory engraved with scrolls at the muzzle and rear of the barrel, as well as surrounding the barrel address: "MANUFAC-TURED BY REMINGTON'S, ILION N.Y./RIDER'S PT. AUG 17, 1858, MAY 9 1859." The frame is fully scroll engraved with scroll engraving on the high parts of the cylinder. Note the excellent original ivory stocks, which have mellowed with age.

Remington-Rider D.A. New Model Belt Revolver, serial #465. This pistol, which is in excellent condition, is fitted with the original full fluted cylinder, as well as the original raised carved ivory stocks. The right stock with an American eagle holding three American flags and clutching the American shield and olive branches. The left stock shows a raised carved Germanic emblem of a crown-topped shield carved with a double-headed eagle clutching a scepter and orb, with a shield on the breast of the eagle showing a man on horseback. The weapon retains a goodly proportion of its original blue.

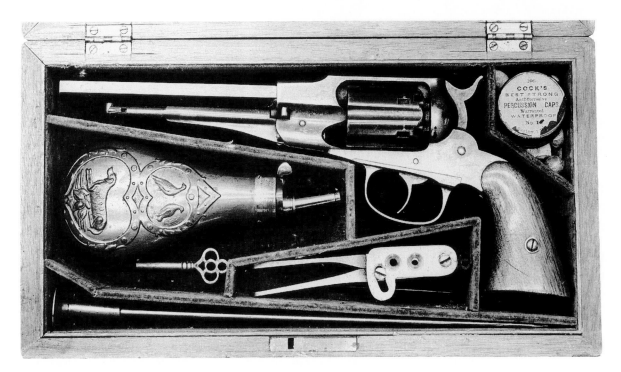

Cased Remington-Rider D.A. New Model Belt Pistol.

Bottom: (previous page)

Cased Remington-Rider D.A. New Model Belt Pistol, serial #691. This pistol is in excellent condition, retaining fully 95 percent of its original bright blue finish; the pistol is fitted with its original full fluted cylinder. Note the excellent varnished stocks. The original varnished walnut case (13.0" x 6.875" x 2.25") lined with faded purple velvet contains the following accessories: a tin of "100 Cock's Best Strong Anti-corrosive Percussion Caps Warrented Waterproof No.1"; several loose bullets; a combination nipple wrench/screw driver; a bright finished two-cavity mold with sprue cutter; a brass handled steel cleaning rod; and a 6.50" lacquered brass powder flask embossed on both sides with two pheasants and a reclining dog.

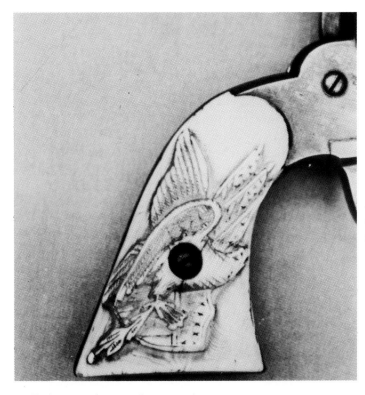

A detail picture of the raised carving of the American eagle with flags, shield and olive branch motif stock.

From top to bottom: (next page)

Remington-Rider D.A. New Model Belt Revolver, serial #1547. This fully-factory engraved revolver has the normal round cylinder associated with this model; the barrel address still retains the Rider patent markings. Note the original ivory stocks. An interesting feature is the Remington New Model Army-type front sight that, upon close inspection, appears completely original to the weapon.

Remington-Rider D.A. New Model Belt Revolver, serial #3455. In excellent condition and retaining the majority of its original bright blue finish, this specimen is fitted with the original ivory stocks, which do much to enhance the appearance of the gun.

Remington-Rider D.A. New Model Belt Revolver, serial #5396. This gun was converted to .38 caliber rimfire, and is fully factory engraved, with the pattern extending approximately the full length of the barrel; the cylinder and frame completely scroll engraved. The triggerguard, backstrap and butt plate are also completely engraved. Note that the pistol is fitted with the original ivory stocks.

Remington-Rider D.A. New Model Belt Revolver, serial #5474. This pistol was converted to .38 caliber rimfire and fully factory scroll engraved overall, including even the loading lever which was rarely, if ever, engraved. In excellent condition, the pistol is fitted with the original ivory stocks; unfortunately, as can be seen in the picture, the left grip is missing a shallow chip from the bottom center.

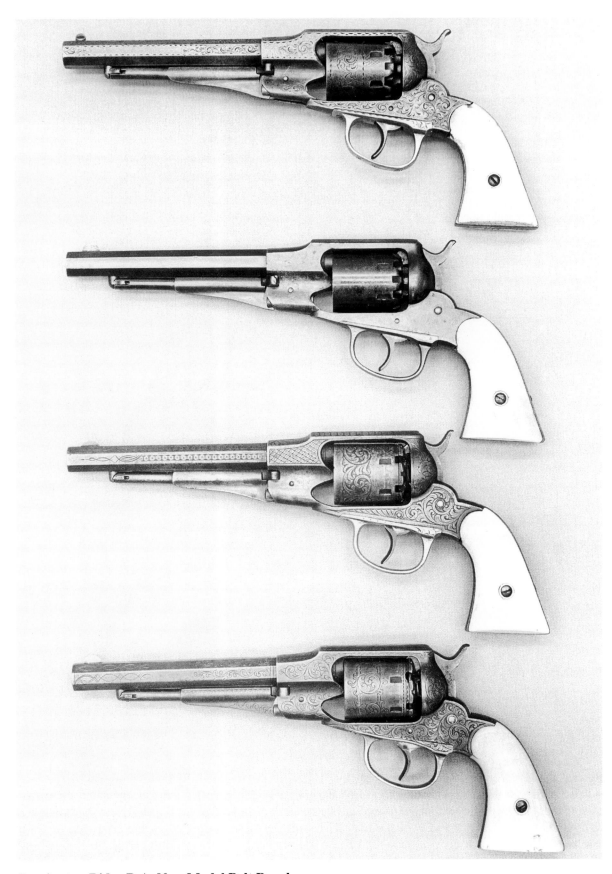

Remington-Rider D.A. New Model Belt Revolvers.

69

REMINGTON NEW MODEL POLICE REVOLVER

The New Model Police Revolver was made c. 1863-1873 in percussion, with subsequent production as factory conversion to metallic cartridge; the total quantity produced is estimated at 18,000 pieces. Percussion, .36 caliber, utilizing a five-shot round cylinder with safety notches on the cylinder shoulder. The octagon barrel came in varying lengths, and could be obtained in 3.50", 4.50", 5.50", and 6.50". An overall blued finish with case-hardened hammer was standard, while other finishes available were overall nickel-plated, or nickel-plated frame with the balance blued. Walnut grips were also standard.

Serial numbers commenced at #1 on up; the barrel markings were as follows: "PATENTED SEPT. 14, 1858 MARCH 17 1863/E. REMINGTON & SONS, ILION, NEW TORK U.S.A./NEW MODEL."

This style revolver was developed as competition with the Colt Model 1862 Police and Pocket Navy Revolvers. This style weapon is actually a scaled down version of the Navy and Belt Model revolvers, with the frame screws entering from the right side.

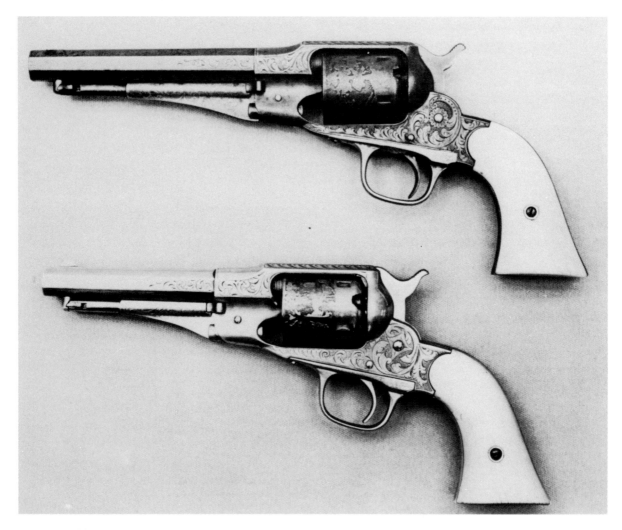

Top and bottom:

Remington New Model Police Revolver, serial #138. This particular fully factory-engraved revolver is fitted with the less common 5.50" barrel. The cylinder is etched with a chase scene of two mounted men firing pistols at one another while galloping through a wooded area; floral-etched loading lever, light scroll engraved at the rear of the barrel around the barrel address. Scroll engraved at front and rear of frame, with herringbone pattern on the top strap, engraved butt strap, butt plate, and bottom of triggerguard. The pistol is fitted with the original ivory stocks. According to Mr. Moldenhauer's files, this is the only known fully factory-engraved 5.50" barreled specimen.

Bottom: (previous page)
Remington New Model Police Revolver, serial #1889. This refinished, fully factory-engraved revolver is fitted with the standard 4.50" barrel. The engraved cylinder is etched with the chase scene of two mounted men shooting at one another while riding through a wooded area; floral etched loading lever, light scroll engraved at the rear of the barrel around the address, scroll engraved at the front and rear of the frame with herringbone pattern on the top strap. The butt strap, butt plate, and bottom of the triggerguard are also engraved, and the revolver is fitted with the original ivory stocks.

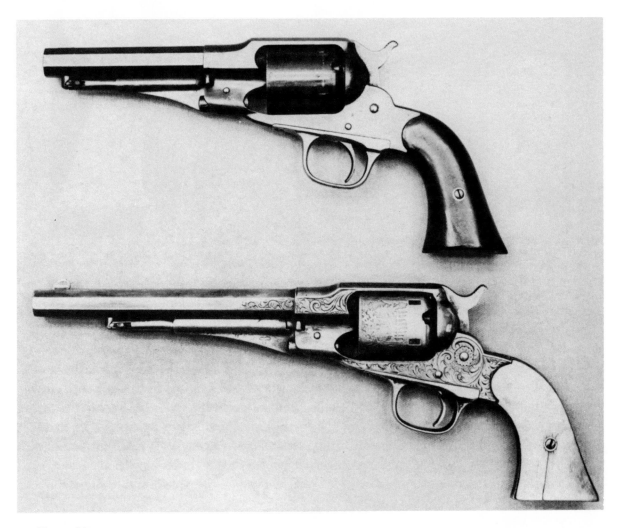

Top and bottom:

Remington New Model Police Revolver, serial #2422. This revolver, which is in excellent condition and showing little, if any signs of wear, has the original factory issue 4.50" barrel and the beautiful, original rosewood stocks.

Remington New Model Police Revolver, serial #2507. This revolver, which has been resilvered, is in very fine condition, and comes with the rare 6.50" barrel. The pistol is fully factory-engraved overall with floral etched loading lever and barrel; the rear of the barrel is lightly scroll engraved, with further scroll engraving around the barrel address. The cylinder is etched with the familiar scene of the policeman and the bandit aiming pistols at one another in a woodland area. Both the front and the rear of the frame are scroll engraved, with the top strap done in a herringbone pattern. Also engraved are the back strap, butt plate, and bottom of the triggerguard. The pistol is fitted with the original ivory stocks.

Cased Remington New Model Police Revolver, serial #2018. This almost mint revolver is fully factory-engraved, with an etched cylinder scene of a policeman and criminal facing off and aiming pistols at one another in a wooded area. Scroll engraved around the rear of the barrel and the barrel address, as well as scroll engraved at the front and rear of the frame with a herringbone pattern on the top strap. The butt strap, butt plate, and bottom of the triggerguard are also engraved. The pistol is fitted with the original ivory stocks. The original purple velvet lined varnished walnut case (10.63" x 5.75" x 2.0") comes complete with the following accessories: a cap tin with green and black label "Eley Bros. 100 Metal-Line Caps, Made Expressly For Remington's Belt and Pocket Pistols, Manufacturers, London"; a correct two-cavity iron bullet mold with sprue cutter; a packet of six .36 caliber skin cartridges; and a 4.0" brass powder flask embossed on both sides with stars and a spread-winged American eagle with shield breast clutching olive branches and arrows over crossed pistols.

Top photo: (next page)
Cased Remington New Model Police Revolver, serial #3094. In near mint condition, with little, if any, signs of use, this revolver is equipped with the rare 6.50" barrel and the original beautiful rosewood stocks. The original red velvet lined case, which is in excellent condition (12.50" x 5.75" x 2.0"), is equipped with the following accessories: a cap tin with green and black label, "Eley Bros. 100 Metal Line Caps, Made Expressly For Remington's Belt and Pocket Model Pistols, Manufacturers, London."; The correct, re-blued two-cavity iron bullet mold with sprue cutter; a combination nipple wrench/screw driver; a packet of .36 caliber skin cartridges; and 4.375" lacquered brass flask embossed on both sides with a single pheasant.

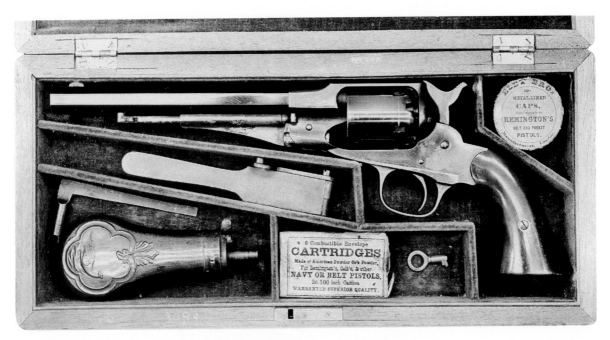

Cased Remington New Model Police Revolver.

Remington New Model Police Revolver, serial #6461. This pistol has the original 3.50" barrel, and has been factory converted to .38 caliber rimfire cartridge. The weapon is seen here with an extra cylinder that is not numbered to the pistol. Note the condition of the original varnished stocks, and the overall fine condition of the gun.

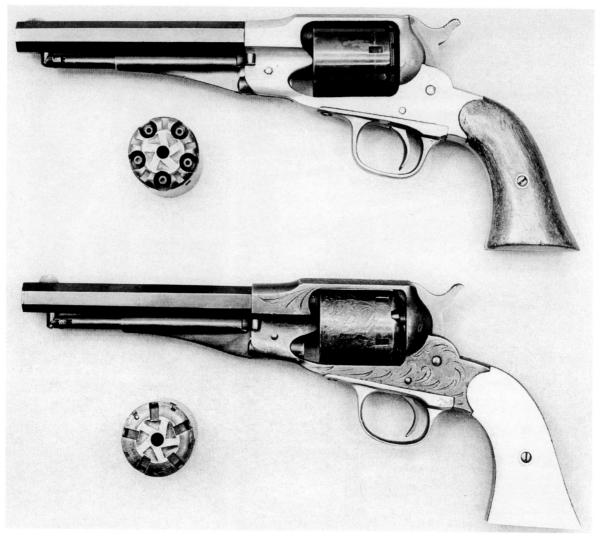

Top and bottom:

Remington New Model Police Revolver, serial #14034. This pistol is in overall excellent condition, with excellent varnished stocks; equipped with the original 5.50" barrel and conversion cylinder to .38 caliber rimfire, the weapon is complete with an unnumbered spare percussion cylinder.

Remington New Model Police Revolver, serial #16624. In very fine, crisp condition, this revolver is fitted with the original 5.50" barrel, and the frame is lightly scroll engraved. The original percussion cylinder is etched with a rare nighttime scene of a mounted policeman pursuing and shooting at a mounted robber in a wooded area, with the stars seen in the sky. Fitted with the original ivory stocks in excellent condition, there is also a plain, spare conversion cylinder not numbered to the gun.

Top photo: (next page)

Cased Remington New Model Police Revolver, serial #9861. In the excellent original red velvet lined case (11.63" x 5.75" x 2.0"), this very fine pistol with 5.50" barrel comes with the following accessories: one tin of "Foil Lined Central Fire Percussion Caps Waterproof/Elm City Mfg. Co/New Haven, Conn;" an "L"-shaped screw driver; the correct iron two-cavity bullet mold with sprue cutter; a package of six skin cartridges by Johnson & Dow's "For Remington's Navy Revolvers Caliber 38-100. Patented Oct. 1st., 1861. Address E. Remington & Sons, Ilion, N.Y.;" a lacquered brass 3.875" powder flask, embossed on both sides with stars, a spread-winged eagle with shield breast clutching arrows and olive branches over crossed pistols. As can be seen, the heavily varnished stocks are in excellent condition, while all of the accessories are in generally very fine to excellent condition.

74

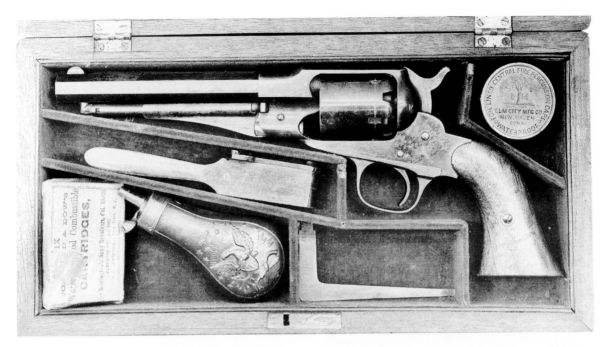

Cased Remington New Model Police Revolver.

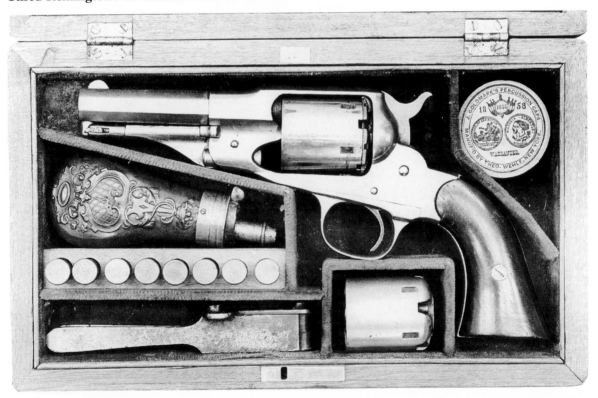

Beautiful cased Remington New Model Police Revolver, serial #381. In a period red velvet lined walnut case (10.0 x 5.75" x 2.0") not original to the gun, this pistol is in generally excellent overall condition, retaining most of the original nickel plating, and complete with the dull case-hardened hammer. The pistol is fitted with the original 3.50" barrel, and has been converted to .38 caliber rimfire. The accessories consist of the following: one packet of Goldmark's percussion caps; an unnumbered spare percussion cylinder; eight .38 caliber rimfire cartridges; one 4.50" lacquered brass powder flask in fine condition with an elaborate embossed pattern on both sides; the correct two-cavity iron bullet mold with sprue cutter.

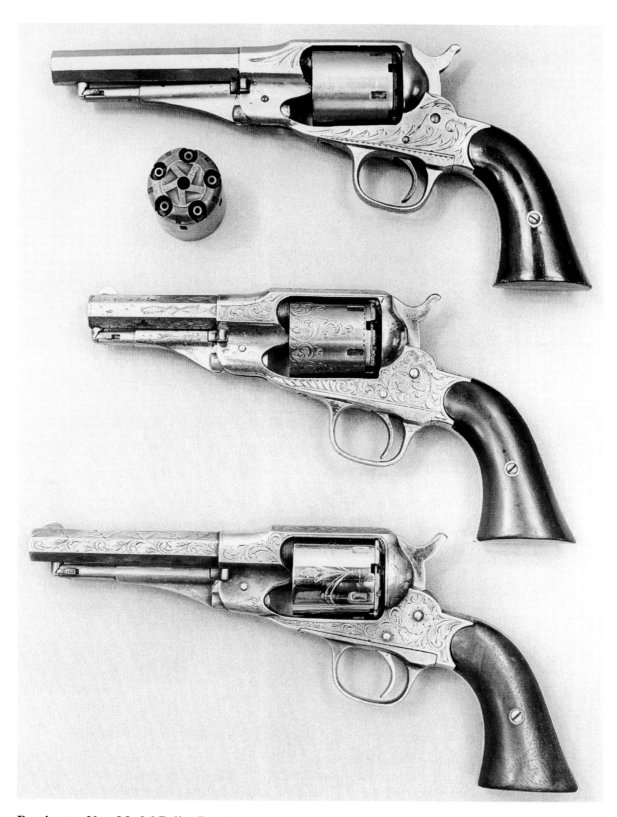

Remington New Model Police Revolvers.

From top to bottom: (previous page)

Remington New Model Police Revolver, serial #16794. This factory conversion to .38 caliber rimfire is fitted with the original 4.50" barrel; the frame bears the sparse original factory engraving. Note the excellent condition of this pistol, which retains at least 98+ percent of the original nickel plate, while the original rosewood stocks are in beautiful condition. The pistol is shown with a spare, non-matching percussion cylinder.

Remington New Model Police Revolver, serial #3395. This pistol retains at least 90 percent of the original nickel plate, with all markings crisp and clear; fitted with a 3.50" barrel and factory converted to .38 caliber rimfire, the piece has been extensively factory engraved overall. The barrel and loading lever have been lightly engraved, while the frame and cylinder have been heavily scroll engraved. The top strap is engraved in a herringbone pattern, with an engraved back strap, butt plate, and bottom of the triggerguard. The lovely varnish-finished rosewood stocks are in excellent condition.

Remington New Model Police Revolver, serial #14490. This factory conversion to .38 caliber rimfire comes with the original 4.50" barrel, and would be considered in very good condition. Note that the pistol has been engraved overall in a most unusual pattern, with the barrel and frame heavily scroll engraved, while the cylinder is lightly engraved in what can only be described as a floral drapery pattern. The original walnut stocks appear to be in good condition.

Remington New Model Police Revolver original walnut case. This the standard red velvet lined case for the New Model Police Revolver showing the correct partitioning. The dimensions of the case are 10.63" x 6.75" x 2.0".

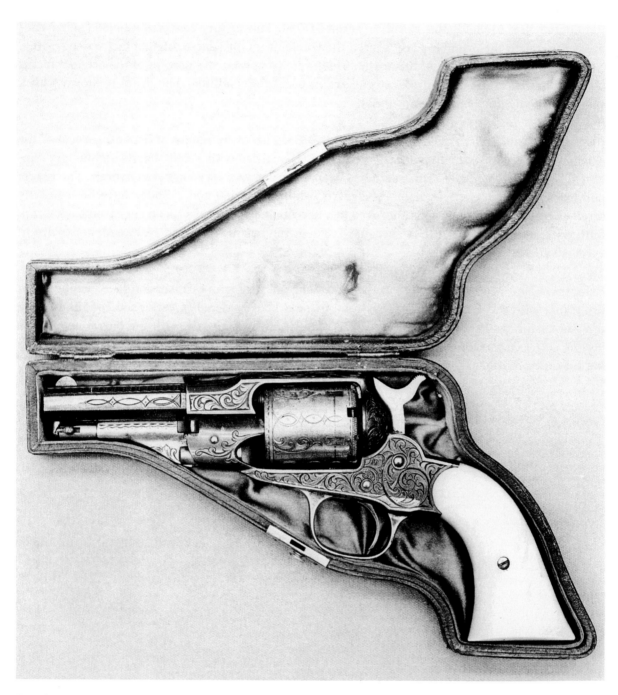

Remington New Model Police Revolver, serial #168. In excellent to mint condition, this 3.50" barrel factory converted to .38 caliber rimfire revolver retains at least 95+ percent of the original light gold wash on the hammer, cylinder, and loading lever, with the balance of the pistol with 98+ percent original silver plate. This pistol is fully period engraved overall, the work being either factory done, or special order by L.D. Nimschke; the back strap is engraved "G W Brown Freehold" in script lettering. The pistol has the original perfect mother-of-pearl stocks. The revolver comes in the original excellent morocco leather covered pipe-style casing, the exterior of the case has gold tooled lines around the edge of the lid, while the interior is lined in sky blue silk.

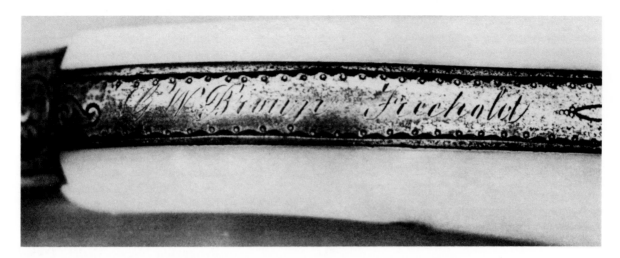

Detail picture of the engraving on the back strap of the preceding pistol.

REMINGTON NEW MODEL POCKET REVOLVER

The Remington New Model Pocket Revolver was made c. 1863-1888; production was in percussion until 1873, with subsequent production as metallic cartridge conversions. The total estimated production was 25,000.

Made in percussion, .31 caliber with a five-shot round cylinder, with safety notches on the cylinder shoulders. Lengths of the octagon barrels are: 3.0", 3.50", 4.0", and 4.50"; the latter two barrel lengths are quite uncommon and command a premium when found.

Stocks are of walnut, while the finish is blue overall with a case-hardened hammer. Alternative finishes included overall nickeled, or nickeled frame, with the balance blued. Serial numbers commenced at #1 on up. Barrel markings as follows: "PATENTED SEPT. 14, 1858 MARCH 17, 1863/E.REMINGTON & SONS, ILION, NEW YORK U.S.A./NEW MODEL."

This pistol is quickly identifiable by its distinctive spur trigger and quite small frame size.

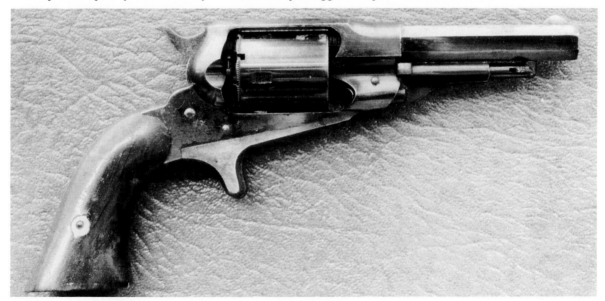

Remington New Model Pocket Revolver, serial #14087. This is the Third Type revolver, with all iron construction, and fitted with a 3.50" octagon barrel in .31 caliber. This pistol is in excellent condition, with at least 95 percent of the original blue finish remaining. The blue finish is beginning to blotch with age, and there are signs of the finish starting to fade. Note the good condition of the varnished stocks, which still retain much of the original varnish. *(Museum of Connecticut History)*

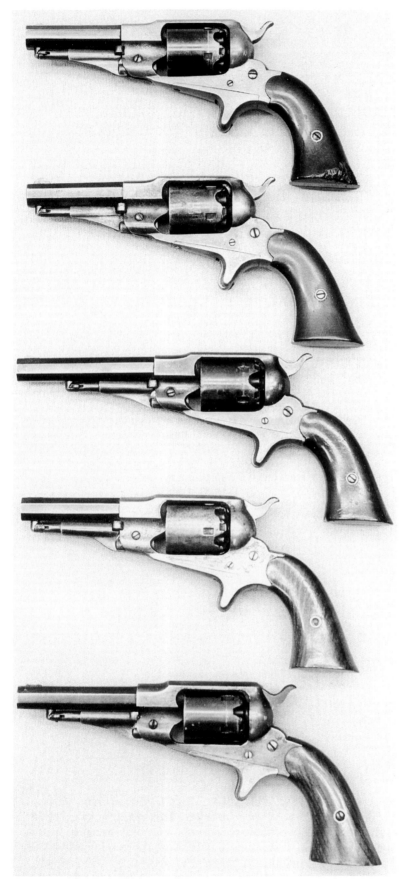

Remington New Model Pocket Revolver, serial #51. This rare First Type with all brass frame and fitted with a 3.0" barrel is encountered up to approximately serial #150. This particular specimen is in excellent shape, with brass frame in lovely condition, and all markings crisp and clear. The original rosewood stocks would rate as excellent, but for the loss of a large chip seen at the rear bottom half of the left stock.

Remington New Model Pocket Revolver, serial #434. This is the Second Type with iron frame and brass sheath triggerguard, fitted with the 3.0" barrel. This pistol is in fine condition, with excellent varnished rosewood stocks.

Remington New Model Pocket Revolver, serial #4365. This pistol, the Third Type with iron frame and iron sheath triggerguard, is fitted with the extremely scarce 4.0" barrel. As can be seen in the photograph, the pistol is in very fine condition, with minimal signs of wear. The original varnish finished stocks are in very fine condition.

Remington New Model Pocket Revolver, serial #4438. This is another of the Third Type with all-iron construction, and fitted with the 3.0" barrel. In very fine, sharp, crisp condition, most of the original silver plate finish is gone from the frame, and practically no finish remains on the cylinder. The original varnished rosewood stocks are in excellent condition.

Remington New Model Pocket Revolver, serial #8223. This Third Type revolver with all-iron construction is in very fine condition, having turned an age-brown with the exception of the cylinder, while the varnished lightly-colored rosewood stocks are in excellent condition.

Left side view of the Remington New Model Pocket Revolver, serial #14087. *(Museum of Connecticut History)*

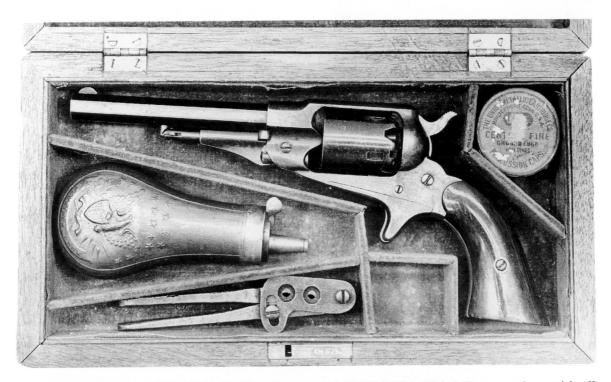

Cased Remington New Model Pocket Revolver, serial #10034. This Third Type revolver with all-iron construction is fitted with the rare 4.50" barrel, and is shown in the original red velvet lined walnut case (10.25 x 5.25" x 2.0"); the pistol is in very fine to excellent condition. The case, as can be seen, is in excellent condition, with only slight fading to the red velvet. The case comes with the following accessories: a cap tin of Union Metallic Cartridge Company percussion caps; the correct style two-cavity iron bullet mold with sprue cutter, and the original lacquered brass powder flask embossed on both sides with stars, spread-winged eagle with shield breast clutching arrows and olive branches over crossed pistols, ribbon with "E Pluribus Unum."

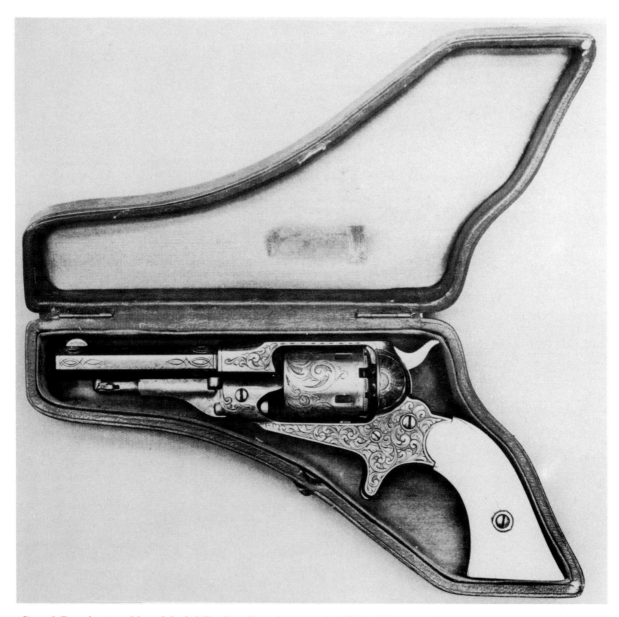

Cased Remington New Model Pocket Revolver, serial #10. This revolver, which has been factory converted to .32 caliber rimfire, is fitted with a 3.50" barrel. The pistol, in very fine condition with the barrel and frame originally silver plated, has been fully-factory engraved, with light engraving to the barrel and heavy scroll engraving to the frame and cylinder. Note the excellent condition of the original ivory stocks. The revolver is shown in its original blue satin lined, brown morocco leather covered pipe-style case, embossed with tooled gold line around the lid, including in fancy gold script "Hiram B. Crosby. New York." This case, as can be seen, is in excellent condition.

Top photo: (next page)
Cased Set of Remington New Model Pocket Revolvers, serial numbers 10014 and 19946. Both pistols are fitted with the rare 4.50" barrel, and are the Third Type with all-iron construction. Both pistols are in excellent condition, and the brass-bound mahogany case (11.50" x 7.75" x 2.75") is lined in the French manner with dark red velvet with blue piping around the pistols and accessories. This case is likely not original to the set, and would appear to be more recent. The accessories consist of the following: a correct style two-cavity iron bullet mold with sprue cutter; a U.M.C. foil lined tin of percussion caps; and a lacquered brass powder flask embossed on both sides with flutes and scroll pattern.

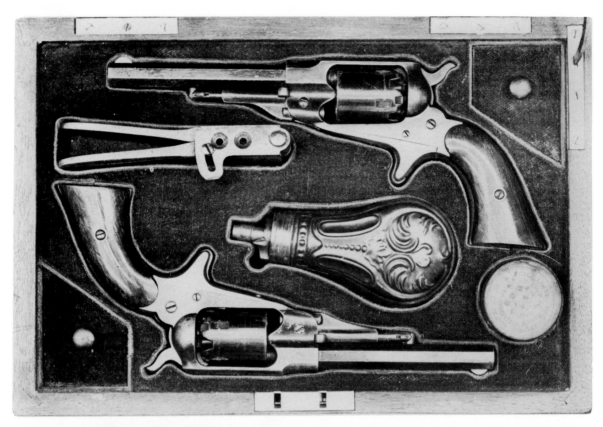

Cased Set of Remington New Model Pocket Revolvers.

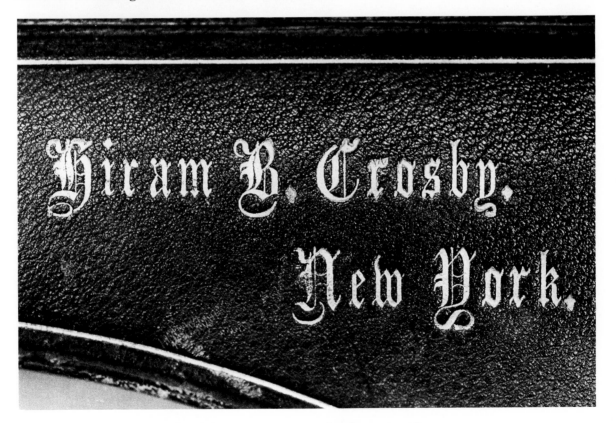

Detail of the script on the lid of the brown morocco leather covered case.

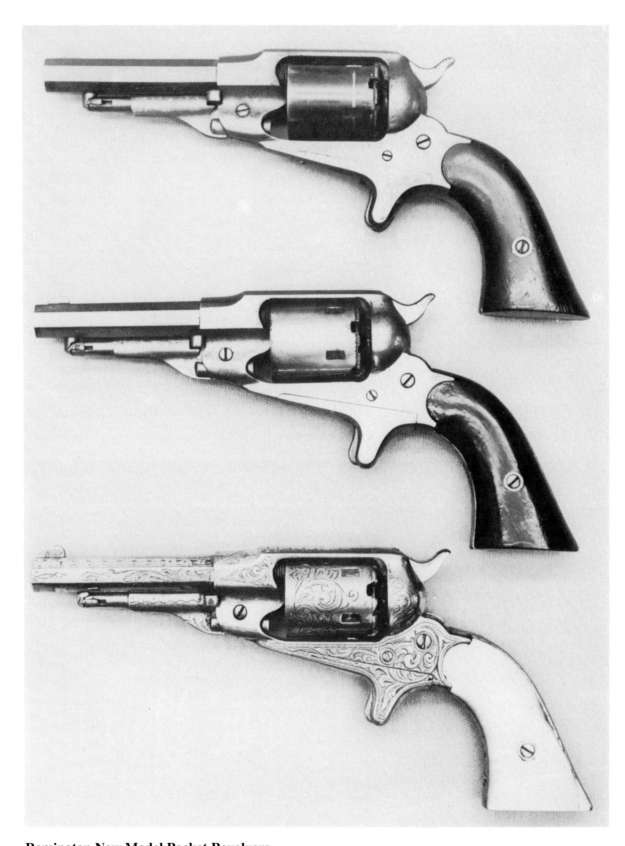

Remington New Model Pocket Revolvers.

From top to bottom: (previous page)

Remington New Model Pocket Revolver, serial #22987. This revolver, which is in fine sharp, crisp condition overall, has been factory converted to .32 caliber rimfire and is fitted with a 3.50" barrel. Slight drag marks may be seen on the cylinder. The original varnished stocks are in very fine condition.

Remington New Model Pocket Revolver, serial #23947. As can be seen, this pistol is in excellent condition; fitted with a 3.50" barrel, it has been factory converted to .32 caliber rimfire. This pistol was nickel-plated originally, and retains at least 95 percent of the finish, while the original varnished stocks are in excellent condition.

Remington New Model Pocket Revolver, serial #24543. In very fine condition, this nickel-plated revolver fitted with 3.50" barrel has been factory converted to .32 caliber rimfire. Fully-factory engraved overall, with profuse coverage on the barrel and loading lever, the balance of the frame and cylinder heavily scroll engraved. The original mother-of-pearl grips are in very good condition.

PATENT MODEL

During the development of the cartridge revolver, one of the largest problems encountered was the problem of shell ejection; many patents were developed and tried, but few met with any commercial success. During the 1860s, this was a major problem, exacerbated by the head spacing and the swelling of the expended shell casings. The patent model described hereafter was obviously modern in concept, and was of great interest to Mr. Moldenhauer; this model was the subject of an article written by him for the 1966 Annual Forum of the Wisconsin Gun Collectors Association, Inc., titled "If." The subject being, if Remington had only continued with the development of this idea conceived by a man who had done considerable work for Remington.

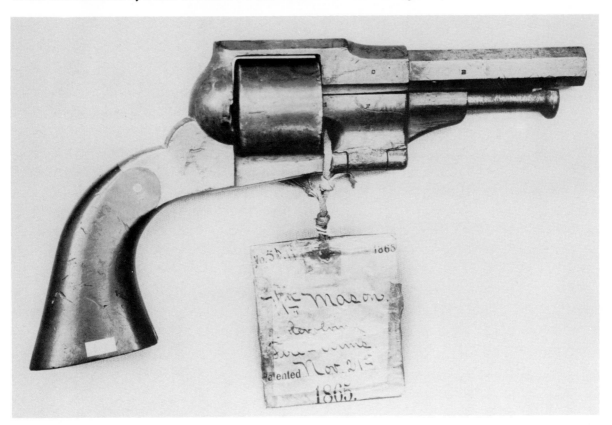

Original Wooden U.S. Patent Model.

Bottom: (previous page)

Original Wooden U.S. Patent Model. Submitted to the U.S. Patent Office for patent number 51117, granted November 21, 1865, to William Mason for an improvement in revolving firearms, basically consisting of a swing-out cylinder and ejection system, much as are known today. This model is 10.75" overall, complete with the original Patent Office tag, and basically is in very fine condition.

REMINGTON-RIDER SINGLE SHOT DERRINGER

Also known as the "Parlor Pistol," the Remington-Rider Single Shot Derringer was made c. 1860-1863, with the total quantity produced estimated at less than 1,000. Percussion, in .17 caliber; the brass 3.0" barrel is integral with the all brass frame. The brass grips are also integral with the frame and barrel. The basis for the patent was the two-piece breech. The standard finish is silver plated throughout.

The derringers were not serially numbered, and the barrels were marked "RIDER'S PT./SEPT 13, 1859." Little data is available about this, the smallest of the pistols produced by Remington. The sole means of propellant was the percussion cap. Apparently there are many spurious specimens on the market, so *caveat emptor*.

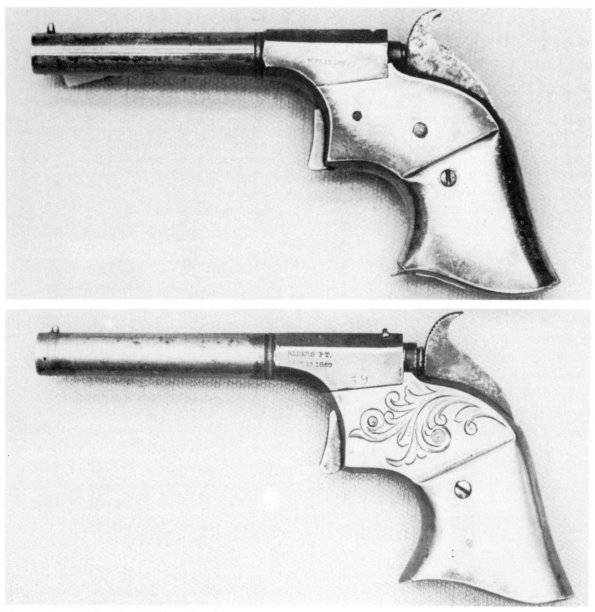

Remington-Rider Single Shot Derringers.

Top to bottom: (previous page)

Remington-Rider Single Shot Derringer. In absolutely beautiful condition, with 99+ percent of the original silver plate, dull case-hardened trigger and hammer, and the breech insert retaining most of its original blue, only the loss of the rear sight mars this otherwise perfect specimen. Marked on the left side of the frame: "RIDER'S PT./SEPT 13, 1859."

Remington-Rider Single Shot Derringer. While carrying the usual markings on the left side of the frame, this derringer also has the number "39" beneath the legend; it was Mr. Moldenhauer's belief that this was a collector's number, and not a serial number. This weapon is in excellent, original condition, including the original breech insert. As a point of interest, this exact pistol is pictured on page 159, picture 142 of Winant's book, *Early Percussion Firearms*.

REMINGTON-ELLIOT ZIG-ZAG 22 DERRINGER

The Elliot derringer in 22RF was also known as "Zig-Zag Pepperbox," and was produced c. 1861-1862, with total production estimated at less than 1,000 .22 caliber rimfire short caliber. Six-shot barrel cluster loaded through a port in the frame at the breech; the barrel group length is 3.375". This is a double action system with concealed hammer and a ring-type trigger; a key part of the revolving mechanism are the zig-zag grooves at the breech end of the barrel cluster.

Produced with a blue finish and hard rubber stocks; there is apparently no continuity in the manner that screws enter the frame, some entering from the right, while other specimens have screws entering from the left. Mainspring set screws also show variations. Pistols are marked as follows: "ELLIOT'S PATENT/AUG.17, 1858/MAY 29, 1860.," and "MANUFACTURED BY REMINGTON'S, ILION, N.Y." Serial numbers are to be found on the left frame beneath the left stock.

Patented by William H. Elliot, one of the more prolific designers and inventors working for Remington, this was the first handgun designed for metallic cartridge ammunition.

From top to bottom: (next page)

Remington-Elliot Zig-Zag 22 Derringer, serial #302. This professionally refinished pistol with silver frame and blued barrel group and trigger is a rare variation with the frame screws entering from the right side of the frame, and no set screw on the mainspring. Note the excellent condition of the gutta-percha stocks.

Remington-Elliot Zig-Zag 22 Derringer, serial #754. This near mint specimen is nickel plated overall, and is in the original chamois leather purse. An interesting note is found in the January 18, 1862, edition of *Harper's Weekly*, which features an advertisement offering this model, referred to as "Elliot's Pocket Revolver" at a retail price of $10.00 for the nickel-plated model with 100 cartridges, while the blued model was priced at $9.50!

Remington-Elliot Zig-Zag 22 Derringer, serial #789. In absolutely mint condition, this derringer retains at least 95 percent of the original bright blue finish, while the plated frame retains at least 99 percent of the original heavy silver plate. The gutta-percha stocks are in excellent to mint condition.

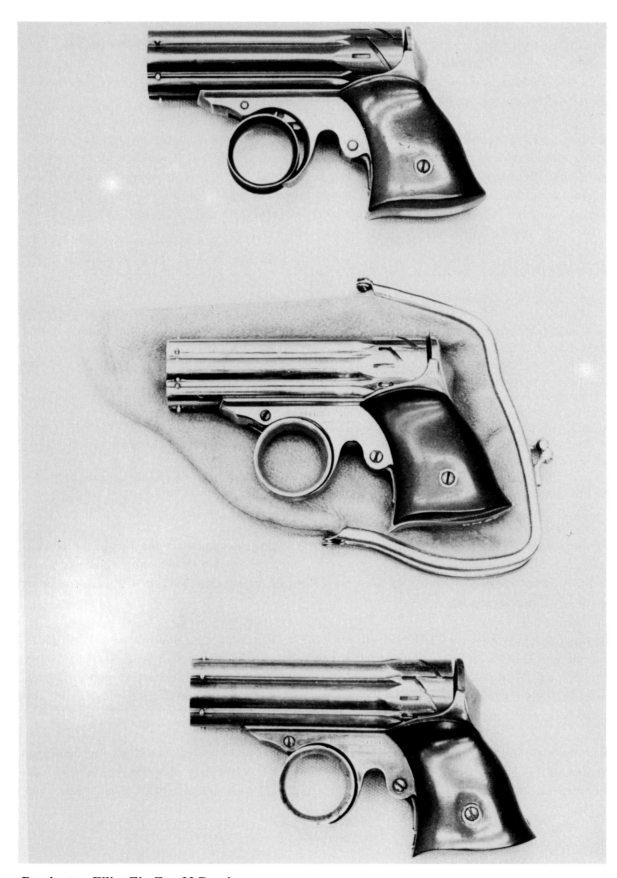

Remington-Elliot Zig-Zag 22 Derringers.

REMINGTON-ELLIOT "PEPPERBOX" DERRINGER

Produced c. 1863-1888, the total quantity made for this model in both .22 rimfire and .32 rimfire is estimated at 25,000. As produced in .22 caliber, there is a 3.0" stationary, fluted five barrel cluster with a revolving firing pin; this barrel group tilts forward for loading and extraction. The trigger is ring-type, and the stocks are of hard rubber. The .32 caliber version differs in having a ribbed stationary four-barrel cluster 3.375" in length; all other features are the same for both versions of this weapon.

Serial numbers are on the bottom of the barrel and inside the frame. Barrel markings are as follows: "MANU-FACTURED BY E. REMINGTON & SONS, ILION, N.Y./ELLIOT'S PATENTS/MAY 29, 1860-

OCT. 1, 1861." An improved version of the Zig-Zag Derringer, this pistol was made in the largest quantity of any Remington ring trigger pistol.

Remington-Elliott .22 Caliber Pepperbox Derringer, serial #670. This derringer is in excellent original condition, with approximately 98 percent of the original blue remaining; the finish is beginning to slightly fade with age and show some light blotches. Mechanically excellent, the original stocks are in almost mint condition, with the exception of one small scratch to the left stock. *(Museum of Connecticut History)*

Left side view of the Remington-Elliott .22 Caliber Pepperbox Derringer, serial #670. *(Museum of Connecticut History)*

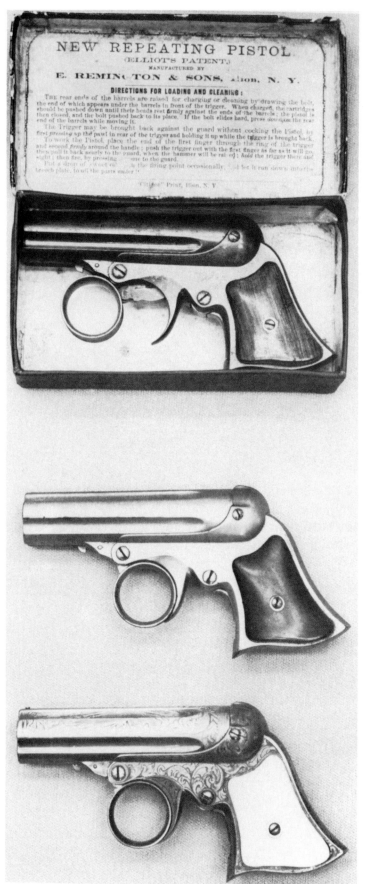

From top to bottom:

Remington-Elliot .22 Caliber Pepperbox Derringer, serial #1507. This derringer is in generally excellent condition, showing virtually no use and only age discoloration; it is in the original cardboard box (5.0" x 2.75" x 1.25") that has a dark purple exterior. Inside the lid are the loading instructions, preceded by "New Repeating Pistol (Elliot's Patent) Manufactured by E. Remington & Sons, Ilion, N.Y." The bottom of the box has the original printed label, "Repeating Pistol 5 Shots No. 22 Cartridge, Plated Frame No. 1507." The interesting thing is that the frame was never plated, nor have there been any corrections to the label. The original wood stocks are in mint condition.

Remington-Elliot .22 Caliber Pepperbox Derringer, serial #1804. With its excellent, original wood stocks, this derringer retains at least 95+ percent of its original nickel plate overall.

Remington-Elliot .22 Caliber Pepperbox Derringer, serial #2162. This derringer, which is in excellent condition, is a rare full factory engraved version, the frame heavily scroll engraved overall, while the barrel group is covered with a floral etched pattern at muzzle and breech, with a trophy of flags in the middle of the barrel. The original ivory stocks are in excellent condition. A most desirable collectible!

From top to bottom:

Remington-Elliot .32 Caliber Pepperbox Derringer, serial #15636. This complete and original derringer is in very fine condition, with excellent gutta-percha stocks. Full factory engraved, the barrel group is covered with a floral pattern, while the frame is fully scroll engraved.

Remington-Elliot .32 Caliber Pepperbox Derringer, serial #16230. As may be seen, this derringer is in excellent original condition, the barrel group retaining most of its original bright blue finish, while the frame has suffered the loss of at least 30 percent of its blue finish. There are little signs of wear to the surfaces or sharp edges of this weapon, and the original varnished rosewood stocks are in outstanding condition.

Boxed Remington-Elliot .32 Caliber Pepperbox Derringer, serial #21706. In very fine condition with thinning blue and excellent varnished rosewood stocks, this derringer is in the original mottled yellow and black cardboard carton (5.375" x 3.125" x 1.50"), the inside lid with the original instruction label, "New Repeating Pistol (Elliot's Patent) Manufactured by E. Remington & Sons, Ilion, N.Y." The bottom of the box has the original label for this particular pistol, "Repeating Pistol, 4 Shots No. 32 Cartridge, Blued. No........"

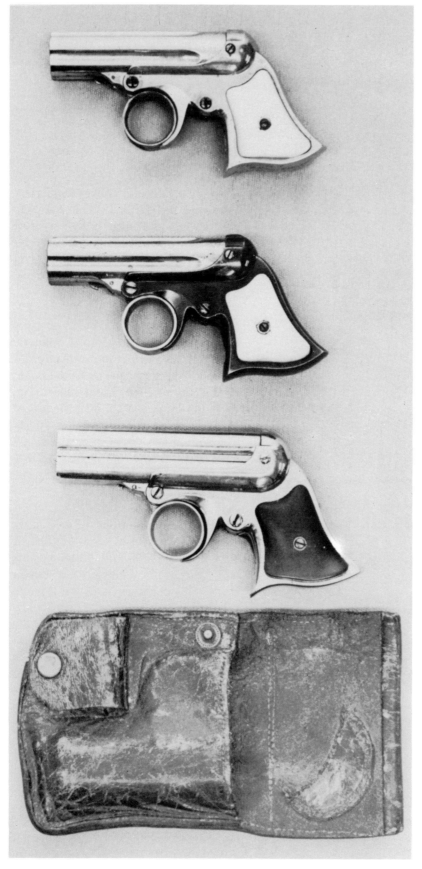

From top to bottom:
Full view of the Remington-Elliot .22 Caliber Pepperbox Derringer, serial #10359.

Remington-Elliot .22 Caliber Pepperbox Derringer, serial #12591. This derringer, which is fitted with lovely, original ivory stocks, is finished in a most unusual manner; the barrel group is nickel-plated, while the frame has a bright, glossy blue finish.

Remington-Elliot .32 Caliber Pepperbox Derringer, serial #392. This derringer retains 99 percent of an old re-nickel plating, and has fine gutta-percha stocks; it comes with the original small leather belt holster that has a pocket for four extra cartridges.

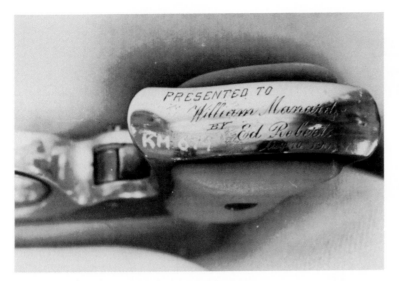

REMINGTON VEST POCKET PISTOL

The Remington Vest Pocket Pistol was also known as "The Saw Handle Derringer," and was manufactured from 1865-1888. The total estimated quantity produced was approximately 25,000 .22 caliber rimfire, single shot with the hammer doubling as a breechblock. The 3.25" round barrel with octagon breech was integral with the frame.

The pistol came with walnut stocks, and could be overall blued or nickel-plate finished. Serial numbers are found on the underside of the barrel and on the grip frame. Barrel markings were: "REMINGTON'S ILION, N.Y. PATENT OCT. 1, 1861." Early production had absolutely no markings anywhere other than serial numbers. This derringer, distintive looking and most unusual, was another of the inventions of William H. Elliot.

Middle pistol: (next page)
Detail showing the engraving "Minnie" on pistol serial #7541.

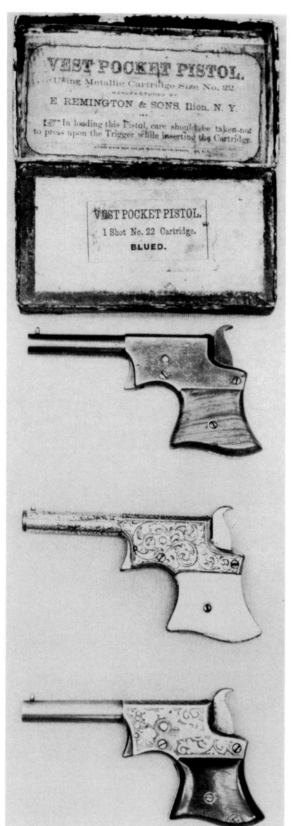

From top to bottom:

Remington Vest Pocket Pistol, serial #3711, with the original cardboard box (4.63" x 2.63" x .875"). The pistol is seen to be in excellent condition, showing minimal wear and with at least 90 percent of the original bright blue finish. Note the grain in the fine original rosewood stocks. The exterior of the box is a purple/black, the inside lid with the original blue label printed in black ink: "Vest Pocket Pistol, Using Metallic Cartridge Size No. 22 Manufactured By E. Remington & Sons, Ilion, N.Y. In loading this pistol care should be taken not to press upon the trigger while inserting the cartridge." The bottom of the box with the original label: "Vest Pocket Pistol, 1 shot No. 22 Cartridge, Blued."

Remington Vest Pocket Pistol, serial #7541. This pistol is in excellent condition, retaining much of the original gold plating on the frame and barrel, while the silver plate on the hammer and trigger are excellent. The frame is extensively covered with scroll engraving, while the top of the frame is engraved with the original inscription "Minnie" in fine script. The original ivory stocks are beautifully age-mellowed.

Remington Vest Pocket Pistol, serial #13288. This pistol is in sharp, crisp condition, but retains little of the original bright blue finish. Marked on the top of the barrel, the frame is completely factory etched with floral decorations. The original rosewood stocks are in fine condition.

From top to bottom:

Remington Vest Pocket Pistol, serial #97. This derringer is one of the early production pieces that was completely unsigned. The pistol, which is in excellent condition, has the original overall scroll and dot pattern engraving on nickel plate, as well as mint mother-of-pearl stocks.

Remington Vest Pocket Pistol, serial #791. In generally excellent condition, with 95+ percent of the original nickel plate, dull case-hardened hammer and trigger, and superb varnished walnut stocks, this is another example of an early, unsigned piece.

Cased Remington Vest Pocket Pistol, serial #912. This very fine specimen is in the original red velvet lined morocco leather covered wooden case (5.0" x 3.0" x 1.0"). This particular specimen is signed on the top of the frame.

Remington Vest Pocket Pistol, serial #1728. This piece, which retains at least 90 percent of its original bright blue finish, is in excellent condition, with fine varnished walnut stocks. The pistol is signed on the top of the frame.

Remington Vest Pocket Pistol, serial #2622. The barrel and frame of this pistol were originally silver plated, but only traces of the finish remain; The hammer, back strap, forestrap, and trigger retain at least 95 percent of the original gold plating. Signed on top of the barrel, the frame is profusely covered with factory scroll engraving. The original ivory stocks are nicely age- mellowed.

Top and bottom:

Remington Vest Pocket Pistol, serial #14608. In excellent condition, this pistol has fine, original rosewood stocks, and is stamped with the legend on top of the frame. Complete with the original cardboard box (4.635" x 2.635" x .875"), the exterior of the box a dark purple/black, with a cream colored label in the lid: "Vest Pocket Pistol, Using Metallic Cartridge Size No. 22 Manufactured By E. Remington & Sons, Ilion, N.Y. in loading this pistol, care should be taken not to press upon the trigger while inserting the cartridge." The bottom of the box with the original label: "Vest Pocket Pistol, 1 Shot No. 22 Cartridge, Blued." It is interesting to compare the colors of the instruction labels used in different boxes (See previous boxed pistol). The box itself is in very good condition, with only the usual scuffing at the edges.

A Pair of Remington-style .22 Caliber Vest Pocket Pistols, no serial numbers. These are quite possibly "lunch box specials," made from original Remington parts; the barrel, trigger, hammer, stocks and stock straps are all apparently original Remington parts. On the other hand, the rounded brass frames are similar to Remington frames, but with some differences. They bear no markings whatsoever and are in a fairly modern case.

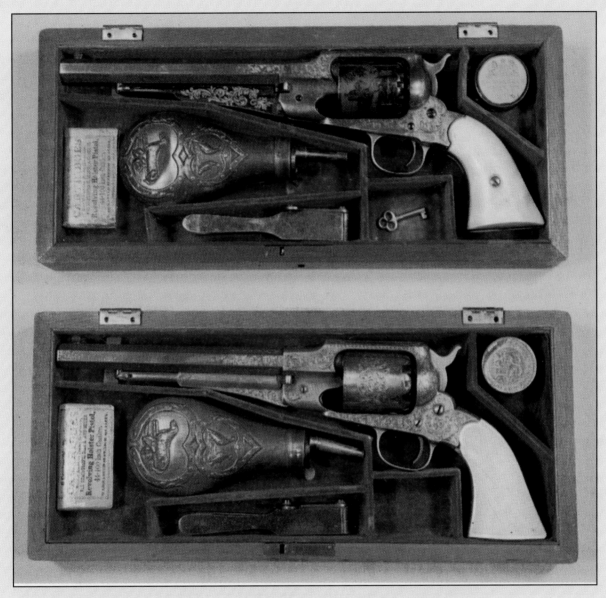

"Two cased special presentation series Remington New Model Army Revolvers."

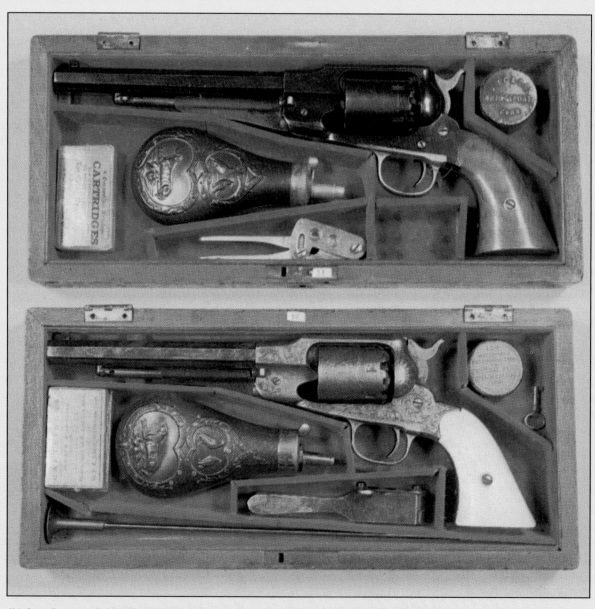

"A lovely cased Civilian Model Remington New Model Army Revolver above, while below is a prime example of a Remington New Model Navy Revolver, fully factory engraved."

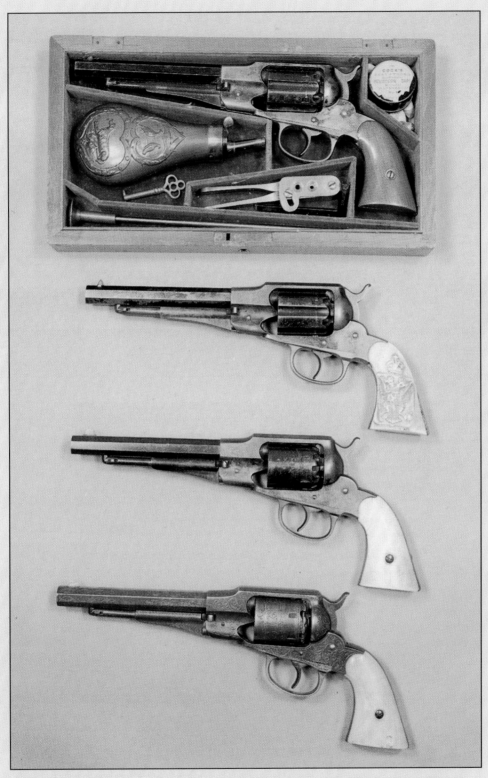

"From top to bottom: A beautiful cased Remington–Rider D.A. New Model Belt Revolver; Remington-Rider D.A. New Model Belt Revolver with full fluted cylinder and original raised, carved ivory grips; Remington-Rider D.A. New Model Belt Revolver with original ivory grips; lastly, a Remington D.A. New Model Belt Revolver fully factory scroll engraved and converted to .38 caliber RF."

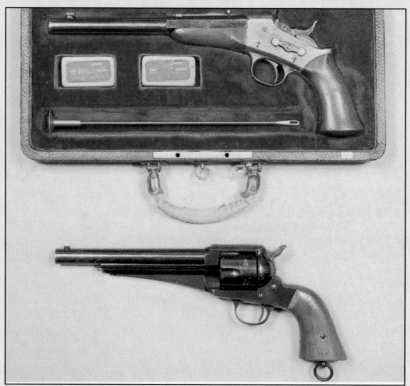

"An exquisite cased fully factory engraved Remington New Model Police Revolver."

Below: "A wonderful cased Remington Model 1891 Target Pistol, beneath which is an outstanding example of the Remington Model 1875 S.A. Army Revolver."

*" Three cased examples of the Remington New Model Police Revolver,
the bottom fully engraved revolver housed in a pipe-style case."*

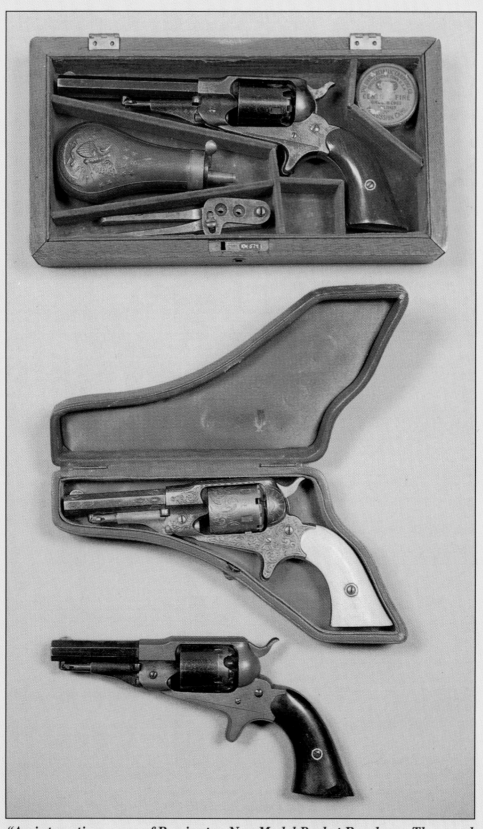

"An interesting array of Remington New Model Pocket Revolvers. The cased piece at the top is the rare 4.50" barrel Third Type with all iron construction, while the middle revolver in the fitted pipe-style case is a fully factory engraved conversion to .32 caliber RF. The bottom revolver is the rare all-brass frame First Type, fitted with a 3.0" barrel.

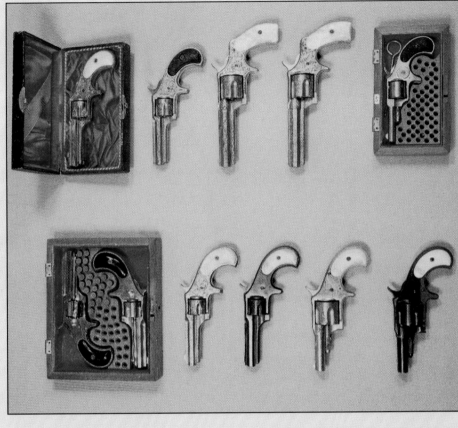

Right Photo: "Illustrated from the top left are: a cased pair of Remington New Model No. 1 Revolvers; a fully factory engraved Remington New Model No. 1 Revolver; a blued finish Remington New Model No. 1 Revolver; a New Model No. 4 Revolver; a Remington New Model No. 4 with original blued finish. From the right top are shown: a cased, fully factory engraved Remington New Model No.2 Revolver; a fully factory engraved New Model No. 2 Revolver; a Remington New Model No.3 Revolver with saw handle; another Remington New Model No.3 Revolver with saw handle; lastly, a cased Remington Iroquois Pocket Revolver with round cylinder."

Left Photo: "From the top to the left bottom are shown a beautiful cased Remington-Rider Percussion Revolver; an exquisite cased Remington-Beals First Model Pocket Revolver, Second Issue; a fine example of the Remington-Beals Second Model Pocket Revolver; lastly; a cased Remington-Beals Third Model Pocket Revolver with rare original floral etched cylinder. On the right, from the top, are three Converted Remington-Rider Pocket Revolvers."

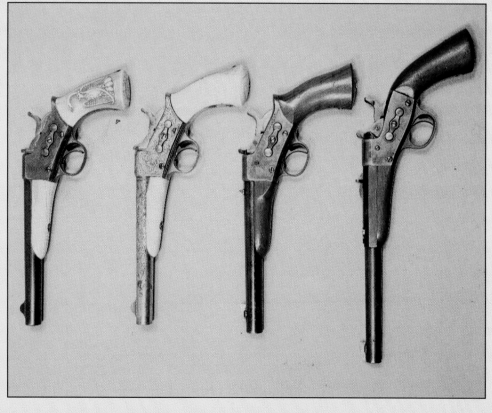

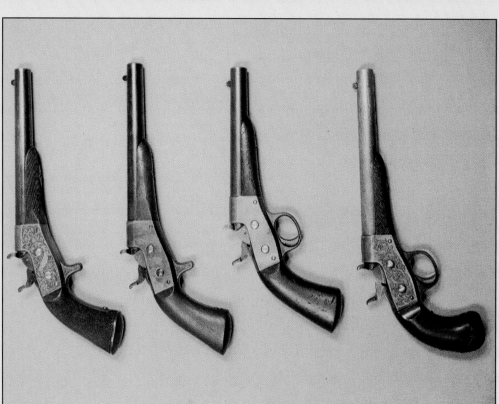

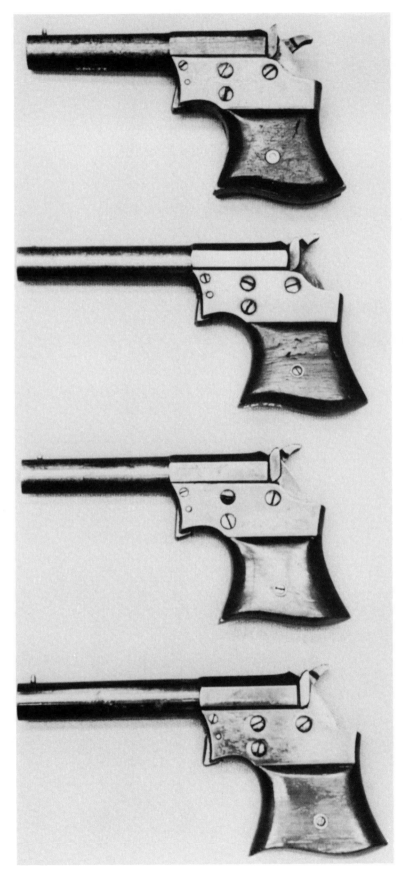

From top to bottom:

Remington Split Breech Derringer, serial #313. This is the early, rare model with brass frame and 3.50" barrel in .30 caliber rimfire in fine condition, naturally age-browned, but still sharp and crisp with good markings. The brass frame, which was originally silver plated, still retains approximately 20 percent of the finish.

Remington Split Breech Derringer, serial #127. Fitted with a .32 caliber 4.0" barrel, this very fine pistol is completely unmarked; while only retaining approximately 40 percent of the original blue finish, there are few signs of wear of any kind. The original rosewood stocks are in fine condition.

Remington Split Breech Derringer, serial #767. In overall fine condition, this derringer, fitted with a .32 caliber 3.50" barrel, retains about 20 percent of the original bright blue finish. The rosewood stocks are in very good condition.

Remington Split Breech Derringer, serial #2341. This derringer is fitted with a .32 caliber 4.0" barrel and is in immaculate condition, showing no signs of wear anywhere. The pistol still retains about 85 percent of the original bright blue finish, and is set off by the beautiful varnished rosewood stocks.

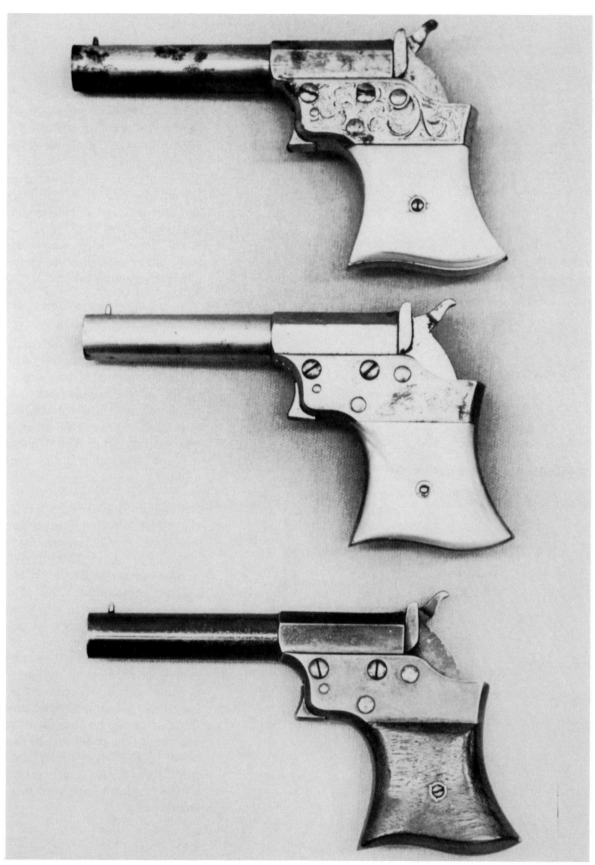

Remington Split Breech Derringers.

REMINGTON SPLIT BREECH DERRINGER/VEST POCKET PISTOL

The Remington split breech derringer, like the Vest Pocket Pistol, was also known as the "Saw Handle Derringer," and was manufactured from c. 1865-1888. The total quantity produced is estimated at less than 10,000. The pistol came in calibers .30, .32, and .41 rimfire (.38 caliber rimfire is sometimes listed, but it is most unlikely that this caliber was ever produced; this is a misconception due to misgauging the .41 caliber model.) For the standard model in .41 caliber, the barrel length was 4.0" part round/part octagon; the iron frame standard models in .30 and .32 caliber had a 3.50" part round/part octagon barrel. The early models with the brass frame are considered quite rare and will often command premium prices.

The pistol came with rosewood stocks, and was available with blued or nickeled finish overall, or any combination of the two. Serially numbered, the barrel markings are: "REMINGTON'S. ILION, N.Y./PATD. OCT 1, 1861. NOV. 15, 1864." These dates refer to both the Elliot and the Rider Patents.

From top to bottom: (previous page)
Remington Split Breech Derringer, serial #169. This pistol, in .41 caliber, is unusual in that the barrel is 4.125" in length. The weapon is factory scroll engraved on the frame only; the frame appears to have been replated many years ago and retains about 90+ percent of this finish. The original ivory stocks have beautifully age-mellowed. As can be seen in the picture, the barrel shows scattered spots of light storage pitting and discoloration.

Remington Split Breech Derringer, serial #1292. Fitted with a .41 caliber 4.0" barrel and original mother-of-pearl stocks, this pistol is in very fine condition with approximately 80 percent of the original nickel plate.

Remington Split Breech Derringer, serial #1622. In excellent condition, this .41 caliber derringer fitted with a 4.0 barrel is a real collector's piece. The barrel and action retain most of their original bright blue finish, while the finish on the frame appears to have mostly flaked away. Excellent varnished walnut stocks.

REMINGTON SPLIT BREECH DERRINGER RIFLE

Is there, or isn't there, such a hybrid as a Remington Split Breech Derringer Rifle? The controversy has apparently gone on for many a year as to whether or not these weapons are a Remington factory product, or the results of a highly competent gunsmith's fancy. The prevailing opinion is that they were the results of the design and execution by one, or several expert gunsmiths during the last quarter of the nineteenth century, using the Split Breech Derringer frame.

Top photo: (next page)
Split Breech Derringer Rifle, no serial number. Fitted with a 9.0" .22 caliber barrel, the weapon measures 10.50" overall; the action has been somewhat modified with the addition of a fitting on the butt, as well as an extension to the trigger. Missing is the folding stock.
Split Breech Derringer Rifle, no serial number. This rifle comes with a 15.50" .22 caliber barrel, and measures 17.50" with the stock folded, and 29.0" overall with the stock in fully extended position. The basic frame has been modified for the attachment of the barrel, the stock fitting, and the folding stock itself. Note that the barrel has been fitted with a rifle-type sight.
Both of these weapons are in generally fine condition, and are indicative of the quality work that went into producing a weapon such as these.

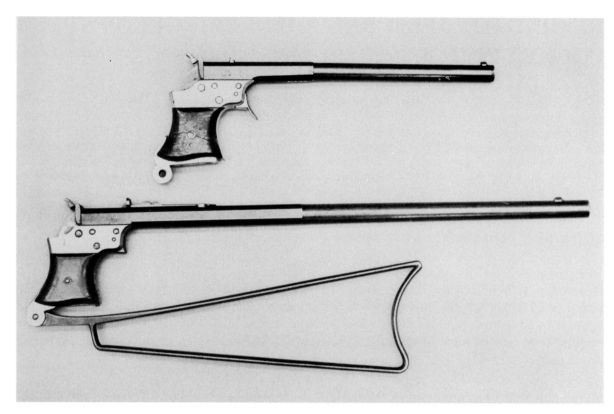

Split Breech Derringer Rifle.

REMINGTON-ELLIOT SINGLE SHOT DERRINGER

The Remington-Elliot Single Shot Derringer was produced c. 1867-1888, with total quantity produced believed to be approximately 10,000. Produced only in .41 caliber rimfire with a 2.50" barrel that screwed into the frame, with a highly ingenious mechanism consisting of a trigger, mainspring, and combination hammer/breechblock. Made with standard walnut stocks, finishes could be either blued, nickel plated, or a combination of both. The derringers are serially numbered under the barrel, and the barrel markings are as follows: "REMINGTONS, ILION, N.Y. ELLIOT PAT. AUG 27, 1867."

Considered one of the most practical and unusual of American derringers, this weapon was the product of William H. Elliot's fertile imagination and inventive genius.

Top and bottom: (next page)
Remington-Elliot Single Shot Derringer, serial #4632. This absolutely gorgeous example of the single shot derringer is in mint condition, with full factory floral engraving and 99+ percent of the original bright nickel plate finish on the frame and the barrel, with a bright blue hammer and trigger. The varnished rosewood stocks are in excellent condition.

Remington-Elliot Single Shot Derringer, serial #6598. An example of a standard pistol off the production line, this derringer is in fine, original condition, with few signs of wear, although the factory blue finish would appear to have flaked off over the years. The varnished rosewood stocks are in fine condition.

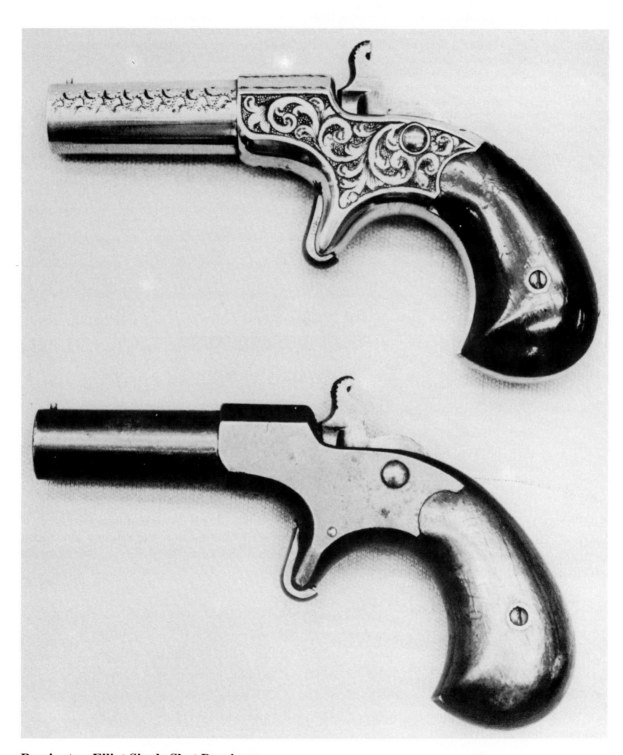

Remington-Elliot Single Shot Derringers.

REMINGTON DOUBLE DERRINGER

The Remington Double Derringer was also known by two other names, "Model 95 Double Derringer," and "Over-Under Derringer." This model was produced between 1866-1935, with the total manufactured estimated at in excess of 150,000. The superposed 3.0" barrels are in .41 caliber; the barrels tip forward for loading and extraction and are locked by a pivoting key on the right side of the frame. The firing pin switches automatically from barrel to barrel.

Stocks could be rosewood, walnut, or hard rubber, and the finish could be blued, nickel plate, or any combination thereof. Barrels are marked on the bottom; serial numbering varied, with some of the numbering sequential, while some groups of derringers were numbered in batches. This makes orderly sequences difficult to determine.

Indisputably one of the best known of American made derringers, this was another design by the talented William H. Elliot; the period of production alone indicates the wide appeal, popularity, and trustworthiness of the design.

Major types of this derringer may be broken down into five basic groups, as follows:

Type I, Early Production. The early models were made without an extractor, and the barrels were marked on the center ribs on each side; "E. REMINGTON & SONS, ILION, N.Y." on one side, and "ELLIOT'S PATENT DEC 12, 1865" on the opposite. Made c. 1865, it is estimated that fewer than 300-400 weapons were produced.

Type I, so-called Transitional Model, c. late 1860s. This model was marked as described above, but was produced with an extractor.

Type I, Late Production, also called the "Third Style;" made c. late 1860s-1888. On this model, the markings are identical, but are in two lines along the top rib of the upper barrel.

Type II. Produced between 1888 and 1911, this type is marked in one line on the top of the upper barrel as follows: "REMINGTON ARMS CO., ILION, N.Y."

Type III. Produced from 1911-1935, this type is marked on the upper barrel in one line, as follows: "REMINGTON ARMS - U.M.C. CO., ILION, N.Y."

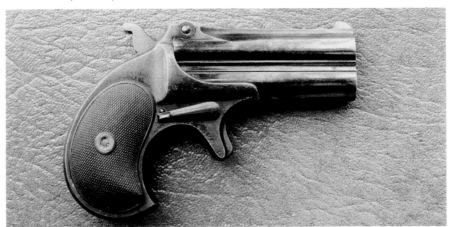

Remington Double Derringer, serial #339. The top barrel flat of this Type II model derringer is marked "REMINGTON ARMS CO., ILION, N.Y." In excellent condition, the original blue finish is starting to to fade and blotch with age, while the original checkered hard rubber stocks are in exceptional condition. In mechanically excellent condition. *(Museum of Connecticut History)*

Left side view of the Remington Double Derringer, serial #339. *(Museum of Connecticut History)*

110

From top to bottom:

Remington Double Derringer, serial #333. This is the extremely rare and desireable Type I, Early Production model made without extractor. This specimen is in fine, original condition, but showing signs of improper storage. It is easy to see that the derringer had minimal usage, as all of the edges are sharp and crisp. The varnished stocks are in fine shape.

Remington Double Derringer, serial #2490. This derringer is the Type I, Late Production model, fitted with an extractor, with the markings on the top rib. This piece is fully-factory engraved overall, with special attention paid to the barrel group. In very fine condition, with the original ivory stocks, this pistol retains virtually all of its old re-nickeled finish.

Remington Double Derringer, serial #3426. This is another Type I, Late Production model, fitted with an extractor and marked on the top rib. This pistol is in very fine condition, with light, original factory engraving on the frame and the rear of the barrel group. Unfortunately, the fine original varnished rosewood stocks show chipping and flaking.

Remington Double Derringer, serial #1. This the Type II model with the top barrel flat marked "REMINGTON ARMS CO., ILION, N.Y." This bright, nickel finish derringer is in mint condition, with blued screws, hammer, trigger, and extractor. This particular weapon comes with the hard rubber stocks. According to Mr. Moldenhauer's records, this is one of three Double Derringers with serial number 1 of which he was aware, indicating that this model was serialized in batches.

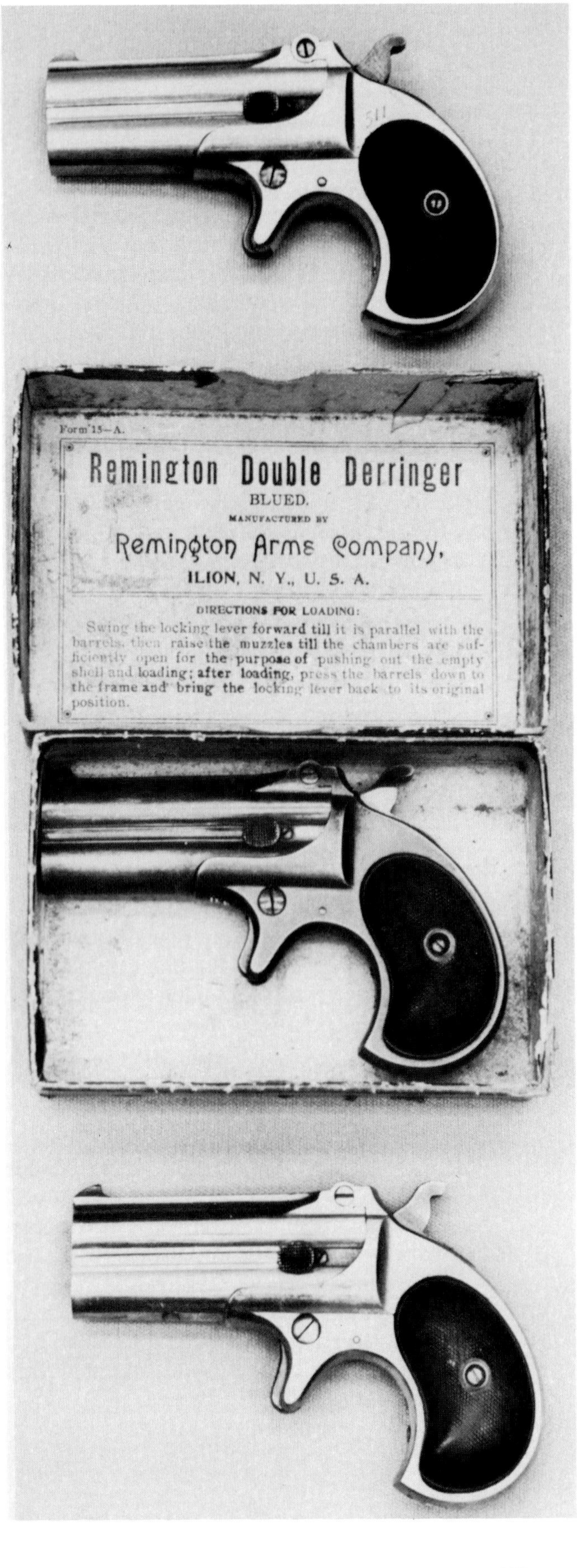

From top to bottom:
Remington Double Derringer, serial #27. The top barrel flat of this Type II model derringer is marked with the "REMINGTON ARMS CO., ILION N.Y." legend. In near mint condition, retaining almost all of its original bright nickel finish, this derringer has excellent hard rubber stocks.

Boxed Remington Double Derringer, serial #406. Although this Type II derringer retains only 25 percent of its original bright blue finish, the pistol shows little, if any, signs of wear, while the original hard rubber stocks are in mint condition. The original dark red cardboard box (5.50" x 3.50" x 1.50") has an end label "Remington Double Derringer, Blued, .41 Caliber Short Rimfire;" while the inside of the lid has the pasted-in instructions, with "Remington Double Derringer/Blued/Manufactured By/Remington Arms Company/Ilion, N.Y., U.S.A."

Unusual Remington Double Derringer, serial #783. The top barrel flat markings indicate that this is a Type II model; in excellent overall condition, it was produced with hard rubber stocks. What makes this derringer unusual and interesting is the fact that the bottom of the barrel group is stamped "U.S. PROPERTY," and the butt is stamped with the flaming U.S. Ordnance bomb. It is common belief that there was never a contract regarding the purchase of any of these weapons by the U.S. Government, but the markings do appear aged and legitimate.

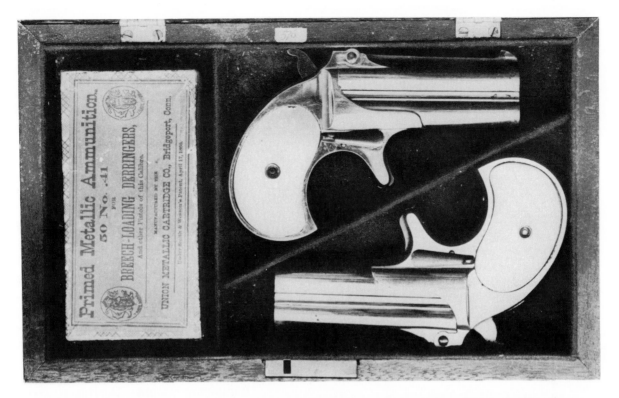

A beautiful cased pair of Remington Double Derringers, serial numbers 741 and 992. Two near mint Type II Double Derringers with bright nickel finish on the barrel groups and frames, blued hammer, screws, trigger, and extractors, both with lovely age-mellowed mother-of-pearl stocks. The old varnished deep blue felt lined walnut case (9.375" x 5.75" x 1.875") comes with a box of early Union Metallic Cartridge Company .41 caliber cartridges marked: "For Breech Loading Derringers, and Other Pistols Of This Caliber."

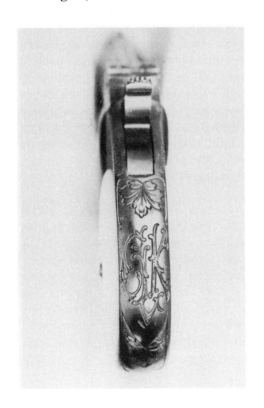

Detail of the back strap engraving on the Double Derringer, serial #155.

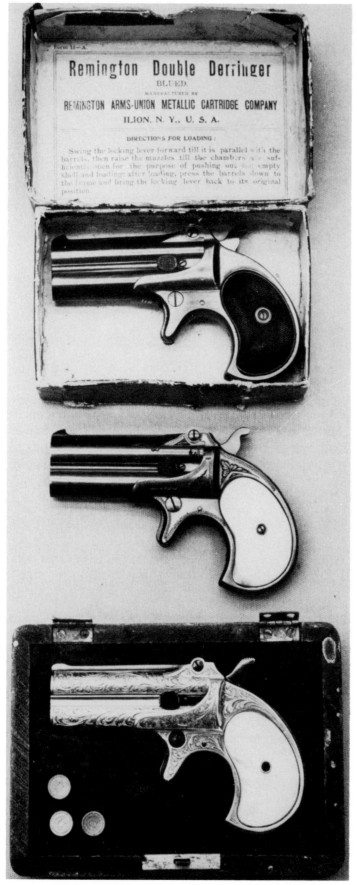

Boxed Remington Double Derringer, serial #70. This Type III model is stamped "REMINGTON ARMS - U.M.C. CO. ILION, N.Y." on the upper barrel flat. In excellent condition, with at least 99+ percent of the original bright blue finish overall, and mint checkered hard rubber stocks. The original cardboard box is labeled at one end of the cover, "Remington UMC Double Derringer Blued 41 Cal Short Rimfire, Remington Arms Works, Ilion, N.Y. U.S.A.," along with an old penciled notation "$6.00". The printed loading instructions are pasted inside the lid, "Remington Double Derringer Blued. Manufactured By Remington Arms - Union Metallic Cartridge Company. Ilion, N.Y., U.S.A."

Remington Double Derringer, serial #155. This is a rare and unique Double Derringer, interesting to both the collector and the student of firearms. This mint Type III model, with perfect original blue finish overall and legend "REMINGTON ARMS - U.M.C. CO., ILION, N.Y.," was specially engraved for Charles Lee Karr, author of *Remington Hand Guns.* Factory engraved, the upper barrel only has been sparsely engraved, as well as the frame with scroll engraving, while the back strap has been finished with ornately entwined initials "CLK." Complete with the original, mint mother-of-pearl stocks, the pistol, interestingly enough, bears British proof marks.

Remington Double Derringer, serial #229. This Type III Derringer is in mint condition, and is completely and elaborately scroll engraved by Kurt Jaeger. Gold plated with blued screws, trigger, hammer, and extractor, the pistol has the original, mint mother-of-pearl stocks. It is displayed in a recent green velvet lined, wooden display case with three extra cartridges.

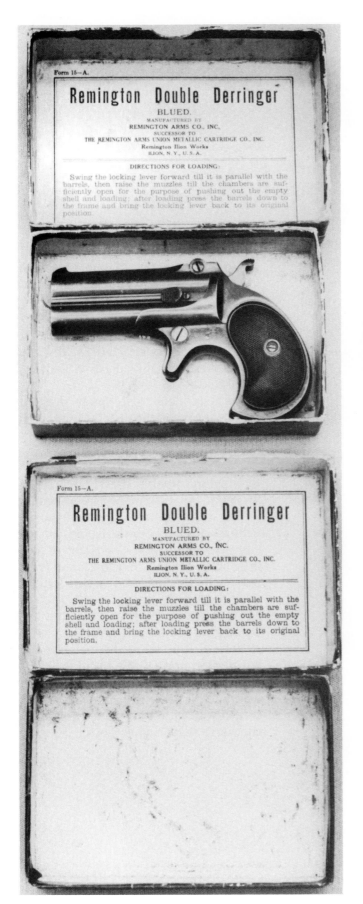

Top and bottom:

Boxed Remington Double Derringer, serial #L99539. In excellent original condition, fitted with the factory standard checkered hard rubber stocks, this pistol is in the original dark red carton (5.50" x 3.50" x 1.50") with the end of the box labeled "Remington Double Derringer, Blued, 41 Caliber Short Rimfire;" the original pasted instruction sheet is in the lid, "Remington Double Derringer/Blued/Manufactured By/Remington Arms Company/ Ilion, N.Y., U.S.A."

An original dark red cardboard carton for the Remington Double Derringer (5.50" x 3.75" x 1.50"), with loading instructions inside the lid, "Remington Double Derringer. Blued. Manufactured by Remington Arms Co., Inc. Successor To The Remington Arms Union Metallic Cartridge Co., Inc. Remington Ilion Works, Ilion, N.Y., U.S.A." The bottom of the box is marked in ink "#992 3rd 5th Issue."

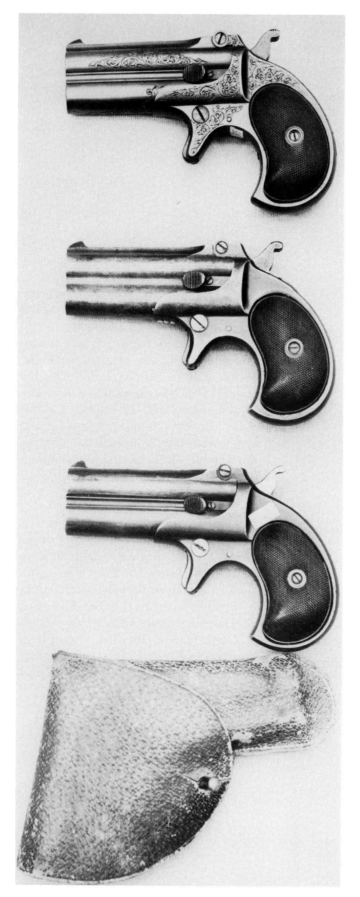

From top to bottom:

Remington Double Derringer, serial #5355. This is a most unusual and outstanding pistol, as it was made for Harry Dunham, the Midwest Representative for Remington Arms; made at the factory circa 1941-1942, the top barrel rib bears the engraved address, "REMINGTON ARMS CO." Very elaborately done with finely detailed scroll engraving, the pistol is fitted with the standard hard rubber factory checkered stocks.

Remington Double Derringer, serial #L76031. An extremely rare variation of the Type III model, manufactured without ribs between the barrels; sharp and crisp otherwise, this pistol retains little of the original blue finish and is fitted with the original hard rubber checkered stocks.

Remington Double Derringer, serial #95926. A Type III model with original flat pigskin holster, this pistol is in fine condition despite the fact that it retains less than 30 percent of its original finish. Fitted with the standard factory checkered hard rubber stocks.

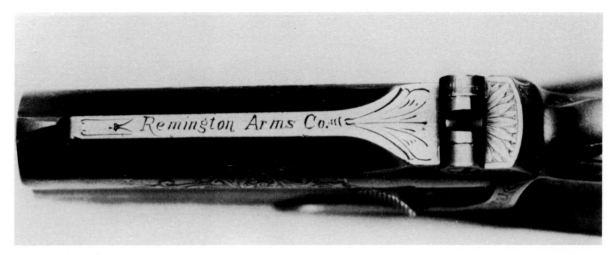

Photo: (top pistol previous page)
Detail picture of the engraved upper barrel flat on Double Derringer, serial #5355.

REMINGTON-RIDER MAGAZINE PISTOL.

The Remington-Rider Magazine Pistol was produced C. 1871-1888, with total production estimated at approximately 10,000. This model was not serially numbered. Made in .32 caliber rimfire extra-short, the five-shot magazine was positioned beneath the 3.0" octagon barrel, loading from the muzzle end, with the breechblock/cartridge carrying mechanism placed adjacent to the hammer. Mother-of-pearl and ivory stocks will often be encountered, although walnut stocks were the standard factory issue.

Most often found with overall nickel plate, specimens have been seen with blued barrels and case-hardened frames, which, being quite scarce, will most often bring a premium. All pistols are marked on the barrel: "E. REMINGTON & SONS, ILION, N.Y./RIDER'S PAT. AUG. 15, 1871."

This is one of the most unusual pocket pistols of the nineteenth century, being one of the first metallic cartridge weapons using a tubular magazine; it is also a tribute to the inventive genius of Joseph Rider. Strange to say, this pistol is most often encountered engraved, while the plain, unengraved weapons are quite scarce. In this instance, scarcity does not appear to increase the value of the pistol.

From top to bottom: (next page)
Remington-Rider Magazine Pistol. This is the extremely rare variation with case-hardened frame and blued barrel. This is probably the best known specimen of this weapon, in almost perfect condition, and fitted with excellent rosewood stocks.

Cased Remington-Rider Magazine Pistol. This pistol, which is in excellent condition, is fully factory engraved and retains at least 98+ percent of the original nickel plate; the original ivory stocks are beautifully age-mellowed, as can be seen by the shading in the photo. The original red flannel lined varnished walnut case is fitted with a cartridge block to hold 12 cartridges, and is in fine condition.

Rare Variation of the Remington-Rider Magazine Pistol. This rarity, which is in fine, crisp condition, with full factory engraving overall, is the blued and case-hardened version. There is much loss of blueing, and the case-hardened color of the frame is mostly gone. With the exception of marring, the original rosewood stocks are in fine condition.

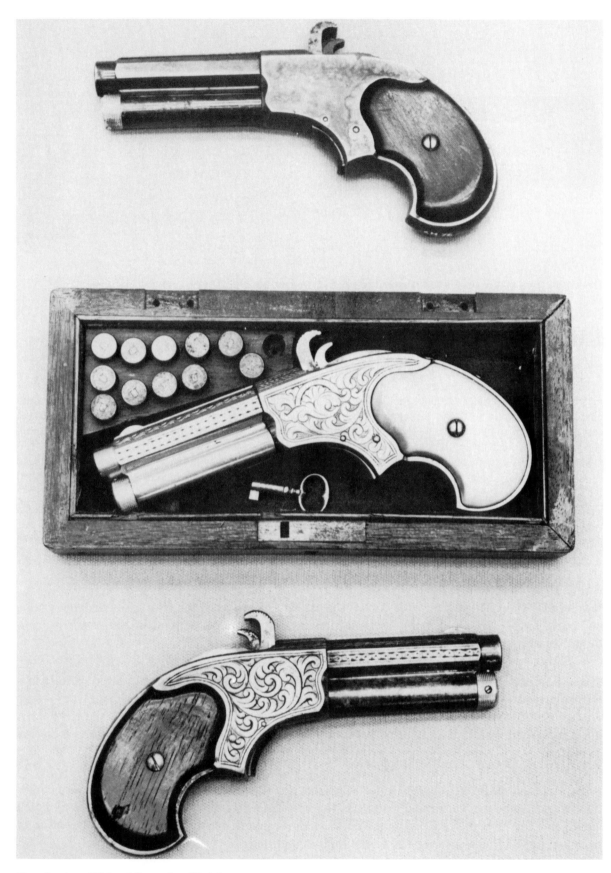

Remington-Rider Magazine Pistols.

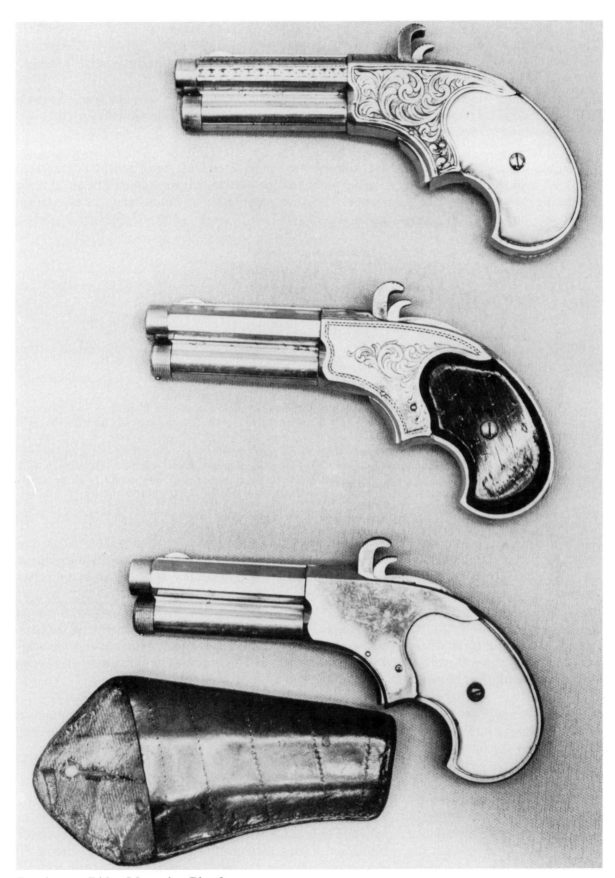

Remington-Rider Magazine Pistols.

From top to bottom: (previous page)
Remington-Rider Magazine Pistol. In excellent plus condition, this factory fully overall engraved pistol retains approximately 98 percent of the original nickel plate, with lovely aged ivory stocks.

Remington-Rider Magazine Pistol. This pistol is in mint condition, with only the frame sparsely engraved. The pistol retains 99+ percent of the original nickel plate finish, while the original varnished rosewood stocks are in fine condition.

Remington-Rider Magazine Pistol. This unengraved model fitted with the original ivory stocks is equipped with the original leather holster designed for attachment to a pants button, thereby facilitating the concealment of the weapon. The pistol and holster, as can be seen, are in excellent condition.

REMINGTON-SMOOT NEW MODEL
No. 1 REVOLVER.

Also termed the No. 1 Revolver-New Model (Smoot's Patent), this revolver is also erroneously known as "New Line Revolver."

No. 1." Produced in .30 caliber rimfire short, the five-shot cylinder is .8125" in length, while the octagon barrel, which is integral with the frame, is 2.8125" in length.

The pistol was made either blued or with full nickel-plate finish, and was supplied with either walnut, composition, or hard rubber stocks. All weapons were serially numbered, and the barrels were marked: "E. REMINGTON & SONS, ILION, N.Y./PAT. W.S. SMOOT OCT. 21, 1873."

This revolver was produced as a competitor to the metallic cartridge pocket revolvers that were being made by Colt; the unusual design of the Remington-Smoot featured a one-piece frame, barrel and ejector housing, and the rod ejector was also special. The rarer early production models featured a revolving recoil shield, while later models were provided with a solid recoil shield permanently affixed to the frame.

From top to bottom: (next page)
Remington-Smoot New Model No. 1 Revolver, serial #644. With at least 90 percent of its original nickel finish remaining, this rare early revolving recoil shield variation is in excellent condition, fitted with the original composition stocks that have the appearance of either ivory or yellow amber.

Remington-Smoot New Model No. 1 Revolver, serial #1524. This revolver, which is in excellent condition, with full factory heavy scroll engraving overall retains at least 99 percent of the original bright nickel finish, with blued screws and trigger. The excellent original mother-of-pearl stocks are beautifully age-mellowed.

Remington-Smoot New Model No. 1 Revolver, serial #1804. In mint condition, with full factory scroll engraving overall and the original mother-of-pearl stocks, this nickel-plate finished revolver is an excellent specimen of its type.

Remington-Smoot New Model No. 1 Revolver, serial #2048. This is a most unusual and rare variation of this revolver, as the pistol is finished in blue as opposed to the nickel-plate version that is most often encountered. The pistol is fitted with original early composition stocks, which are formed, using as a foundation, a metal plate into which holes are drilled upon which the composition is poured and molded, the composition flowing through the holes to form the base of the stocks. Aside from some age discoloration to the frame, the pistol appears to show little evidence of use.

Remington-Smoot New Model No. 1 Revolvers.

121

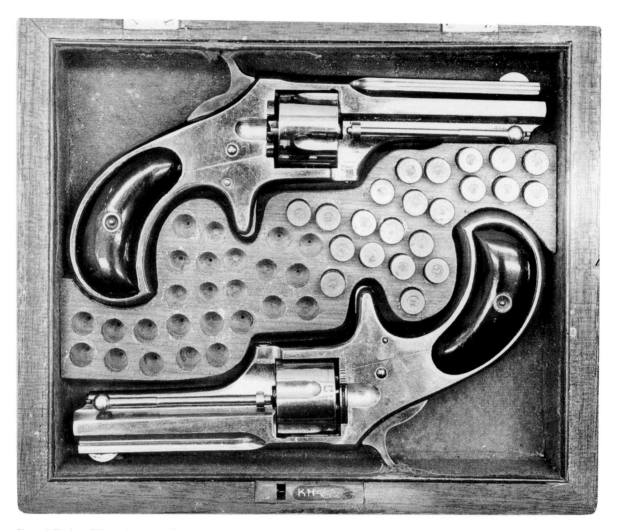

Cased Pair of Remington-Smoot New Model No. 1 Revolvers, serial numbers 452 and 654. Both of these revolvers are in mint condition, with at least 99.5 percent of the original nickel finish remaining, bright case-hardened hammers, triggers, and blued screws, with absolutely excellent original rosewood stocks. #452 is the rare variation with the revolving recoil shield. Cased in the original red flannel lined, varnished walnut case (8.0" x 6.63" x 2.0") with an elaborate outlined cartridge block, complete with 22 of the raised "H"-head stamped cartridges. This cased set was originally in the collection of the late William M. Locke.

REMINGTON-SMOOT NEW MODEL
No. 2 REVOLVER.

The No. 2 Revolver-New Model (Smoot's Patent) is most easily termed the Remington-Smoot New Model No. 2; it is also erroneously called the "New Line Revolver No. 2." Produced c. 1878-1888, with a continuing controversy regarding the number made, which is considered to be approximately 20,000. There is also some confusion as to the caliber of the pistols produced; long thought to have been produced in .32 caliber short rimfire only, several examples in this section are unquestionably in the original .30 caliber rimfire! The cylinder measures .875" long, while the 2.75" octagon barrel is forged integral with the frame.

The pistol was supplied with checkered hard rubber stocks, and the finish was either blued or nickel plated, the hammer was case-hardened and the trigger blued in all cases. All guns were serially numbered, and the barrel address was identical to the New Model No. 1. It is believed that all weapons were produced with a solid recoil shield, however, the possibility exists that some could have been manufactured with a revolving recoil shield; this naturally would make any such specimen a desirable rarity.

From top to bottom:

Remington-Smoot New Model No. 2 Revolver, serial #704. What is interesting about this pistol is the fact that the original cardboard box is marked "No. 1, 32 CTG. FULL PLATE," as well as the penciled notation "#704.", while the pistol is in .30 rimfire short. The original carton (7.50" x 3.0" x 1.25") has a light green exterior with a gold line around the top edge; inside the cover are the original instructions for use of the pistol. The nickel-plated pistol is in excellent condition, as are the checkered hard rubber stocks.

Remington-Smoot New Model No. 2 Revolver, serial #977. This absolutely mint condition nickel-plated revolver in .30 caliber rimfire short is shown in the original cardboard box (7.50" x 3.0" x 1.25") with a dark green exterior incorporating a lighter green stripe around the top edge of the box; the interior of the lid has the pasted-in instructions for use of the weapon. Complete with case-hardened hammer, blued screws, trigger, and absolutely perfect hard rubber stocks.

Remington-Smoot New Model No. 2 Revolver, serial #1360. Full factory engraved in excellent condition, this nickel-plated revolver is in .32 caliber rimfire short; the hammer retains the distinctive case-hardened colors, while the screws and trigger are bright blue finished. Excellent hard rubber checkered stocks. Shown in the original cardboard box (7.50" x 3.0" x 1.25") with green exterior and the pasted-in instructions for use of the pistol. "Manufactured by E. Remington & Sons, Ilion, N.Y. (Smoot's Patent.)," the bottom of the box stamped "FULL PLATE No......Ctg."

123

Cased Remington-Smoot New Model No. 2 Revolver.

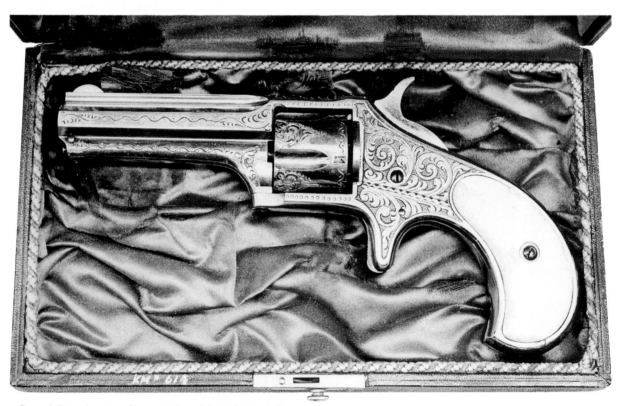

Cased Remington-Smoot New Model No. 2 Revolver.

124

Top photo: (previous page)

Cased Remington-Smoot New Model No. 2 Revolver, serial #63. This nickel-plated .32 caliber rimfire short pistol is in mint condition, with 99 percent of the original finish remaining; the hammer is case-hardened and the trigger blued. The original mother-of-pearl stocks are beautifully age-mellowed. The original red flannel lined varnished walnut case (8.0" x 4.875" x 1.75") is partitioned for inclusion of a box of cartridges, cleaning equipment, or oil bottle.

Bottom photo: (previous page)

Cased Remington-Smoot New Model No. 2 Revolver, serial #134. This beautiful mint condition .32 caliber rimfire short specimen is fully factory scroll engraved overall; nickel-plated with bright blue screws and trigger, the revolver has the original mother-of-pearl stocks. The deluxe dealer style case, of the type used by Schuyler, Hartley, and Graham (7.25" z 4.25" x 2.0"), has a morocco leather covered beveled lid, and is lined with red satin, with a diagonal gold satin ribbon in the lid. The bottom of the case is lined with red and cream colored cord piping.

REMINGTON-SMOOT NEW MODEL No. 3 REVOLVER

The No. 3 Revolver-New Model (Smoot's Patent) is more familiarly known as the Remington-Smoot New Model No. 3 Revolver, while also termed erroneously "New Line Revolver No. 3". Manufactured c. 1878-1888, the total production, including both styles of grip, is estimated at about 25,000. Produced in .38 caliber rimfire short; some pieces were made in .38 caliber centerfire, which will command a premium.

The five-shot cylinder is 1.813" in length, while the 3.75" octagon barrel is screwed into the frame. Serially numbered, the barrel markings are identical to Models No. 1 and No. 2; the finish was blued or full nickel plate, and the stocks were checkered hard rubber. The pistol was produced with two styles of grip; the saw-handle version and the bird's head grip style.

From top to bottom: (next page)

Remington-Smoot New Model No. 3 Revolver, serial #13531. In .38 caliber centerfire, this bird's head grip version without barrel rib is in mint condition; full factory engraved overall, the nickel-plate finish is immaculate, as are the checkered hard rubber stocks.

Remington-Smoot New Model No.3 Revolver, serial #17183. This revolver is the bird's head grip variation with barrel rib in .38 caliber centerfire. This revolver is in mint condition with bright nickel finish, blued screws and wonderful checkered hard rubber stocks.

Remington-Smoot New Model No. 3 Revolver, serial #23244. This is the saw-handle version with barrel rib in .38 caliber rimfire, with extensive full factory engraving overall; fitted with the original age-mellowed mother-of-pearl stocks. In mint condition with at least 99 percent of the original nickel-plate finish and blued screws.

Remington-Smoot New Model No.3 Revolver, serial #24306. In mint, nickel-plated condition with blued screws, this saw-handled version with barrel rib is fitted with the original mother-of-pearl stocks.

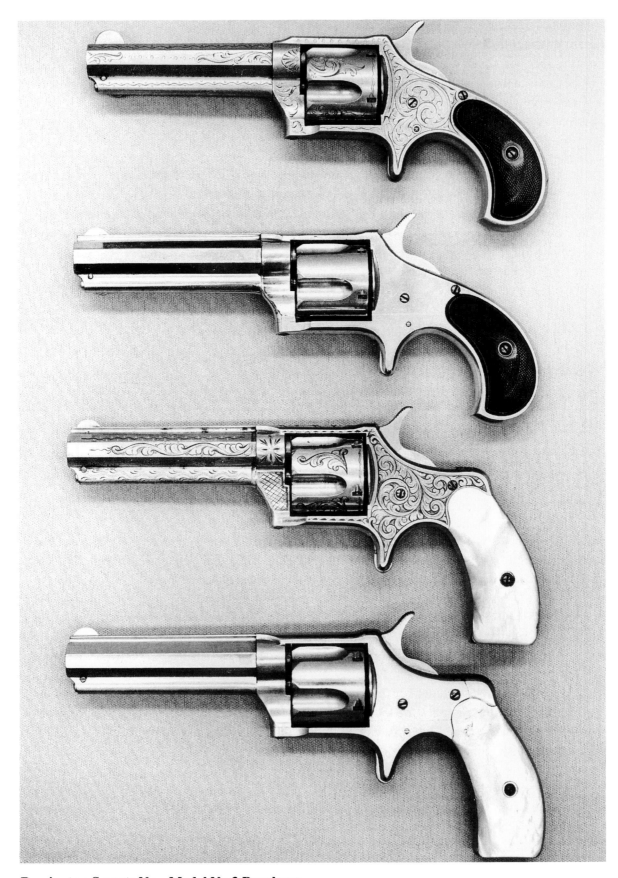

Remington-Smoots New Model No.3 Revolvers.

126

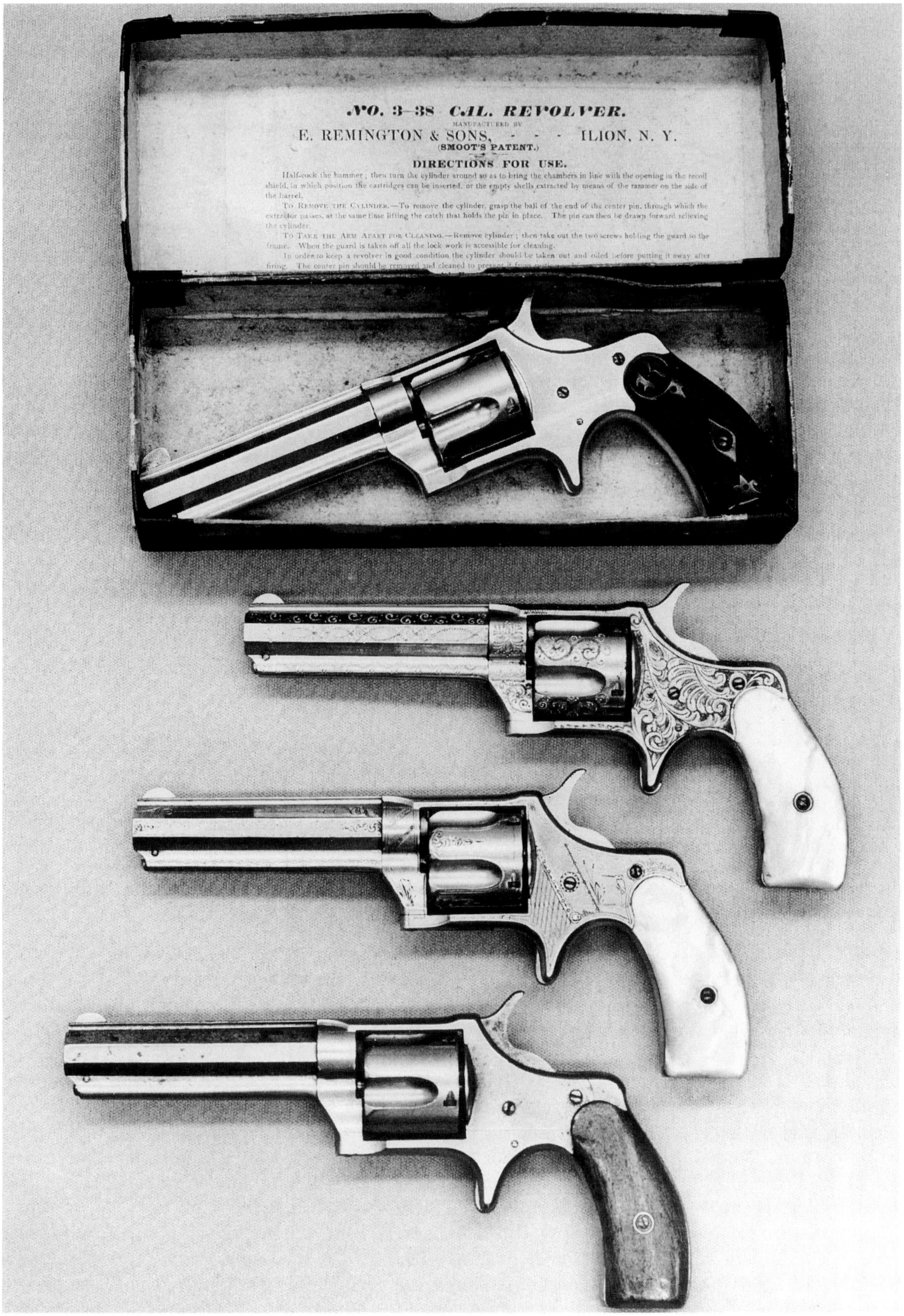
NO. 3—38 CAL. REVOLVER.
MANUFACTURED BY
E. REMINGTON & SONS, - - - ILION, N. Y.
(SMOOT'S PATENT.)
DIRECTIONS FOR USE.
Half-cock the hammer; then turn the cylinder around so as to bring the chambers in line with the opening in the recoil shield, in which position the cartridges can be inserted, or the empty shells extracted by means of the rammer on the side of the barrel.
TO REMOVE THE CYLINDER.—To remove the cylinder, grasp the ball of the end of the center pin, through which the extractor passes, at the same time lifting the catch that holds the pin in place. The pin can then be drawn forward relieving the cylinder.
TO TAKE THE ARM APART FOR CLEANING.—Remove cylinder; then take out the two screws holding the guard to the frame. When the guard is taken off all the lock work is accessible for cleaning.
In order to keep a revolver in good condition the cylinder should be taken out and oiled before putting it away after firing. The center pin should be removed and cleaned to

Boxed Remington-Smoot New Model No. 3 Revolvers.

Boxed Remington-Smoots New Model No. 3 Revolver, serial #24351. This saw-handle model with barrel rib is in excellent nickel-plated condition, with mint, checkered hard rubber stocks, sporting a fancy "R" monogram. Shown in the original green cardboard box (8.63" x 3.25" x 1.50") with instructions on the inside of the lid; "No. 3 - 38 Cal Revolver. Manufactured by E. Remington & Sons, - - - Ilion, N.Y. (Smoot's Patent.)." Note that the edges of the box have been repaired at some time in the past with black masking tape.

Remington-Smoot New Model No. 3 Revolver, serial #27409. This saw-handle variation with barrel rib in .38 caliber rimfire is full factory engraved in a most pleasing scroll design, retaining at least 98+ percent of the original nickel plate. The mother-of-pearl stocks, which are original, have beautifully age-mellowed.

Remington-Smoot New Model No. 3 Revolver, serial #27455. This is the saw-handle model in .38 caliber centerfire. Note the unusual overall factory engraving; light scrollwork is visible on the barrel and cylinder, while the left side of the frame shows an unusual panel with a heron in a marsh. On the right side of the frame are geometric patterns, scrollwork and a small view of marshland. The revolver is in immaculate condition, with at least 99+ percent of the original nickel-plate finish, and mint age-mellowed mother-of-pearl stocks.

Remington-Smoot New Model No. 3 Revolver, serial #27837. This saw-handle model is in .38 caliber centerfire, fitted with plain varnished wood stocks. Originally marked on the butt "27837 U.S.A.". As can be seen, the original nickel plate finish is in a fine, smooth condition, with at least 90+ percent of the finish remaining.

REMINGTON-SMOOT NEW MODEL No. 4 REVOLVER.

Known as the Remington New Model No. 4 Revolver, but also mistakenly termed the "New Line Revolver No. 4," this revolver was produced from 1877-1888, with the total quantity manufactured estimated at approximately 10,000.

Made either in .38 caliber rimfire or centerfire short, or in .41 caliber rimfire or centerfire short, with a cylinder measuring 1.625" in length, and a round barrel 2.50" long that screwed into the frame. Made without an ejector rod.

Finishes were either blued or full nickel plate, with all pieces serially numbered. Barrel markings are "E. REMINGTON & SONS, ILION, N.Y."

Remington-Smoot New Model No.4 Revolver, serial #691. This nickel-plate version of the No. 4 revolver is lightly factory engraved, and is in .38 caliber rimfire; in very fine condition overall, the original hard rubber stocks are excellent.

Cased pair of Remington-Smoot New Model No. 4 revolvers, serial numbers 4676 in .38 caliber rimfire, and 7392 in .41 caliber rimfire. While not matching or consecutively numbered, the two nickel-plated revolvers are identically full factory engraved with the same scroll and leaf patterns. In both cases, the pistols are fitted with ivory-like composition stocks. The purple velvet lined, partitioned case (5.635" x 8.375" x 2.125"), while undoubtedly a pistol box, is not a period piece.

Remington-Smoot New Model No. 4 Revolver, serial #4849. This nickel-plate, full factory engraved specimen in .38 caliber rimfire, is in excellent condition. The stocks, in this case, are a dark brown hard rubber in mint condition. Notice the slight differences in the engraving on the frame as compared with pistol serial #691 at the top of the picture. While the concept is consistent, the factory engraving would sometimes vary from piece to piece.

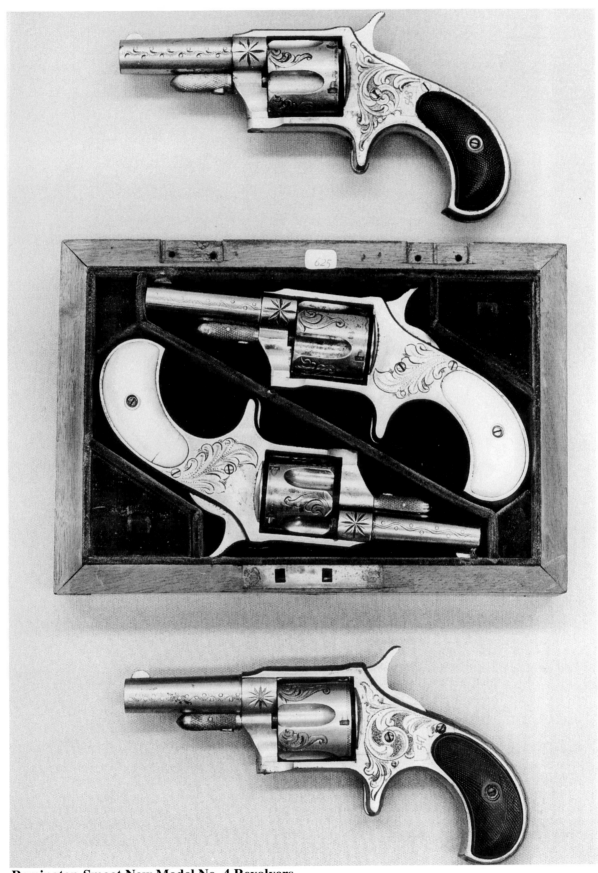

Remington-Smoot New Model No. 4 Revolvers.

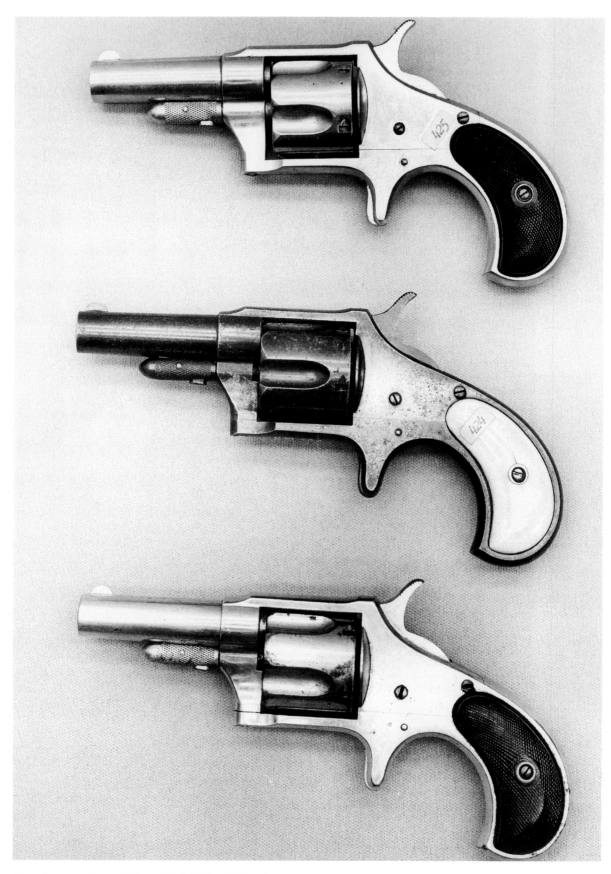

Remington-Smoot New Model No. 4 Revolvers.

130

From top to bottom: (previous page)

Remington-Smoot New Model No 4. Revolver, serial #9747. Apparently this cylinder was re-nickeled at some time in the past, with an excellent job being done; the remainder of the pistol shows the original nickel plate to good advantage, setting off the blued screws. The checkered hard rubber stocks are in mint condition, showing virtually no wear.

Remington-Smoot New Model No. 4 Revolver, serial #10273. This pistol, in .38 caliber centerfire, is another rare variation with full blue finish overall, original genuine ivory stocks, and British proof marks. As can be discerned, the original blue finish has mixed with flaking and brown age patina, which does not take away from the fine appearance of the weapon.

Remington-Smoot New Model No. 4 Revolver, serial #11193. Retaining at least 85 percent of the original nickel plate, this revolver is in very fine to excellent condition; the hard rubber black checkered stocks are in fine shape. Note the trace of finish loss on the cylinder.

From top to bottom: (next page)

Remington-Smoot New Model No. 4 Revolver, serial #12119. With approximately 98 percent of the original nickel finish remaining, this revolver in .38 caliber rimfire is in excellent-plus condition, with the original fine black checkered hard rubber stocks.

Remington-Smoot New Model No. 4 Revolver, serial #13948. With excellent checkered hard rubber stocks, this overall nickel-plated revolver in .41 caliber centerfire retains approximately 95 percent of the original nickel plate. Due to a light, professional cleaning, it is virtually impossible to determine where the nickel plate ends and begins. The original checkered hard rubber stocks are in very fine condition.

Remington-Smoot New Model No. 4 Revolver, serial #18492. This revolver, in .38 caliber rimfire, is perhaps a unique variation with a rebated cylinder and flat-head oversized frame screws that enter from the left side of the frame (the usual screws are roundhead and smaller). The original finish is no longer evident, with the entire pistol now a smooth, even natural steel coloration; the checkered black hard rubber stocks are original to the gun. This piece was at one time a part of the William M. Locke collection.

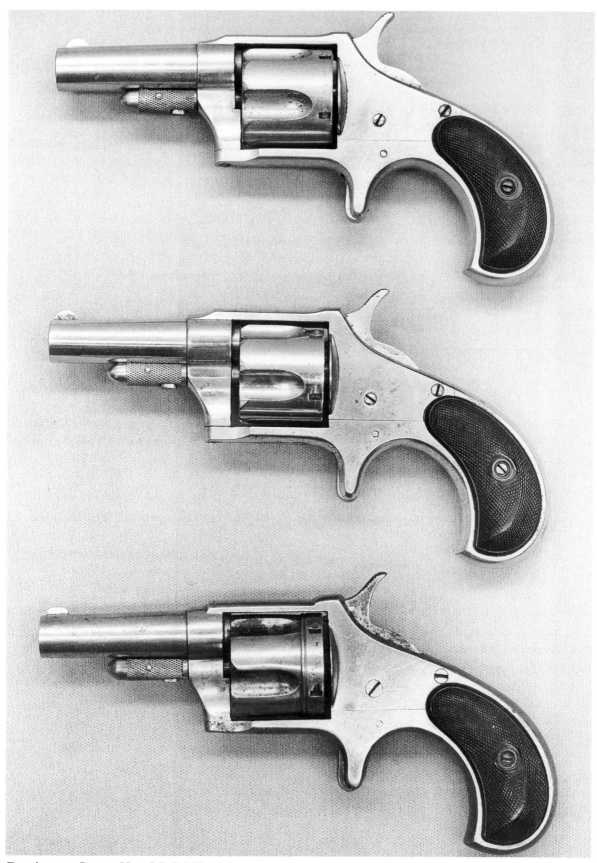

Remington-Smoot New Model No. 4 Revolvers.

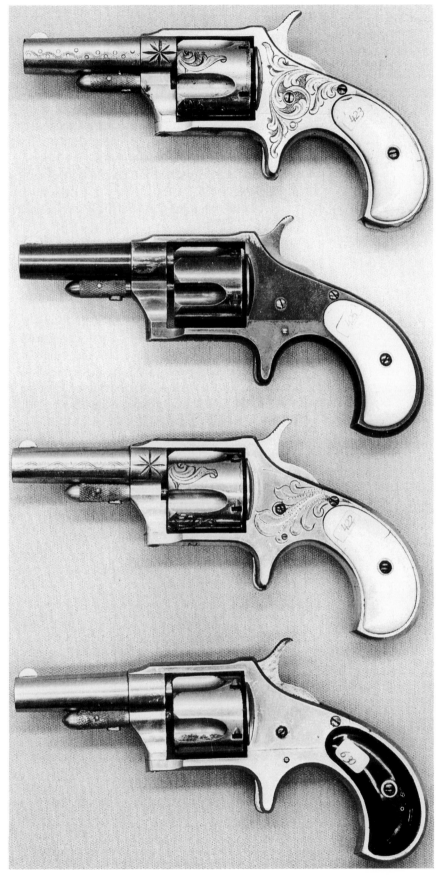

From top to bottom:

Remington-Smoot New Model No. 4 Revolver, serial #5423. In .38 caliber rimfire, this nickel-plated, overall factory engraved revolver is in excellent, complete condition. The very fine, age-mellowed ivory-like composition stocks are original to the pistol. Note the pleasing flow of the scroll engraving on both frame and cylinder.

Rare Variation Remington-Smoot New Model No. 4 Revolver, serial #5996. This pistol, in .41 caliber centerfire, is stamped with British proofs, an extremely rare variation with excellent original blued finish. The stocks are the ivory-like composition variety as originally furnished.

Remington-Smoot New Model No. 4 Revolver, serial #7272. Overall factory engraved and fitted with original ivory-like composition stocks, this .38 caliber rimfire pistol is in near mint condition. The revolver retains 99 percent of the original nickel plate finish, with bright blued screws. Compare the graceful lines of the engraving on this piece with the top revolver; both are elegant in their own manner.

Remington-Smoot New Model No. 4 Revolver, serial #9561. In .41 caliber rimfire, this revolver is in excellent condition, with at least 95+ percent of the original nickel plate remaining; the finish is only marred by the stripe of age discoloration seen on the cylinder. The black composition stocks, which are in fine condition, are similar to the ivory-like composition used.

133

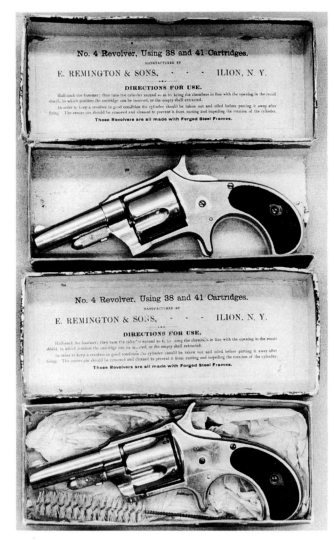

Boxed Remington-Smoot New Model No. 4 Revolver, serial #19542. This is an absolutely mint condition pistol in .38 caliber rimfire, with full bright nickel-plate finish, blued screws and the original checkered black hard rubber stocks. The original green cardboard box (7.50" x 3.0" x 1.50") is complete with the directions in the lid, "No. 4 Revolver, Using 38 and 41 Cartridges. Manufactured by E. Remington & Sons - - - Ilion, N.Y.," the bottom of the box rubber stamped "FULL PLATE. NO. 4 - 38. Rim Fire."

Boxed Remington-Smoot New Model No. 4 Revolver, serial #22528. This pistol is in mint, unfired condition, still in the original tissue paper lining the box. In .38 caliber rimfire, this pistol is perfect, with 100 percent bright nickel finish, blued screws, and checkered black hard rubber stocks. In the original green colored cardboard box (7.50" x 3.0" x 1.50"), with a yellow stripe around the top edge, and directions for use inside the lid, "No. 4 Revolver, Using 38 and 41 Cartridges. Manufactured by E. Remington & Sons,- - - Ilion, N.Y.," rubber stamped on the bottom of the box, "FULL PLATE. NO. 4 - 38. Rim Fire." The number 22528 is marked in pencil. Complete with original wire brush.

REMINGTON IROQUOIS POCKET REVOLVER.

The Iroquois Pocket Revolver was produced from 1878-1888, with the total quantity manufactured estimated at approximately 10,000. Actually a scaled-down version of the Remington-Smoot New Model No. 4, this pistol was produced as competition to the Colt New Line .22 caliber revolver, which it outwardly resembled.

Made in .22 caliber rimfire, the seven-shot cylinder was produced in either plain or fluted form, while the 2.25" round barrel screwed into the frame; this model was made without an ejector rod. Available in either all blue or nickel-plate finish, the standard stocks were checkered hard rubber.

These pistols were not serially numbered, and were usually, but not always, marked on the top of the barrel "IRO-QUOIS," and on the side of the barrel "REMINGTON, ILION, N.Y." These pistols will often be found unmarked, and correctly so, while others will be encountered with just the "IROQUOIS" barrel marking, omitting the Remington markings.

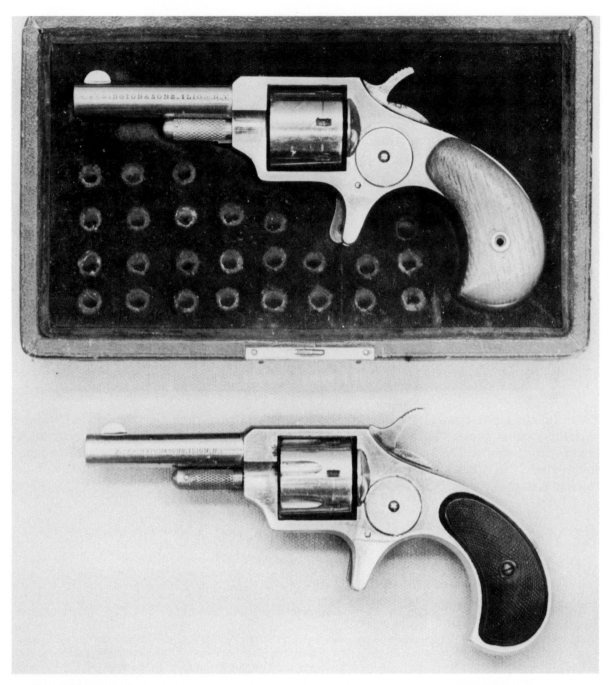

Top and bottom:

Cased Remington Iroquois Revolver. This round cylinder variation pistol has the large address on the barrel, and is generally in excellent condition. The pistol retains at least 98 percent of the overall nickel-plate finish, with the hammer dulled and the trigger and frame screw blued. Both the cylinder pin and the wooden stocks are extremely well made replacements; unfortunately, the attachment screw for the stocks is missing. The attractive bright purple lined, black leather case with integral cartridge block is in excellent condition.

Remington Iroquois Revolver. This fluted cylinder version revolver is in immaculate condition, retaining at least 98 percent of the original bright nickel-plate finish; the case-hardened hammer shows its distinctive colors to advantage, while the blued trigger can just be seen. The checkered black hard rubber stocks are in fine plus condition.

135

Cased Remington Iroquois Revolver. This excellent nickel-plated specimen of the round cylinder variation retains at least 98 percent of the original finish, while the checkered hard rubber stocks are in crisp condition. The dull case-hardened hammer and trigger can be seen to good advantage in this photo. The original red flannel lined walnut case (6.75" x 4.0" x 1.63") is complete with the original walnut cartridge block as well as simple steel 4.125" cleaning rod.

REMINGTON MODEL 1875 SINGLE ACTION ARMY REVOLVER

The Remington Model 1875 Single Action Army Revolver was manufactured c. 1875-1889, with the total quantity produced estimated at approximately 25,000.

This was an attempt by Remington to compete with the Colt Single Action Army Revolver, although this effort was hindered by Colt's early advantage in government sales. No records exist to show that there were sales to U.S. military organizations, although many collectors have theorized on this possibility. In the year 1883, the Interior Department purchased approximately 1,300 nickel-plated pistols for use by the Indian Police on the various reservations scattered across the West; unfortunately, no records exist today to show exactly how these pieces were marked. One martial contract that was obtained in 1875 was from the Egyptian government for troop use in the Sudan; these revolvers were to see much use in the future Sudanese campaigns.

Throughout most of the production of this series, the pistol was made in standard .44 caliber Remington center-fire; later production saw the introduction of some specimens in .44-40 caliber, which command a premium from collectors. Apparently, the Remington catalogs of the period list some revolvers in .45 caliber Government; however any weapons encountered in this caliber should be examined by an expert, as they were extremely scarce.

Between 1879 and 1889, the Mexican government purchased an estimated 1,000 Model 1875 Remington Revolvers in .45 caliber to supplement the .45 caliber Colt Single Action Revolvers previously purchased. Known as the "Improved Army," they were supplied with a nickel-plate finish and were equipped with a lanyard ring. Barrels were marked "E. REMINGTON & SONS, ILION, N.Y., U.S.A.," while the Mexican government then added the Mexican Liberty Cap on sunburst over "R" and "M". Cylinders were marked "R de M" between the locking notches, while the web below the ejector rod was marked on the right side "R de M", with acceptance marks "R" on the left side of both frame and barrel. ".45" was stamped on the back of the cylinder.

The six-shot cylinder was fluted, with a standard 7.50" round barrel; a few pieces were made in the original 5.50" barrel length. However, once again these should be examined carefully before buying, as many that are found on the market are fakes that have been carefully doctored to appear original. One of the distinctive features of the Model 1875 is the web-like contour on the underside of the ejector housing.

Manufactured with walnut stocks, pistols may be found with or without lanyard rings at the butt. The finish available was blued with case-hardened hammer and loading gate, or an overall nickel-plate finish. Serial numbers were batched, thus many pistols will be found with low serial numbers. The barrels were marked "E. REMINGTON & SONS, ILION, N.Y. U.S.A."

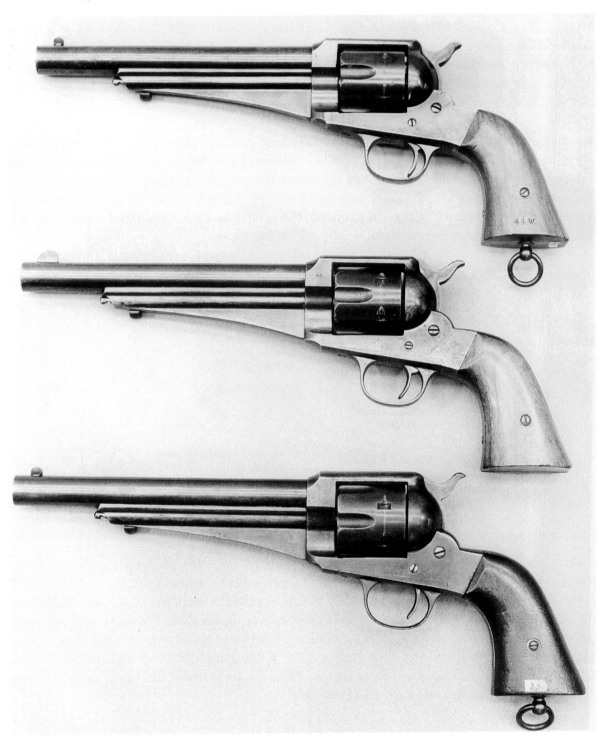

Remington New Model 1875 Single Action Army Revolvers.

From top to bottom: (previous page)

Remington New Model 1875 Single Action Army Revolver, serial #145. As may be seen, this pistol, in .44-40 caliber, is in virtually mint condition, showing little, if any, signs of use. The bright blue finish is excellent, with only slight tracking to be seen on the cylinder. The case-hardened hammer shows to good effect, while the oil-finished walnut stocks are near perfect. Marked on the left stock, "44.W." and the butt is fitted with a lanyard ring.

Remington New Model 1875 Single Action Army Revolver, serial #856, in caliber .44-40. This is another example of this weapon in excellent condition, showing few signs of use, other than tracking on the cylinder. The finish shows fading and would rate at approximately 85 percent remaining. The case-hardened hammer is most distinctive, and the oil-finished walnut stocks rate as excellent. Note the stamped "44" on the left front of the frame.

Remington Model 1875 New Model Single Action Army Revolver, serial #8923. This sharp, crisp, martially marked specimen is in overall excellent condition, showing few signs of usage. The finish has faded and turned an age-brown, while the case-hardened hammer can be seen with its distinctive dulled color. Fitted with a lanyard ring on the butt, the left side of the barrel is marked with a star and "R", with another "R" on the left front of the frame and one also on the cylinder. The left stock bears an indistinct inspection mark within a cartouche.

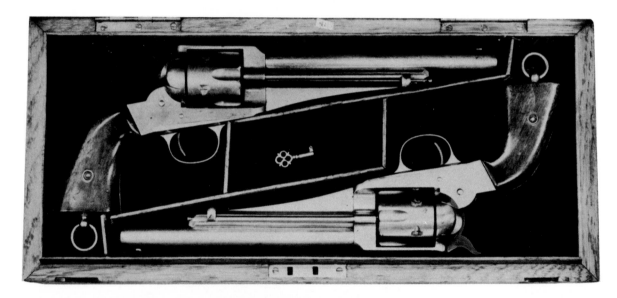

Cased Consecutively Numbered Pair of Remington Model 1875 New Model Single Action Army Revolvers, serial numbers 13207 and 13208, both nickel-plated weapons in caliber .44 Remington centerfire. Both pistols retain approximately 90+ percent of the original nickel plate, and where the nickel plate ends, a lovely natural steel color begins. In excellent condition, neither pistol shows much usage, and both show bright blued hammers and heavily varnished walnut stocks. The purple velvet lined case (16.50" x 7.50" x 2.375"), which appears to be period English-style, is, in all likelihood, not original to the pistols. Properly partitioned, the center section would appear to hold either cleaning tools or cartridges.

Remington New Model 1875 Single Action Army Revolver. No serial number. This revolver, in .44-40 caliber is in excellent overall condition, retaining approximately 98 percent of the original fading blue finish; in certain areas of the frame, the finish has taken on a straw effect. The stocks show little ill usage, and, while fitted for a lanyard ring, the ring itself is missing. *(Museum of Connecticut History)*

Left side view of the Remington New Model 1875 Single Action Army Revolver without serial number. *(Museum of Connecticut History)*

REMINGTON MODEL 1890 SINGLE ACTION ARMY REVOLVER.

The Remington Model 1890 Single Action Army Revolver was manufactured c. 1891-1894, with total production in the area of 2,000. Mr. Moldenhauer's records indicate that he had observed serial number 2012.

It was produced only in .44-40 centerfire, with a six-shot cylinder. Barrels were available either in 5.50" length, or 7.50" length, both lacking the prominent web beneath the ejector rod housing so common to the Model 1875. Stocks were of checkered hard rubber with the monogram "RA" in a panel at the top, while the finishes available were either blued or full nickel plate.

Pistols were numbered from serial number 1 on up, while the earliest models produced were marked on the barrel, "E. REMINGTON & SONS, ILION, N.Y. U.S.A.;" later production models were marked "REMINGTON ARMS CO., ILION, N.Y."

This extremely scarce revolver is undoubtedly one of the most sought after by Remington collectors.

An interesting and almost unknown variation that was presumedly produced between 1891 and 1895 is what is referred to as the Remington Model 1891 Revolver, made only for the government of Mexico. This pistol was supposedly manufactured with a bronze frame, fires both single and double action, is top break like a Smith and Wesson, and made only in .38 caliber centerfire. Cylinder capacity is five rounds; the overall length and weight of the pistol are unknown, as no proven specimen has been found to this day. Sights are a blade front sight with a notch rear sight; stocks are presumed to be a checkered hard black rubber, with an old English "R" in a circle at the top. Barrel markings would have been "REMINGTON ARMS CO., ILION, N.Y.," while the Mexican government would have applied their own markings to the pistol.

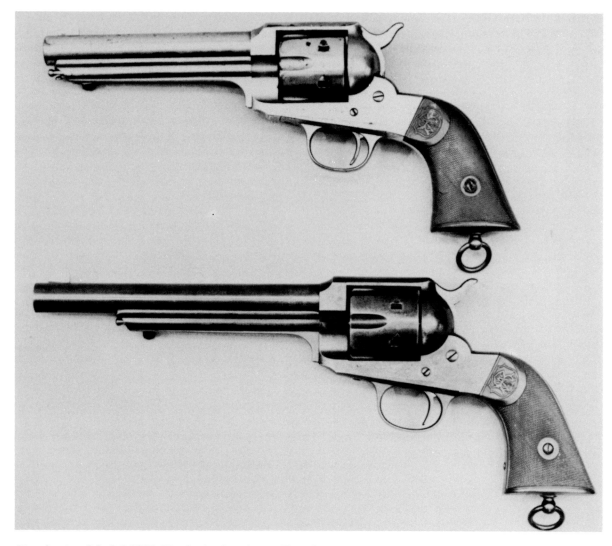

Remington Model 1890 Single Action Army Revolvers.

Top and bottom: (previous page)

Remington Model 1890 Single Action Army Revolver, serial #525. Although showing some wear and signs of usage, this revolver is generally in very fine condition, with approximately 90 percent of the original nickel-plate finish remaining. Evident in the picture is some spotty discoloration at the muzzle, with some further discoloration around the face of the cylinder. Made with the 5.50" barrel, the revolver has monogrammed stocks and is fitted with a lanyard ring.

Remington Model 1890 Single Action Army Revolver, serial #1810. While this pistol appears to have lost the majority of its original blue finish, the weapon is in sharp, crisp, condition, with excellent, checkered brown hard rubber monogrammed stocks. Made with the 7.50" barrel, the butt is fitted with a lanyard ring. A truly fine example of a most hard-to-find weapon.

REMINGTON MODEL 1865 NAVY ROLLING BLOCK PISTOL

The Model 1865 Navy Rolling Block Pistol, a distinctive weapon because of the spur trigger and rolling block action, was manufactured from 1866-1870; it was originally believed that production totaled approximately 1,000 pieces. Research, however, points to the conclusion that there were originally 6,500 weapons made, with about 5,500 being converted to the Model 1867. Thus, a shortage exists of true Model 1865s.

This single-shot pistol, considered one of the strongest actions ever designed and called the "Rolling Block" due to the pivotal action of the breechblock and the hammer, which acted in unison to form a postive locking action at the time of firing, was made in .50 caliber rimfire with a round 8.50" barrel. Its most distinctive feature is the spur trigger. Manufactured with walnut stocks and forend, the barrel was blued, while the frame, breechblock, trigger, trigger sheath, and hammer were all case-hardened. The pistols were serially numbered under the barrel ahead of the forend, with the frame marked "REMINGTONS, ILION, N.Y. U.S.A. PAT. MAY 3d NOV. 15th, 1864, APRIL 17th, 1866."

Martially marked models also bear inspector marks "P" and "FWC" on the right side of the frame, while inspector's initials will be found on the left stock, as well as an anchor on top of the barrel near the breech. Civilian models are identical with the exception of the inspector's markings.

Centerfire models will be found with breechblocks adapted for centerfire only. While it is considered possible that some specimens were made this way, it is assumed that many others were altered by interchanging later centerfire breechblocks.

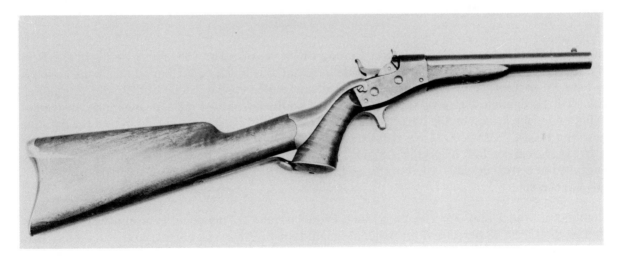

Experimental Model 1865 Navy Rolling Block Pistol Carbine.

Bottom: (previous page)

Experimental Model 1865 Navy Rolling Block Pistol Carbine, without serial number on either pistol or stock. The pistol has no other marking except for a Naval anchor on the breech of the barrel, possibly indicating a weapon for experimental development by the Navy. The pistol and stock are in excellent overall condition, retaining the greater part of the original blue finish, while the brass mounts on the stock are in beautiful shape, nicely age-toned. The attachment of the stock to the weapon is especially interesting, a screw being attached to each side of the rear of the frame, forming the mounts for the curved stock attachments. The butt of the pistol has a mounted oval steel plate with a small teat projecting from the rear that fits into a groove in the top of the screw mounted on the bottom of the stock. The mountings on the stock are finely crafted from brass, while the screws are made of steel. A most unusual and appealing specimen, and one a collector would give a right arm to own!

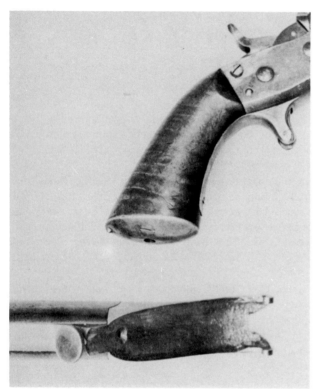

Detail picture of the stock and butt attachment of the Experimental Remington Model 1865 Navy Rolling Block Pistol Carbine.

From top to bottom: (next page)

Engraved Remington Model 1865 Navy Rolling Block Pistol, serial #35. This pistol is in excellent condition, retaining at least 55+ percent of the original blue finish on the barrel, while the action is at least 90 percent; the frame has nearly all of the dulled case-hardened finish still remaining. Interestingly enough, the serial number is located on the left side of the top stock tang, instead of being under the forend on the barrel. The barrel marking is also most unusual in that the one-line marking reads: "REMINGTONS ILION. N.Y. PATd OCT. 1. 1861. NOV. 15 1861;" There is also a heavy Naval anchor inspector's mark. The frame, trigger, and backstrap are beautifully engraved in a style possibly attributable to L.D. Nimschke, while the forend has been professionally checkered.

Remington Model 1865 Navy Rolling Block Pistol, serial #2. This pistol is in almost mint condition, with at least 98 percent of the original bright blue finish on the barrel, with at least 95+ percent of the original dull case-hardened finish on the frame. The rolling block action and hammer are in perfect condition, as are the oil-finished walnut stocks. The pistol is deeply marked with a naval anchor at the breech end of the barrel.

Bottom pistol: (above)

Remington Model 1865 Navy Rolling Block Pistol, unnumbered. This pistol is unusual in that, according to the records of Mr. Moldenhauer, it is the only specimen encountered with six-groove rifling. The pistol is in very fine condition, with the barrel sharp and clean. Surprisingly, the barrel at one time was coated with a thin black lacquer or paint, which was later removed, but is still visible under the forend and near the muzzle. (Protection from salt corrosion?) The excellent stocks bear faint inspector's marks still visible. The top of the barrel is marked with the naval anchor, while the left side of the barrel is marked "USN." The right side of the frame is stamped with the inspector's marks "P/F.C.W.," while the left side of the stocks bear the "F.C.W." inspection marking.

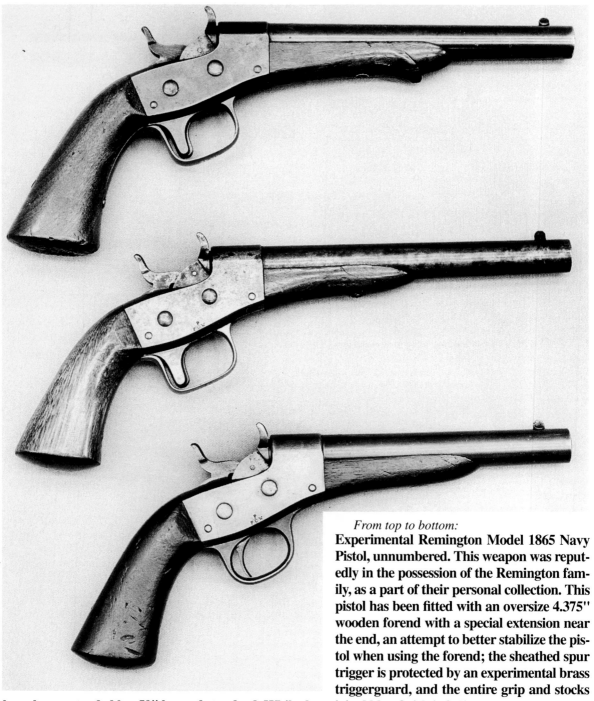

From top to bottom:

Experimental Remington Model 1865 Navy Pistol, unnumbered. This weapon was reputedly in the possession of the Remington family, as a part of their personal collection. This pistol has been fitted with an oversize 4.375" wooden forend with a special extension near the end, an attempt to better stabilize the pistol when using the forend; the sheathed spur trigger is protected by an experimental brass triggerguard, and the entire grip and stocks have been extended by .50" beyond standard. While the original blue finish is fading, the pistol is in fine original and complete condition. While some chipping is noticeable on the forend, and some marring is to be seen on the stocks, this does not detract from the overall appearance of this unique weapon.

Experimental Pattern Remington Model 1865 Single Shot Pistol, serial #3205, one of five specimens known with a brass triggerguard. While showing loss of finish and storage staining, this pistol is otherwise in fine original condition, the brass triggerguard being nicely age-mellowed, while the excellent varnished walnut stocks still show clear inspectors markings. The right side of the frame is stamped with the inspector initials "P/F.C.W.," while the top of the barrel is marked with the naval anchor. The left stock is stamped with the inspector's mark "F.C.W." The experimental brass triggerguard is stamped with the following: "PATTERN GUARD./ ORDER JANY. 28, 1870/ ORD. DEPT. U.S.N.Y./ P.C."

REMINGTON 1867 NAVY ROLLING BLOCK PISTOL.

The Model 1867 Navy Rolling Block Pistol was manufactured in the early 1870s, with the total quantity produced an unknown; many experts theorize that the 1867 model was never manufactured, but was actually the result of conversion of Model 1865s...this in turn would help account for the scarcity of Model 1865s!

This single shot pistol was produced in .50 caliber centerfire and was equipped with a 7.0" round barrel. The finish was blued with a case-hardened frame and triggerguard, while the hammer and breechblock were finished bright; the stocks and forend were made of walnut.

Serial numbers are to be found under the barrel ahead of the forend, while assembly numbers are under the stocks. The frame is marked as follows: "REMINGTONS ILION N.Y. U.S.A./PAT. MAY 3d NOV. 15th, 1864 APRIL 17th, 1866."

A modification of the Model 1865, apparently all of the Model 1867s were contracted for by the government and will bear martial markings consisting of "P" and "F.C.W." on the right side of the frame, while inspector's initials will be in script on the left stock. If found without martial markings, these would naturally command a collector's premium.

Bottom pistol: (previous page)
Remington Model 1867 Navy Rolling Block Pistol, serial #2505. This Model 1867 pistol is in excellent condition, retaining approximately 80 percent of the original blue finish, while the frame reflects little loss of the dull case-hardened color. The stocks are in beautiful condition, with sharp, clear inspector's marks. Fully martially marked, with the barrel showing inspection marks "I.H.B." and the naval anchor, while the right side of the frame is stamped "F.C.W."

Detail of the markings on the triggerguard of the center pistol in the previous photo.

From top to bottom: (next page)
Experimental or Special Presentation Order Remington Model 1867 Single Shot Navy Pistol, no serial number. The Model 1867 triggerguard is marked with the number "910," with the only other number showing, a "78" on the top strap. This pistol most likely was made with the original sheath trigger, but was later converted by the factory to incorporate the triggerguard. The pistol is fitted with an 8.50" round barrel with the naval anchor marking, and the barrel address "REMINGTON'S ILION. N.Y. PATd. OCT. 1. 1861 NOV. 15 '86."

This weapon bears the original scroll engraving on the frame signed "LN" for the famous engraver, L.D. Nimschke; the walnut forend is checkered and the original special order curved rosewood stocks are checkered at the butt only.

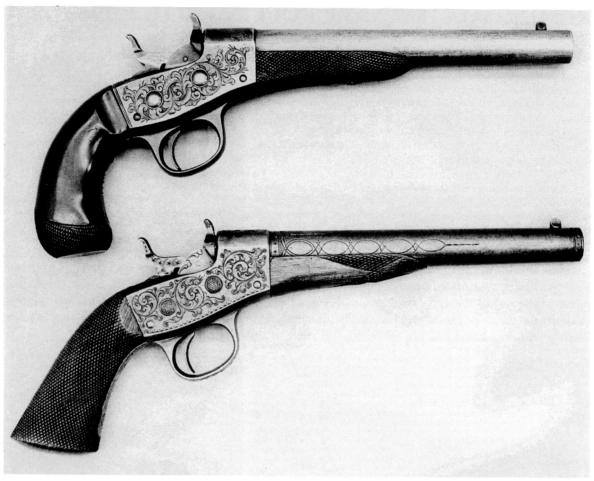

Remington Model 1867 Single Shot Navy Pistols.

REMINGTON MODEL 1867 ROLLING BLOCK PISTOL, TRANSITIONAL TYPE

The Model 1867 Transitional Type Pistol with 8.50" round barrel is identical to the Remington Model 1867 Navy Rolling Block Pistol with one distinguishing difference. This feature is the grip screw that enters through the rear frame strap, passing through the stock and threaded into the backstrap itself, as opposed to the normal stock fastening with two wood screws. This is a civilian model and will not be found with martial markings, although many specimens with British proof marks do appear.

Bottom pistol: (above)
Remington Model 1867 Pistol, Transitional Type, serial #1007. This pistol is in excellent condition, the barrel retaining at least 50 percent of the original thinning blue finish, while the case-hardened colors on the frame and trigger are excellent; the blued action would rate at 90 percent. Mr. Moldenhauer was of the opinion that this was not a conversion of the Model 1865, but was definitely a model made as a result of a government contract in 1867. This specimen has been fully engraved overall in the manner of the master, L.D. Nimschke, and was originally in the collection of the late William M. Locke.

146

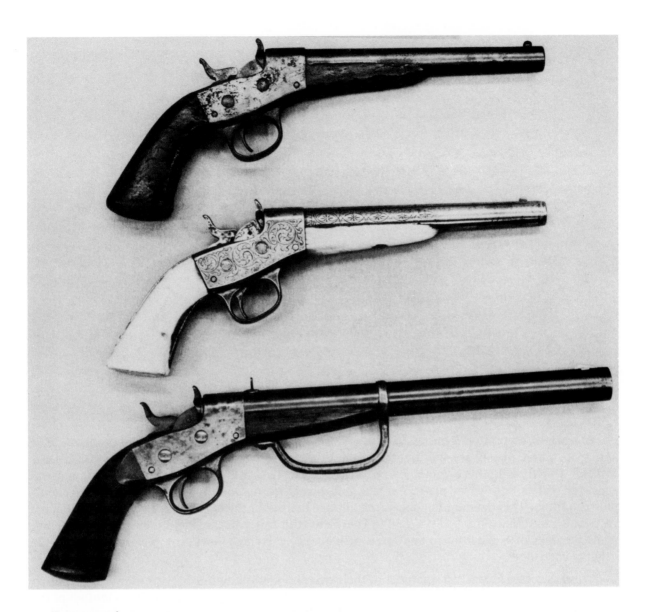

From top to bottom:

Remington Model 1867 Pistol, Transitional Type, serial #1223. What makes this an unusual pistol is the fact that it is original rimfire, not often encountered. In fair to good condition, the pistol shows evidence of age spotting and medium pitting overall. The walnut stocks still appear to be in good condition.

Remington Model 1867 Pistol, Transitional Type, serial #1689. This pistol was originally nickel-plated, of which only slight traces are discernable, and, while in very good condition, the pistol has been cleaned overall. Equipped with the original ivory forend and stocks, this specimen has lovely overall scroll engraving. At the joints between steel and ivory, the ivory has turned a dark brown with age staining, a not unusual happening.

Remington Model 1867 Pistol, Transitional Type, no serial number. This completely re-worked pistol is in fine condition, having been professionally fitted with a heavy 10.0" round barrel in .50-70 caliber with a rifle-style keyed front sight and an old, crude replacement rear sight. The barrel and the forend have been fitted with a hand forged iron carrying handle, encircling the barrel and screwed into the forend. The checkered stocks are just discernable, and appear to be in fine condition. While the action retains approximately 95 percent of the original age-dulled case-hardened finish, the barrel retains only 50 percent blue finish. An interesting and unusual variant of this pistol.

Cased Set of Presentation Remington Model 1867 Pistols, Transitional Type, serial numbers 1539 and 1616. These pistols are well known to the world of Remington collectors as the "Gold Dust Twins." Fitted with the original ivory stocks, these two fully deluxe, overall scroll pattern engraved pistols, with silver-plated barrels, gold-plated frames and blued actions are in excellent-plus condition. This outstanding pair of pistols are housed in the original red velvet lined, deluxe rosewood case (15.625" x 9.75" x 2.50"), complete with fancy brass shield escutcheon in the lid, while the interior is partitioned and fitted with a large cartridge block, completely filled with the original cartridges.

Both pistols retain at least 98+ percent of their original gold-plate finish, with the same retention for the bright blued actions. The barrels would rate approximately 80 percent for retention of the silver plate. This set of pistols was awarded the silver medal of excellence by the National Rifle Association of America at its annual meeting in Chicago, Illinois, April 3, 1966. These pistols are a collector's dream, and deservedly so!

REMINGTON MODEL 1871 ARMY ROLLING BLOCK PISTOL

The Remington Model 1871 Army Rolling Block Pistol was manufactured c. 1872-1888, with the total quantity produced estimated at 6,000 plus. The Model 1871 evolved from improvement in the preceding Navy models, producing the distinctive profile, of which the hump at the rear of the frame is the most noticeable.

This pistol is single-shot, with a .50 caliber centerfire 8.0" round barrel. The finish is blued, with a case-hardened frame and triggerguard, while the hammer and the action are finished in the bright. The stocks and forend are made from walnut. All weapons are serially numbered, with the frame marked "REMINGTONS ILION, N.Y. U.S.A./ PAT. MAY 3d NOV. 15th, 1864 APRIL 17th, 1866 P S."

The majority of these pistols (about 5,000) were sold to the U.S. government and will be found martially marked, including the government inspector's initials on the barrel and stocks (usually C.R.S.). Civilian models are to be found, but do not bring a premium from the collector.

148

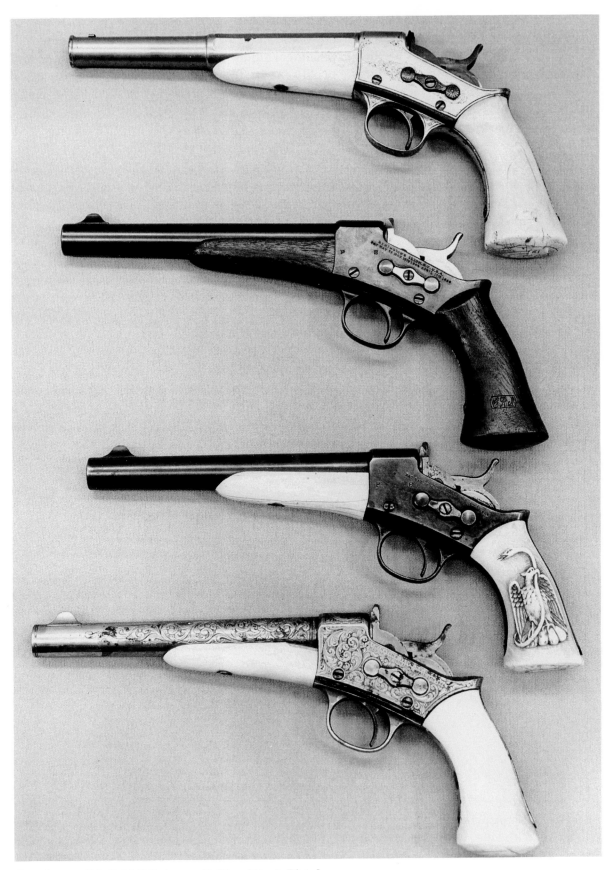

Remington Model 1871 Army Rolling Block Pistols.

From top to bottom: (previous page)

Remington Model 1871 Army Rolling Block Pistol, serial #124. This custom, special order, nickel-plated pistol is in complete and original excellent condition, fitted with an 8.50" half round/half octagonal barrel with cannon muzzle in .50 caliber centerfire. The frame has been lightly scroll engraved, incorporating a panel scene at the top of the frame of a wildcat pouncing on a snake, while the right side of the frame is hand engraved "Remington." The pistol is fitted with excellent age-mellowed original ivory stocks.

Remington Model 1871 Army Rolling Block Pistol, serial #3112. This .50 caliber centerfire specimen is fully martially marked and in excellent original condition, with approximately 99 percent of the original blue and case-hardened colors. The stocks are in mint condition with crisp, sharp "C.R.S." inspector's marks, while the frame markings are especially sharp and clear.

Remington Model 1871 Army Rolling Block Pistol, serial #4338. This customized pistol is in excellent original condition, with approximately 95 percent of the original blue finish on the barrel, while the frame, which is struck with "PS" inspection marks, retains at least 90 percent of the original case-hardened colors. The pistol was fitted with an ivory forend that has mellowed with age; the forend also shows some long, stained cracks, also from aging.

Remington Model 1871 Army rolling block Pistol, serial #5898. This .50 caliber centerfire pistol retains at least 95+ percent of the original overall nickel plate and is in generally excellent condition, with blued frame screws and trigger. The original ivory stocks are excellent, missing only a small chip on the left side where the barrel and the frame meet. The pistol is profusely scroll engraved on the barrel and frame either by L.D. Nimschke, or by someone imitating his style.

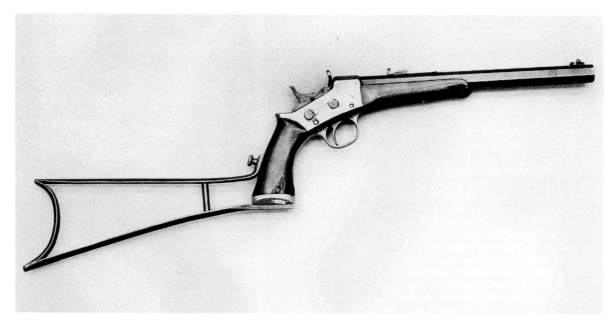

Remington Model 1871 Army Rolling Block Pistol, not serially numbered. This .32 caliber rimfire pistol has been professionally rebuilt by a competent gunsmith, and now incorporates a full octagon barrel with rifle sights. The flattened butt is equipped with a slotted brass stock attachment for a hand-forged Stevens-type wire shoulder stock. The pistol and stock are in overall good to fine condition.

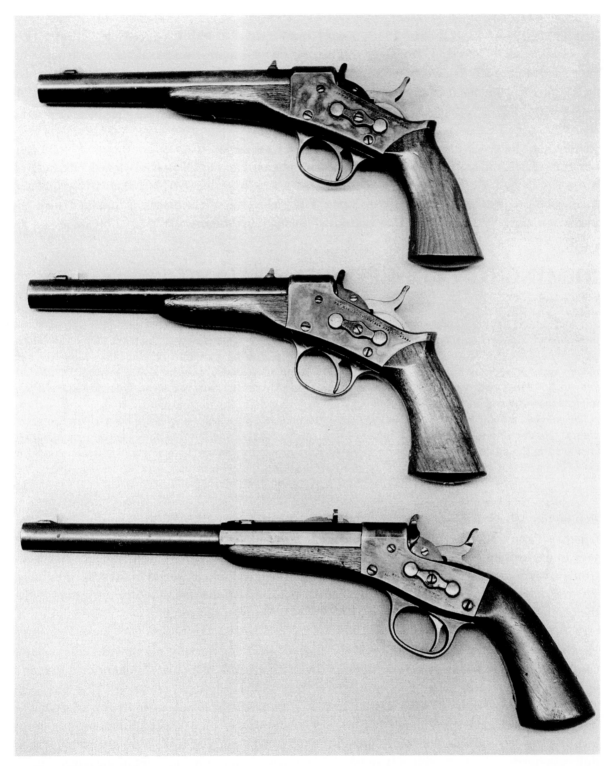

From top to bottom:

Remington Model 1887 Rolling Block Target Pistol, serial #194. This pistol is constructed on a Model 1871 frame, with a .22 caliber, 8.0" barrel. This pistol would rate in mint condition, with little, if any, loss to the bright blue finish on the barrel, or of the bright case-hardened finish on the frame and triggerguard. Note the excellence of the original varnished walnut stocks.

Middle and bottom pistols: (previous page)

Remington Model 1887 Rolling Block Target Pistol, serial #1400. Produced on a Model 1871 frame with an 8.0" barrel in .22 caliber rimfire, this pistol is in near mint condition, with beautiful varnished walnut stocks. The pistol retains at least 95+ percent of the original bright blue finish on the barrel, while the frame and triggerguard retain at least 98 percent of the bright case-hardened colors.

Remington Model 1887-style Rolling Block Target Pistol, serial #1724. Manufactured in .22 caliber rimfire, with a special 10.0" half round/half octagon barrel (The barrel signed "Remington Arms Co. Ilion, N.Y.") on a Model 1865 frame. The barrel is equipped with a blade front sight and a rifle-style adjustable Buckhorn rear sight. The right side of the frame is stamped with the inspection mark "P/FCW," while the bottom of the barrel is stamped "22 6155 1724 22".

REMINGTON ROLLING BLOCK TARGET PISTOLS

It was in 1887 that E. Remington & Sons began to fail as a company. Thus it is a reasonable assumption that these target pistols were made from the large stockpile of Model 1871 parts created in anticipation of unrealized government contracts, as an income producing measure to stave off their creditors. First advertised in 1887, the models were based on the Model 1871 Army Pistol, and were offered in .50 caliber, .32 S&W, and .22 caliber, all with an 8.0" barrel made with a blade front sight and modified fixed Buckhorn rear sight. These pistols have been referred to by Remington collectors as "Remington Plinker Models."

The company went into receivership in 1888, and was reorganized the same year as the "Remington Arms Co." with M. Hartley serving as president. The new organization also believed in using parts that were on hand, and continued in the production of "Plinker" pistols. At least two specimens are known marked "Remington Arms Co." The interesting thing about both of these pistols is the fact that they were made on a Model 1865 frame!

From top to bottom: (next page)

Remington Model 1887-style Rolling Block Target Pistol, serial #5033. Made on a Model 1865 frame, with an original 10.0" half round/half octagon barrel in .22 caliber rimfire, this pistol is in very fine condition, with the original blue starting to thin on the barrel, while the case-hardened frame and triggerguard still retain their finish. The plain walnut stocks are in excellent condition. The only markings that occur on the pistol are a small dot on the barrel under the forend, while the frame is stamped with inspection marks "P.F.C.W." on the right side.

Remington Model 1887-style Rolling Block Target Pistol, not serially numbered. This pistol is constructed on the frame of a Model 1865, fitted with an 8.0" barrel in .22 caliber rimfire; it is equipped with a blade front sight and a fixed rear sight, the barrel stamped "REMINGTON ARMS CO., ILION, N.Y.," while the right side of the frame is struck with the same legend. No inspector's marks are to be found. This particular pistol is in very fine condition, in spite of the fact that the original blue finish is thinning; the frame and triggerguard retain almost all of their dull case-hardened colors, with only some slight storage discoloration in front of the triggerguard. The plain walnut stocks are in excellent condition.

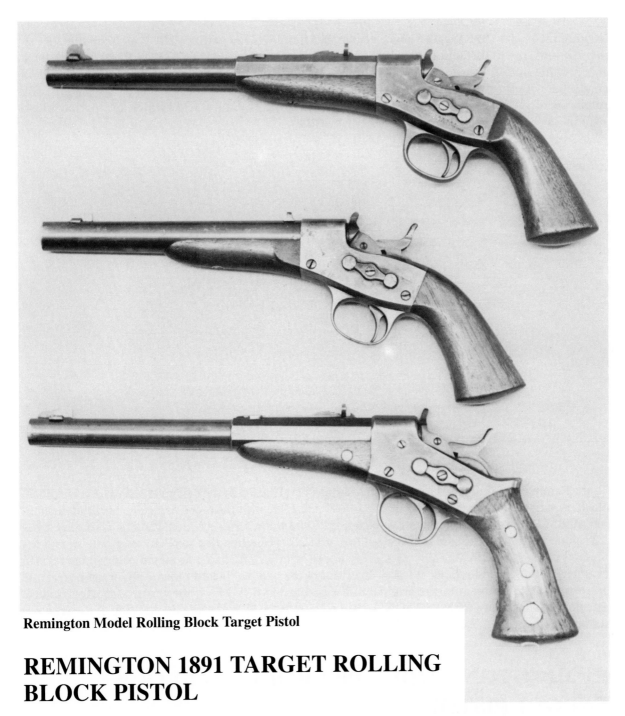

Remington Model Rolling Block Target Pistol

REMINGTON 1891 TARGET ROLLING BLOCK PISTOL

Made between 1892 and 1898, factory records show that only 116 pieces were produced. However, it is entirely possible that greater numbers were manufactured. Calibers available were .22 caliber long and short rimfire; .25 caliber Stevens, and .32 caliber S&W rimfire and centerfire. Made only as a single shot, barrel lengths available are 10.0", 8.0", and 12.0" half round/half octagon, with the latter two sizes bringing a collector's premium.

Stocks and forend are of plain walnut, while the finish is bright blue with case-hardened frame and triggerguards, with the hammer in the bright. Front sights are blade type, while the rear sight is a modified Buckhorn style. For some unknown reason, while serially numbered, the numbering system is indecipherable. The barrels are marked "REMINGTON ARMS CO., ILION, N.Y.," while the left frame is marked "REMINGTONS ILION, N.Y. U.S.A./ PAT, MAY 3d NOV. 15th, 1864 APRIL 17th, 1866 P S," the latter two marks indicating a military receiver.

Since these weapons are so scarce, and extremely difficult to find, great care must be taken that, if one does turn up on the market, it is not the work of some competent gunsmith. It must be understood that there were overruns on the production of Model 1871 Army contract receivers.

Bottom: (previous page)

Remington Model 1891 Target Pistol, serial #30. Manufactured with a 10.0" long barrel in .25 caliber Stevens, the half round/half octagon barrel is stamped "REMINGTON ARMS CO., ILION, N.Y.," while the left side of the frame bears the five-line patent stamping. The pistol is in excellent condition, with the original blue finish fading on the barrel, while the frame and triggerguard still retain all of the dull case-hardened colors. The original walnut stocks, which are period inlaid with mother-of-pearl discs, are in excellent condition.

Cased Remington Model 1891 Target Pistol, serial #121. Housed in the original heavy red velvet lined, black pigskin leather covered case (16.25" x 7.75" x 2.25"), with the piped cartridge partition lined in red satin. This partition contains two boxes of "Remington Arms - Union Metallic Cartridge Co." .22 caliber cartridges. The case is also fitted for an 11.25" brass-handled steel cleaning rod, the rod not original to the gun. This .22 caliber pistol, equipped with a 10.0" half round/half octagon barrel is in excellent condition and retains at least 98 percent of the original bright blue finish on the barrel and approximately 50 percent of the original dull case-hardened finish on the frame and triggerguard. The barrel is marked "REMINGTON ARMS CO., ILION, N.Y.," while the left side of the frame is stamped "REMINGTON'S ILION, N.Y. U.S.A./PAT. MAY 3d, NOV. 15th, 1864 APRIL 17th, 1866."

REMINGTON MODEL 1901 ROLLING BLOCK TARGET PISTOL

The Remington Model 1901 Rolling Block Target Pistol was manufactured between 1901 and 1909, with a total of only 735 pistols being produced; this was the last of the Remington Rolling Block production, the curtain coming down with the last piece produced. Records indicate that 1 was made in 1900; 190 were made in 1901; between 1902 and 1904, 462; 72 in 1905; 2 in 1906; 1 each in 1907 and 1908, and a grand total of 6 in 1909.

The single-shot pistols were available in the following calibers: .22. short and long rifle rimfire; .25-10 rimfire, and .44 S&W centerfire. The barrel is 10.0" in length, and is half round/half octagon.

All metal parts are blued, while the barrel and frame markings are the same as the Model 1891, with the exception of the "P" and "S" inspector's markings. The stocks and the forend are elaborately checkered. Notice that the the thumb lever on the rolling breechblock is offset horizontally so that it will not interfere with the line of sight. The rear sight is mortised into the frame, while the ivory bead type, wide blade front sight is mortised into the front of the barrel.

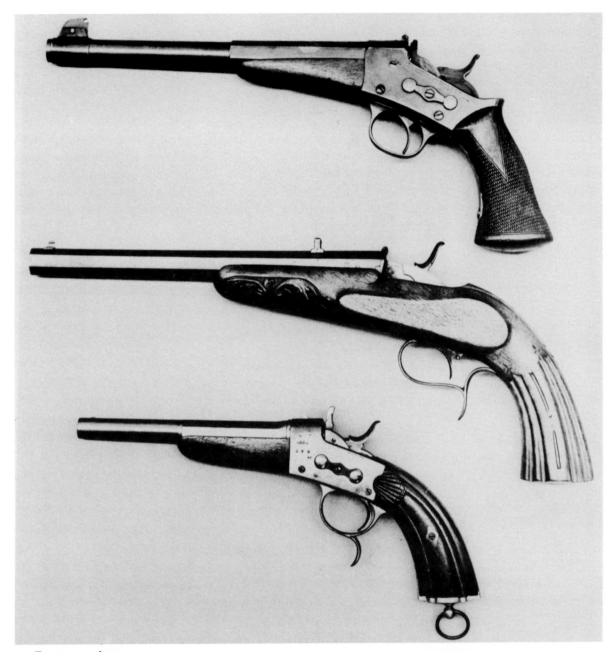

From top to bottom:

Remington Model 1901 Target Pistol, with a mixed bag of serial numbers. The 10.0" half round/ half octagon barrel, in .44 S&W RF, is marked with serial #2139, the lower frame with #1450, the upper frame with #3810, gun and stock numbers 1808; an unusual mixture, but all parts are original Remington. The barrel is marked "REMINGTON ARMS CO., ILION, N.Y. U.S.A.," and is fitted with replacement front sights and the correct Model 1901 rear frame sight. The gun is in very fine original condition, with about 40 percent of the original thinning blue; the triggerguard and frame retain almost all of the original dull case-hardened colors. The uncheckered forend is an old Remington replacement, while the oversize stocks are original Remington equipment.

IMITATION IS THE SINCEREST FORM OF FLATTERY

During the more than 44 years that Rolling Block action weapons were in production, imitators worldwide hastened to take advantage of the strongest action on the market by making their own versions. Several are illustrated here in order to acquaint the collector with what may be encountered.

155

Middle pistol: (previous page)

Belgian Salon Pistol, 15.5" overall, with a 9.50" full; octagon barrel; the caliber is approximately 7mm centerfire. Proof marked "ELG" and "BREVET REMINGTON 256" on the left side of the barrel, the triggerguard and tang are scroll engraved, while the fine grained walnut half stock is relief carved. The fluted butt is missing the butt cap.

Bottom pistol: (previous page)

European Rolling Block Pistol, no serial number. 11.0" overall, with a .380 caliber 6.50" half round/half octagon barrel. The gun is stamped with an "R" proof, while the left side of the frame is marked "DF" with an arrow through the initials, "380" and "*K" proof. Equipped with a plain walnut forend and fluted butt with steel butt cap with lanyard ring. This gun is in very fine condition, and still retains approximately 80 percent of the original nickel-plate finish. The stocks can be seen to be in excellent shape despite their years.

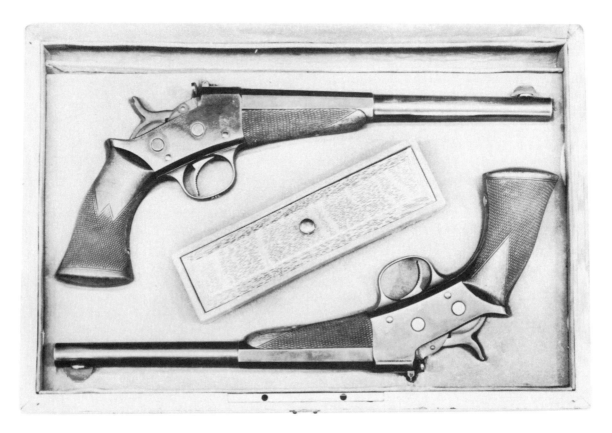

Cased Pair of Remington Model 1901 Target Pistols, serial #2134 in .22 long rifle, and #3028 in .22 caliber short. The pistols are presented in the original tan chamois leather lined, varnished oak case (16.0" x 10.75" x 2.75"), with lidded partition still in excellent condition after all these years. Both pistols are in excellent condition, as may be seen in the picture; #2134 retains at least 95 percent of the original bright blue finish, while the stocks are in sharp, crisp condition. #3028 has about 80 percent of the original blue finish remaining on the barrel, with the frame, action, and triggerguard retaining much more of the bright blue. As with its companion piece, the stocks are in immaculate condition.

REMINGTON-UMC MODEL 1911 .45 CALIBER AUTOMATIC PISTOL

The Model 1911 Automatic Pistol, Military Series, was manufactured between 1912 and 1957, with total production of approximately 2,695,000 pistols. Made in .45 ACP caliber, the magazine had a capacity of seven shots, with an extra cartridge in the chamber, if so desired. Barrel length was 5.0".

The Remington-UMC Model 1911 pistol serial number range was from 1 to 21,676, and all pistols had Colt and Remington-UMC slide markings, while the inspector's stamps were either "E" or "B".

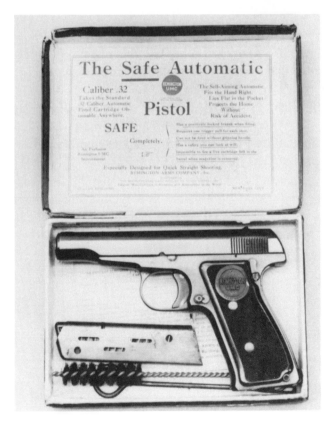

Top and bottom:

Remington-UMC model 1911 .45 caliber Automatic Pistol, serial #340. This pistol has the early bright commercial-style finish associated with early production models, rather than the later softer blue usually found on World War I production pistols; the pistol retains practically all of its original finish, and would be considered to be in excellent condition. The stocks are sharp and crisp, showing little, if any hard usage.

The left side of the frame is marked "UNITED STATES PROPERTY" with the flaming bomb ordnance marking, while the right side of the frame bears the number "340." The left side of the slide bears the usual Colt and Remington-UMC legends.

REMINGTON MODEL 51 AUTOMATIC PISTOL

The Remington Model 51 Automatic Pistol was produced in two different calibers, which will be discussed separately. The basic pistol was made with a 3.50" round barrel, complete with grip and manual safeties, as well as a magazine safety. The finish was a blue-black overall, while the stocks were a checkered hard rubber with Remington-UMC markings in a circular panel.

Markings on weapons under serial number 63,000 were "THE REMINGTON ARMS - UNION METALLIC CARTRIDGE CO. INC./REMINGTON ILION WKS. N.Y. U.S.A. PEDERSEN'S PATENTS PENDING." Guns with a serial number higher than 63,000 were marked "REMINGTON ARMS CO. INC. ILION WKS N.Y. U.S.A./PEDERSEN'S PATENT, (with a 1920-1921 patent date.)"

There were approximately 54,500 guns manufactured in caliber .380, serially numbered from 1 to 60,800; under serial number 40,000, the grasping portion of the rear of the slide has 9 grooves, while above that figure, there are 15 grooves, and the Remington trademark has been added to the frame and the caliber stamped on the barrel. As made in .380 caliber, the magazine contained 7 cartridges.

The Model 51 was made in caliber .32 between 1921 and 1934, with an approximate total produced of 10,200; these broke down into two distinct series of serial numbers, running from number 60801 to 70280, and from number 90501 to 92627. The .32 caliber model was capable of holding 8 cartridges in the magazine.

Bottom photo: (previous page)
Boxed Remington Model 51 Automatic Pistol, serial #PA66712. This gun is in .32 caliber; the pistol and the accessories are in absolutely mint condition, the weapon appearing to have never been fired. Complete in the original cardboard box (7.125" x 5.0" x 1.50") with the owner registration card, cleaning brush and cleaning rod. Note the original factory label.

From top to bottom: (next page)
Remington Model 51 Automatic Pistol, serial #PA90567. Made in caliber .32, this pistol is in excellent plus condition, retaining virtually all of the original slightly dulled overall blue finish.

Remington Model 51 Automatic Pistol, serial #PA16096. Produced in caliber .380. While in overall excellent condition, the finish on this particular gun is starting to thin, and approximately 20 percent of the finish is gone. Note the 9 grasping grooves on the slide indicating earlier manufacture.

Boxed Remington Model 51 Automatic Pistol, serial #PA23873. This .380 caliber pistol is in excellent-plus condition, with approximately 98 percent of the original bright blue factory finish overall. It is shown in the original factory cardboard box (7.125" x 5.0" x 1.50"), which is in excellent shape, complete with factory label in the lid. This, too, is an earlier production model with 9 grasping grooves on the slide.

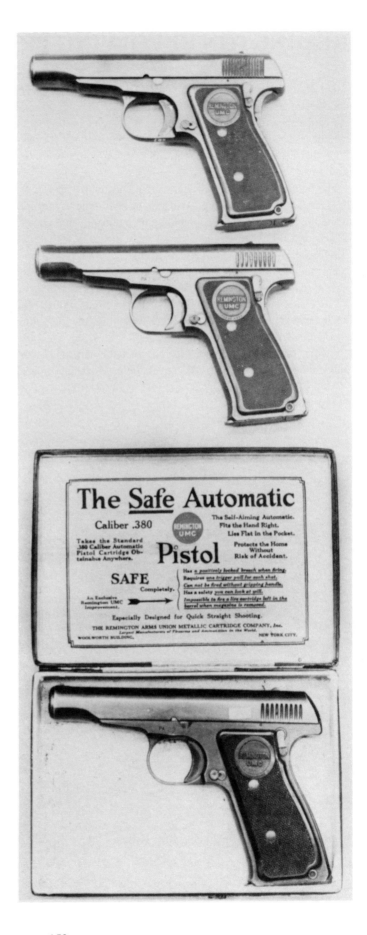

**Remington Model 51
Automatic Pistols.**

REMINGTON REVOLVING PERCUSSION RIFLE

The Remington Revolving Percussion Rifle was manufactured between 1866 and 1879, with the quantity produced estimated at less than 1,000 pieces. Made in both .36 caliber percussion (the type most encountered) and in .44 caliber percussion, which is extremely scarce and will demand a premium if found on the market. The round cylinder is six-shot, with safety notches at the shoulder. Barrels are in 24.0" and 28.0" standard lengths, although 26.0" barrels were advertised; the full octagon barrel was normal production, although some half octagon/half round barrels were produced.

The buttstock is made of walnut, and comes with either of two crescent butt plate types; flat and pointed. The triggerguard is the scroll type, with a spur below the trigger bow. The frame and the hammer are case-hardened, while the rest of the finish is blued. Serial numbers commenced from #1 on up, with none being known to-date in excess of 1,000. The standard barrel markings are: "PATENTED SEPT. 14, 1858/E. REMINGTON & SONS, ILION, NEW YORK, U.S.A./NEW MODEL." Built on the frame of the New Model revolver series, the cylinder is normally 2.1875" in length, making it .1875" longer than the New Model Army Revolver cylinder; the loading lever is also a special extra length, thus providing another means of identification of authentic rifles.

These rifles will be found with two styles of rear sights, either a folding leaf type, or an open buckhorn type, while front sights are blade type. Stock mountings are most often found in brass, although iron mountings will be encountered.

Factory conversion to breech-loading metallic cartridges will be found, with .38 caliber RF believed to be the only caliber thus converted; this conversion necessitated a specially installed cylinder.

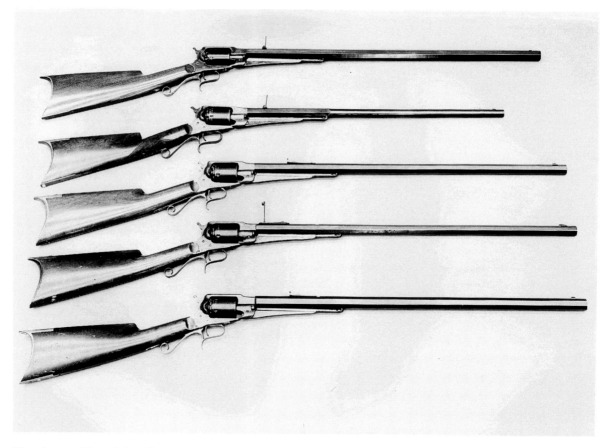

Remington Revolving Percussion Rifles.

Remington Revolving Percussion Rifle, serial #734. This particular rifle is possibly the finest known specimen of the Remington Revolving Percussion Rifle, with a minimum of at least 95+ percent of all of the original finishes. The barrel and the cylinder retain at least 98 percent of the original bright blue, while the case-hardened lever and frame retain a minimum of 95 percent of their original bright coloring; the triggerguard and the butt plate show 98 percent of the original silver plate, and the varnished walnut stock is in mint condition. The 28.0" full octagon barrel in .36 caliber is fitted with a standard blade front sight and folding leaf rear sight, and shows the standard markings for this model.

Remington Revolving Percussion Rifle, serial #60. Fitted with the rare 24.0" half round/half octagon barrel converted to .38 caliber rimfire, there is a folding leaf rear sight and an open front sight; the markings on the barrel are standard for this model. The triggerguard and butt plate are in brass, while the varnished walnut stock is checkered at the wrist. Interestingly, the triggerguard is stamped "34" on the left side. The rifle is in fine condition, however there are only suggestions of the original bright blue finish, the balance of the metal showing an overall age patina. The case-hardened colors on the frame and loading lever have completely faded out, leaving a "silvered" look to the metal; the conversion cylinder and ring do show approximately 30 percent of the original blue finish.

Remington Revolving Percussion Rifle, serial #123. This rifle is fitted with a 28.0" full octagon barrel stamped with the serial number, but without a standard barrel address; the barrel fitted with a blade front sight and a Buckhorn-style rear sight. This rifle was factory-converted to .38 caliber rimfire. The fittings are all silver-plated brass. The rifle is in excellent condition, however most of the original finish has disappeared with time, leaving an age-brown patina; the case-hardened colors on the frame and loading lever are mere suggestions of their former selves. The wood is in excellent shape, retaining much of the original varnish.

Remington Revolving Percussion Rifle, serial #128. This rifle is a factory conversion to .38 caliber rimfire, equipped with a 28.0" full octagon barrel, with only the serial number on the barrel, omitting the barrel address. Fitted with a blade front sight, and slotted for the original rear sight, but now equipped with an elaborate folding leaf rear sight that presumedly was installed at some later period. The triggerguard and butt plate are beautifully cared-for brass, while the varnished walnut stock is well preserved. With 80 percent of the original bright blue finish on the barrel, the balance remaining has turned a smooth age-brown patina, while the case-hardened colors on the frame and loading lever are age-dulled, with only 20 percent remaining.

Remington Revolving Percussion Rifle, serial #525. Fitted with an unusually heavy original 28.0" full octagon barrel with blade front sight and Buckhorn-style rear sight, this barrel bears no address markings; only the serial number is shown. The rifle has been factory converted to .38 caliber rimfire; the mountings are all nickel-plated brass in crisp condition, while the varnished walnut stock is in fine original shape. The barrel retains approximately 45 percent of the original bright blue finish, with the balance a light age-brown patina; the case-hardened finish on the frame and loading lever is practically all present, with about 10 percent of the color remaining, the balance age-stained and dull. The nickel-plate finish on the brass triggerguard and butt plate are in excellent condition, having lost only 10 percent of the finish.

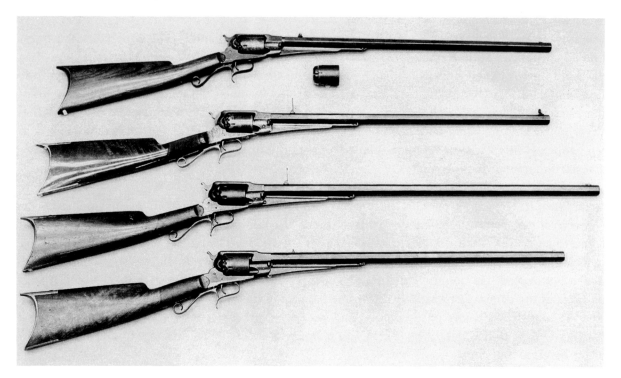

From top to bottom:

Remington Revolving Percussion Rifle, serial #118. In .44 caliber, this rifle is fitted with a 24.0" full octagon barrel; for some unknown reason, the barrel is turned round .250" next to the frame, but it is original; the barrel has the standard markings and folding leaf rear sight and blade front sight. The mountings, including the butt plate, are iron, and the left side of the triggerguard has been marked "42" while the rear tang of the triggerguard is marked with the serial number "118." This rifle is shown with an original conversion cylinder. In excellent overall condition, the blued finish has turned a lovely brown patina with age, while the wood is in very fine condition. Unfortunately, the loading lever is missing from this specimen.

Remington Revolving Percussion Rifle, serial #315. This fully-factory engraved rifle is a unique specimen in very fine condition; the rifle is in .36 caliber percussion, with a 24.0" octagon barrel, fitted with Beech's combination folding leaf rear sight and front sight, with the usual barrel markings. The frame, barrel, and the silver-plated triggerguard and butt plate are heavily scroll engraved in the style of L.D. Nimschke. The checkered burled walnut stock is beautifully varnished, and is in excellent condition. While the metal is in excellent condition, less than 70 percent of the original blue finish remains, with only traces of case-hardening remaining on the frame.

Remington Revolving Percussion Rifle, serial #374. This rifle is in .36 caliber, has a 28.0" full octagonal barrel with blade front sight and folding leaf rear sight, with all silver-plated brass fittings, the buttstock sporting original checkering at the wrist. The gun is in very fine condition, with all of the original blue having turned a beautiful even blue-brown patina overall. The triggerguard and butt plate still show traces of the original silver plating. Barrel markings are standard for this weapon.

Remington Revolving Percussion Rifle, serial #469. This weapon goes to prove that there is an exception to every rule; an original revolving rifle, the cylinder is the normal 2.0" overall New Model revolver cylinder that is completely original for this size frame. The rifle also is fitted with a full octagon .44 caliber barrel that is 24.25" in length, .25" longer than standard. All of the mountings are brass, which is in fine condition, while the burled walnut stock is checkered at the wrist. While difficult to see in the picture, the lever plunger is an old, poorly made replacement.

REMINGTON RIFLE CANE

The Remington Rifle Cane, also known as the "Cane Gun" was made in percussion from 1858 to 1866; after 1866, it was produced for breech loading metallic cartridges until 1888. Recent research tends to indicate that approximately 1,000 such cane guns were manufactured. There were two single-shot cartridge models made, the No. 1 model in .22 caliber rimfire, and the No. 2 Model in .32 caliber rimfire. The cane gun had the operating mechanism located in the gutta-percha handle, with a concealed button trigger on the underside of the shaft; loading and cocking was accomplished by pulling back on the handle, inserting the cartridge and returning the handle to its former position. The barrel length was approximately 26.0", with the shaft encircled by a German silver band just below the handle; the shaft was usually covered with gutta-percha. The muzzle of the cane gun was covered with a screw-on metal cap. Cane handles came in three distinctive styles; a gutta-percha handle of smooth design completely unembellished in any respect, a gutta-percha handle in the shape of a dog's head, and a gutta-percha ball-and-claw handle. Values are usually determined by the handle of the cane, with the ball-and-claw handle the most desirable. An oddity, and what many considered Remington's first metallic cartridge longarm; another point of interest is the fact that Remington was the only arms manufacturer to produce a cane gun.

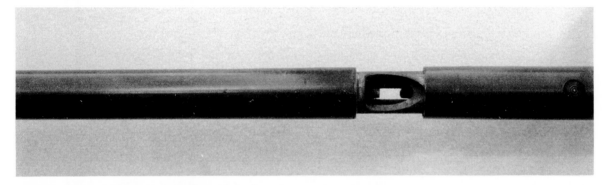

Remington Cartridge Cane Gun, showing the action open and ready for the insertion of the cartridge. *(Museum of Connecticut History)*

Remington Cartridge Cane Gun, showing the screw-on metal muzzle cover and markings. *(Museum of Connecticut History)*

From left to right: (next page)
Two excellent examples of the Remington Cane Gun,

Remington Cartridge Cane Gun, serial #66. This excellent specimen fitted with a dog's head handle is in .32 caliber rimfire and measures 35.50" overall. As is the case with most cane guns, age cracks will have developed in the gutta-percha. The metal muzzle cover is marked "F THOMAS/ PATENT/FEB'Y 9 1858/REMINGTON & SONS/ILION, N.Y./66."

Remington Percussion Cane Gun, serial #17. This lovely percussion specimen is fitted with a ball-and-claw handle, is 33.0" in length overall, and comes in .44 caliber. Again, age cracks are to be found in the gutta-percha, and, in this particular cane, the German silver ring was re-soldered at some time in the past. The metal muzzle cover is marked "F F THOMAS./PATENT/FEB'Y 9, 1858/REMINGTON & SONS/ILION, N.Y./17."

Remington Cartridge and Percussion Cane Gun

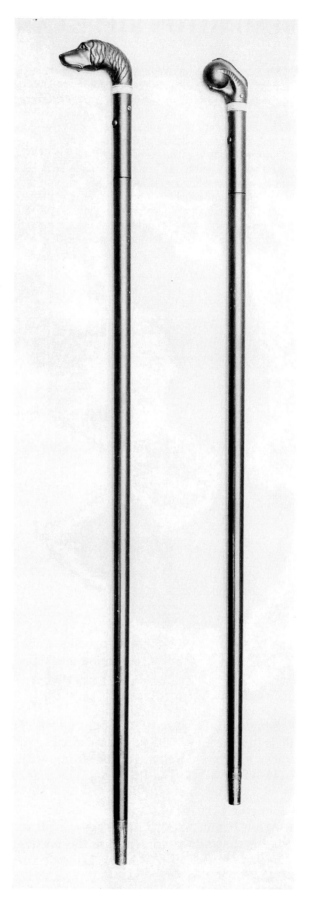

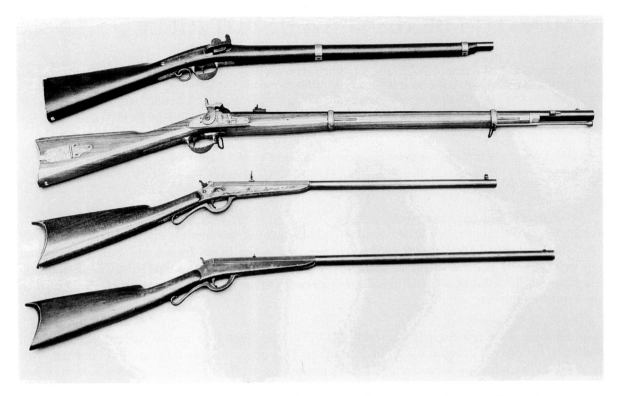

This picture illustrates several styles of longarms that were produced by Remington under contract.

From top to bottom:

Remington-Jenks Percussion Breechloading Carbine, otherwise known as "The Mule-Ear Carbine." Developed by N.P. Ames of Springfield, Massachusetts, approximately 4,250 of these carbines were produced in .54 caliber percussion between 1841 and 1846. This was a single-shot, side hammer breechloader, the action being opened by pulling up and back on the hooked lever located on the breechblock. Fitted with a 24.25" browned barrel with two barrel bands, all mountings were in bright finished brass, the lockplate and breech lever were case-hardened; full walnut stock with sling ring fitted on the rear section of the trigger plate.

This lock is fitted with the Maynard tape primer and is marked "REMINGTON/HERKIMER/ N.Y.," and the barrel is marked "CAST STEEL 1847 U.S.N. RP P W JENKS P." In absolutely mint condition, the barrel retains at least 98 percent of its original glossy brown finish, while the case-hardened lock, breech lever, and stock are in excellent condition with crisp, sharp inspector's marks. This was the only mule-ear style weapon officially accepted by the U.S. military.

Remington Model 1863 Percussion Contract Rifle, known as the "Zouave Rifle." This particular weapon is a replica, and is included for representation purposes. Serial #2223, this gun was made in Italy. The 1863 Contract Rifle was made between 1862 and 1865, with a total production of 12,501. Produced as a .58 caliber, single shot muzzleloader with a 33.0" round barrel fastened by two barrel bands. The mountings were all of brass, while the barrel was blued, the lock case-hardened and all brass parts finished bright.

The lock markings were the American eagle over small "U.S." ahead of the hammer, while under the bolster in two lines is "REMINGTON'S /ILION, N.Y.," and behind the hammer is the horizontal date "1863." The breech of the barrel is dated and marked "V/P(eaglehead)" proof and inspector's initials and "STEEL." "U.S." is marked on the tang of the buttplate.

Well designed and made, the Zouave Rifle is a favorite with Civil War collectors, with most of them being found in very good condition, possibly suggesting that they were held in reserve.

165

REMINGTON-BEALS SINGLE SHOT RIFLE

The Remington-Beals Single Shot Rifle was a sporting-style weapon produced between 1866 and 1868, with the total quantity manufactured estimated at less than 900 examples. Available in both .32 caliber and .38 caliber long rimfire, standard half round/half octagon barrel lengths were 24.0", 26.0", and 28.0", fitted with a blade front sight and a sporting-style folding leaf rear sight. The action of this unusual weapon is based on the lever principle, moving the barrel forward for loading and extracting when lowered.

All mountings were of iron, while the metal was blued; fitted with a walnut stock and made without a forend. Frames were mostly of brass, although iron frames will be found once in a great while, bringing a premium from collectors. All guns were serially numbered, and the barrels were marked "BEALS PATENT JUNE 28, 1864. JAN. 30, 1866/E. REMINGTON & SONS, ILION, NEW YORK."

Second from bottom: (previous page)
Remington-Beals Single Shot Rifle, serial #18. This unusual specimen is fitted with a 24.25" half round/half octagon barrel in .30 caliber rimfire, while the brass frame and butt plate retain approximately 95 percent of the original silver plate. Apparently, the barrel was professionally refinished in the distant past, and thus retains virtually all of its finish. The barrel is marked with the standard address.

Bottom: (previous page)
Remington-Beals Single Shot Rifle, serial #867. This the rare iron frame variant, fitted with a 28.0" half round/half octagon barrel in .32 caliber. This gun is in very fine condition overall, with the original finish having turned a light brown age patina, while the varnished stock is in very fine condition.

REMINGTON ROLLING BLOCK ACTION RIFLES

One of the most famous, often imitated, and almost universally used (no South American revolution could start without them!) weapons system is the Remington Rolling Block action. Manufactured in astounding quantities (well over a million military and carbine models made!) from 1864 to 1934, in one form or another.

A man by the name of Leonard M. Geiger patented the principle for the rolling block breech in 1863, shortly before he went to work for Remington; Joseph Rider, Remington's in-house genius, improved upon the action and developed the split-breech carbine. Working in concert, Geiger and Rider continued to work upon and improve the basic mechanism until it was perfected in April of 1866 and further modified by patent in August of 1867 and November of 1871.

The Rolling Block action has been popular, not only for its simplicity, but at the same time, for being one of the strongest actions ever developed through an interlocking system of hammer and breech. The hammer is cocked, and the breechblock is rolled backwards and down by thumb pressure on the lever projecting from the right side of the block, simultaneously extracting the spent cartridge; inserting a fresh cartridge, the action is rolled back up, and the gun is ready to fire. At the moment of firing, the hammer locks the breechblock into postion by cam action, producing almost unbelievable strength of action.

For collecting purposes, there are two distinctions, i.e., military and sporting guns; within each group, there are sub- catagories, especially within the sporting section. Basically, there are four different basic action sizes, which, for the most part, are also the model number designations.

No. 1 Action, which is 1.250" wide, is the largest of the rolling block actions, incorporating a wide range of chambering, from the smallest bore to the largest and heaviest calibers available. This action was used on Remington's Model No. 11/2 rifle.

No. 2 Action, which is 1.125" in width, generally used to chamber various sizes of less potent cartridges, including pistol size cartridges. The arched or curved contour at the rear sides of the action where it joins the stock readily identify this model.

No. 3 Action. This was the Remington-Hepburn, a falling block action, not a rolling block action.

No. 4 Action. This is a lightweight rolling block action that is quite short in size, made in rimfire calibers .22, 25/10 Stevens and .32. The forward section of the receiver is quite noticeably narrower than either Models No. 1 or 2.

No. 5 Action. Introduced in 1898, this was a large action made expressly for "Smokeless High Powered Cartridges," and is equipped with an extractor for rimless cases. This was the last of the large frame rolling blocks.

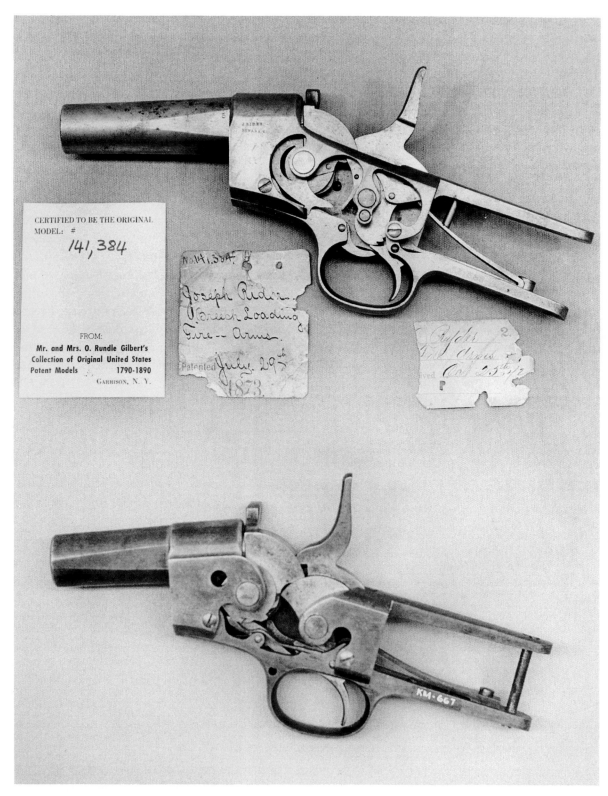

Original patent model upper action.

The upper action in this picture is the original patent model for U.S. Patent No. 141384, awarded to Joseph Rider for an improvement on the rolling block action on July 29, 1873. This was an attempt to improve the locking mechanism of the action in order to prevent accidental discharge. To Mr. Moldenhauer's knowledge, this was never incorporated into any production weapons. This all steel action is deeply marked "J. RIDER/NEWARK. O." The original patent model tag is shown attached, accompanied by a certificate, "Certifying the Original Model #141384 From Mr. and Mrs. O. Rundell Gilbert's Collection of Original United States Patent Models. 1790-1890. Garrison, New York."

Probably one of the most complicated tool room cutaways ever manufactured, according to the notes of Mr. Moldenhauer. This was done on a New York State contract musket, serial #338, and functions as follows: The hammer is drawn back to the full cock position; as the breechblock drops, it engages the spring loaded extractor, and as it continues, the extractor is given a quick snap to throw the empty casing clear of the breech. At the same time, the hammer is released and held in the safe position by means of a positive sear hook arrangement; a new cartridge is then inserted and the action returned to battery. The hammer boss rides on the breech until the breech is almost in the closed position; at this point, the hammer falls forward approximately .0625 of an inch, which puts the hammer boss under the breech boss by a like amount, thus locking the breech. This is a safe position, and the gun will not fire until the hammer is drawn back slightly to full cock, allowing the gun to fire. The rear upper tang is marked "REMINGTON ILION NY USA/PAT. MAY 3d NOV 15th 1864 APRIL 17th 1868/ AUG 27th 1867. NOV. 7th 1871."

REMINGTON SINGLE-SHOT BREECH-LOADING CARBINE

This single-shot breech-loading carbine, the predecessor of the "Rolling Block" design, is also known as the "Split Breech Remington," manufactured between 1864 and 1866 in both caliber .46 and .50 rimfire. Approximately 5,000 guns in .46 caliber were made for government contract by 1865, while 14,999 pieces in .50 caliber were delivered to the government between 1864 and 1865. The majority of the .50 caliber carbines are believed to have been unissued and later sold to France, accounting for their scarcity on the collector's market.

Both weapons are fitted with a 20.0" barrel held by one barrel band, all mountings are iron, the finish is blue with a case-hardened action, and the butt stock and forend are of oil finished walnut. All pieces were serially numbered, and the tang of the breech is marked "REMINGTON'S ILION, N.Y./PAT. DEC.23, 1863 MAY 3 & NOV. 16, 1864." This was one of Remington's earliest production longarms made for metallic cartridge ammunition.

In order to differentiate between the two models, let's call the .46 caliber carbine Type I, while the .50 caliber carbine is termed Type II.

The Type I has a small size action, with a long breech and a short hammer; the trigger is quite curved, and it has a short forend. A sling ring is attached to the left side of the frame, while inspector's marks are found on the left side of the stock.

Type II carbines have a much heavier action than the Type I, with a short breech and a long hammer; there is a sling ring and bar on the left side of the frame. The carbine is fitted with a rifle style butt plate, while some weapons have been found with sling swivels on both the buttstock and the barrel band. The forend measures 9.75" in length

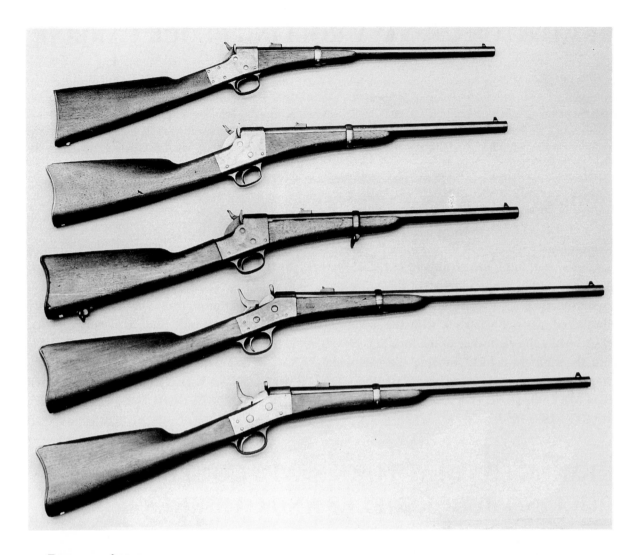

From top to bottom:

Remington Split Breech Saddle Ring Carbine. In .46 caliber, this carbine is martially marked with small single letter sub-inspection marks on the barrel band, barrel, frame, butt plate, and saddle ring bar; the stock has two script cartouches with inspector's marks "CGC" and "TB" (?), with other block stamping on top of the comb of the stock near the butt. In the case of this particular carbine, the case-hardened colors on the action have turned a silver color, the barrel has achieved a fine age patina, and the walnut stock is in excellent condition.

Remington Split Breech Military Carbine. This .50 caliber carbine is in very fine condition, with approximately 40 percent of the original blue finish remaining, while the case-hardened action and butt plate show traces of the original colors. The carbine is fitted with a saddle ring and bar on the left side, while the butt plate is stamped "US," the only markings on the weapon.

Remington Split Breech Saddle Ring Carbine. With but minor usage marks, this carbine is in very fine original condition. The weapon is a variant fitted with a sling swivel mounted on the front band, with the rear swivel inletted into the stock. The butt plate is deeply stamped "US," while the barrel, frame, and saddle ring bar are stamped with a single small letter sub-inspection mark.

REMINGTON U.S. NAVY ROLLING BLOCK CARBINE

The U.S. Navy Rolling Block Carbine was produced from 1868 to 1869, with the total quantity manufactured estimated at 5,000. This carbine was made in .50-70 centerfire caliber, with a short forend held to the 23.25" barrel by a single barrel band; the barrel has a short single leaf rear sight. All of the mountings are of iron, the barrel is blued, with a case-hardened frame, and there is a bar and sling ring fixed to the left frame. On others, swivels will be found on the barrel band and inletted into the buttstock. Markings are on the upper rear tang behind the hammer, "REMINGTON'S, ILION, N.Y. U.S.A./PAT. MAY3d. NOV. 15th 1864, APRIL 17th 1866," while inspector's marks are on the right frame, "P/FCW/(anchor)." There will also be found an inspector's cartouche at the wrist of the stock.

Second from bottom: (previous page)
Remington U.S. Navy Rolling Block Carbine, serial #4729. This carbine is in excellent to mint condition, retaining practically all of its original bright blue finish, while the case-hardened butt plate and action retain most all of their original bright coloring. The forend and buttstock are in exceptionally good condition, with all edges and markings crisp and clear. The barrel is serially numbered, as well as struck with the naval anchor; the top of the butt plate is deeply marked "US," while the right rear of the forend is clearly marked with the inspector's cartouche "FCW," and the right buttstock showing the cartouche "ESA" at the wrist. Interestingly enough, the markings on the upper tang are "REMINGTON ARMS COMPANY, ILION, NY/PAT. MAY 3rd 1864 MAY 7th JUNE 11th NOV 12th DEC. 24th 1872/DEC. 31st 1872, SEPT. 9th 1873 JAN. 12th MARCH 18th 1874."

REMINGTON NEW YORK STATE CONTRACT ROLLING BLOCK RIFLES AND CARBINES

The New York State Contract Rolling Block Rifles and Carbines were made for the New York State National Guard circa 1872, with the total quantity made estimated at 15,000. The rifle is fitted with a 36.0" barrel held by three barrel bands, while the carbine has a barrel 22.0" in length, held by a single barrel band to the shortened forend; the finish is blue, and the mountings are iron, with sling swivels on the rifle and a ring bar and sling ring on the carbine. The stocks of both weapons are oil finished walnut. The guns are marked with the Remington three-line markings and patent dates on the upper tang; the distinguishing feature of the inspector's markings on the left side of the stock at the wrist is a "banner" cartouche and the initials "H.B.H." inside the banner. Others can be found with "U.S. N.Y." on the right side of the butt, with two markings by inspectors at the left wrist. Many will be found with regimental letters and number markings on the top of the comb.

Bottom: (previous page)
Remington New York State Contract Saddle Ring Carbine. This carbine is fitted with the 22.0" barrel in .50-70 caliber, the entire weapon being in excellent condition, retaining at least 90+ percent of the original bright blue finish, with traces of the original case-hardened colors still to be seen. The wood is in exceptional condition, but for one deep bruise on the top rear comb of the buttstock. The butt plate is deeply stamped with the rack or weapon number "80," while on the left side of the stock is stamped in large block letters, "TROUP 'C' N.Y.," accompanied by the fancy banner cartouche with the letters "H.B.H." inside.

REMINGTON ROLLING BLOCK MILITARY RIFLES AND CARBINES.

Remington Rolling Block Rifles and Carbines were manufactured between 1867 and 1902, with well in excess of 1,000,000 weapons produced. The majority of the weapons made appear to be of Remington manufacture; however, in many cases, actions alone were supplied for foreign sales, with the entire weapon being assembled overseas. In other cases, the entire gun was produced abroad under license from Remington. This situation has produced variations almost to the point of infinity, with barrel lengths ranging from 30.0" to 39.0" on rifles, to any variation in length of carbine barrels from 19.0" to 22.0", rifle forends are held either by three or two bands, with carbine barrels held by a single band to the short forend; foreign markings will be encountered that include, but are not limited to, English, Arabic, Turkish, Chinese, Spanish and a host of others.

Officially adopted by Denmark in 1867, this adoption was closely followed by Norway and Sweden in 1868, and by Spain in 1869 (both the carbine and the rifle helped immensely in the pacification of the Philippines and Cuba); Egyptian troops found themselves facing the natives of the Sudan with their official rifle and carbine after 1870, while post 1879, the rolling block rifle and carbine were helping the Argentinians pacify the natives of the Pampas. France continued to order the Remington Rolling Block Rifle in 8mm Lebel until well into the first World War, when it was used to arm rear area and line-of-communication troops.

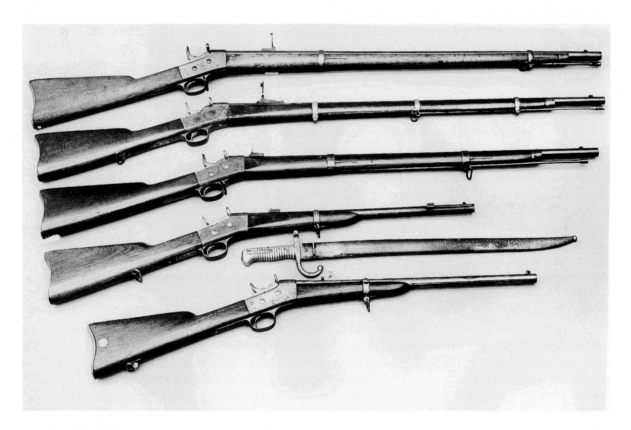

Top rifle: (above)

U.S. Model 1871 Remington Rolling Block Rifled Musket. This gun was manufactured under license at Springfield Armory; in very fine condition with all the metal parts a light steel color beginning to show age coloring, while the wood shows little usage. Fitted with a .50-70 caliber barrel, the right side of the frame is stamped with a spread-winged eagle, "U.S./SPRINGFIELD/ 1872," while the left side of the frame is stamped "REMINGTONS PATENT/PAT. MAY 3d NOV 15th 1864 APRIL 17th 1868."

Civilian Remington Rolling Block Musket. This rifle is 50.25" in overall length, fitted with a 35.0" full round barrel in .45-70 caliber. The steel-tipped forend is secured by three barrel bands, with the middle barrel band fitted with a swivel; there is also a sling swivel inletted into the bottom of the buttstock. The upper tang is marked "E. REMINGTON & SONS ILION, N.Y." with the usual patent dates through March 16th, 1874. In excellent condition, the barrel retains at least 90 percent of the original blue finish, while the action and butt plate show at least 90 percent of the original case-hardened colors. The wood, while exhibiting storage and handling dings, is in otherwise excellent condition.

Extremely rare Remington Military-Style Rolling Block Rifle. This rifle was made in .58 caliber Berdan. Fitted with a 32.0" round barrel, with a rifled musket rear sight, and measuring 48.0" overall, the barrel is held to the 25.75" steel-tipped forend by two flat barrel bands held by retaining springs mounted ahead of the bands. According to Mr. Moldenhauer's records, this is the only rifled musket that he had ever discovered in this caliber; there is a definite possibility that this was a prototype for a proposed military contract. There are no inspection marks to be seen, and the upper tang is marked "REMINGTONS ILION N.Y. U.S.A./PAT. MAY 3d NOV 15th 1864 APRIL 17th 1866." Condition of this piece is mint throughout, with only the slightest handling marks to mar what would be otherwise be a perfect specimen.

Unusual Remington Rolling Block Carbine. This carbine is in complete, excellent original condition. Fitted with an 20.50" round barrel with bayonet lug in .44 caliber centerfire, the carbine measures 35.50" overall. The 9.50" forend is secured to the barrel by a single barrel band with sling swivel, a sling swivel also being inletted in the bottom of the buttstock. The upper tang is marked "REMINGTON ILION N.Y. U.S.A./PAT. MAY3d NOV 15th 1864 APRIL 17th 1866". The correct 27.50" sword bayonet, with 22.50" blade and blued scabbard are shown with the weapon. This carbine came with the original gun bag marked "Dr. Belisario D. Romero/La Paz". The barrel retains at least 95 percent of the original bright blue finish, while the case-hardened action and butt plate retain at least 90 percent of their bright coloring; the oil finished stock and forend are also in excellent condition, showing that while used presumedly in the wilds of Bolivia, the gun was well cared for.

Remington Brevette Carbine, serial #13743. Fitted with a 21.0" barrel in .44 caliber centerfire, proofed profusely, including "ELG" and the date "1871", the left side of the action is marked with the serial number and "BREVET/REMINGTON EM & L NAGANT A LIEGE". It would appear that at some point in time, the carbine was equipped with some form of folding bayonet that attached through a hole in the base of the front sight; the single barrel band is seen to have a clip attachment on the right side for the blade, indicating the use of a spring-loaded bayonet. The gun is in very fine condition; note the circular arsenal or inspection stamping on the lower right side of the stock.

Model 1879 Argentinian Rolling Block Rifle. Adopted in 1879 by the Argentine Armed Forces in .43 caliber Spanish (11mm), the weapons saw much use by Argentinian troops in the pacification of the indigenous population of the Pampas during the 1880s. These weapons were also used to good effect during the constant alarms on the Chilean/Argentinian border during the closing years of the nineteenth century. Paraguayan rebels in the Revolution of 1904 were equipped with Argentine Rolling Block rifles when they crossed the border from Argentina to Paraguay; these were later incorporated into the Paraguayan arsenal at the conclusion of hostilities. Fitted with a barrel 34.50" in length, the rifle measures 51.0" overall and is fitted with a side mounted bayonet lug. The barrel is held to the forestock with three barrel bands, the central band incorporating a sling swivel, with a sling swivel inletted into the lower buttstock. Markings are on the upper tang, "REMINGTON ARMS COMPANY, ILION, N.Y. U.S.A., and patent dates ending in MARCH 16th, 1874;" the octagon portion of the barrel forward of the receiver is marked on the top flat "MODELO ARGENTINO 1879 E.N." This particular weapon was arsenal refinished prior to sale, with scattered slight pitting evident under the re-blue, with the wood in excellent condition. *(Author's collection)*

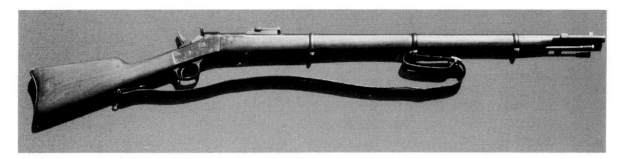

Model 1879 Argentinian Rolling Block Rifle. *(Author's collection)*

View of the Argentinian markings on the top flat of the barrel. *(Author's collection)*

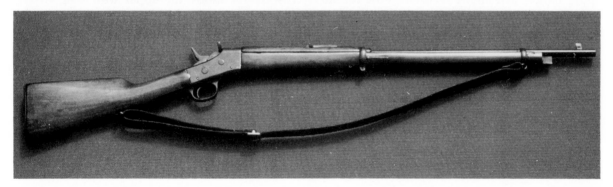

Mexican Model 1897 Remington Rolling Block Rifle, serial #2618. Fitted with a 28.25" round barrel with sliding leaf rear sight in caliber 7mm, the rifle measures 45.0" overall. Note the bayonet lug for the short model Remington bayonet. Markings on this weapon include the three-line address with "REMINGTON ARMS COMPANY ILION, N.Y. and patent dates ending with MARCH 16th 1874," and the Mexican "REPUBLICA MEXICANA/(eagle looking right clutching snake in its beak)". Many such weapons were marked on the barrel in front of the handguard "7mm S.M." for 7mm Spanish Mauser. The serial number is marked on the lower tang. Mexico first ordered the Remington Rolling Block weapons in 1876, with the acquisition of both rifles and carbines; due to the ease and simplicity of operation, as well as strength of action, orders continued for decades, ending with the Model 1897. These weapons, as well as others, were the backbone of Mexico's many uprisings culminating in the revolution of 1910. This rifle was obviously well cared for, as it retains 95+ percent of the original bright blue finish on the barrel, while the casehardened action has dulled with the years. Unfortunately, like many such actions from Central and South American countries, screw slots have been "buggered" in many cases. The wood is in surprisingly good condition, considering its probable history. The barrel is held to the forestock by two barrel bands, the upper band with sling swivel, while a similar sling swivel is inletted into the buttstock. *(Author's collection)*

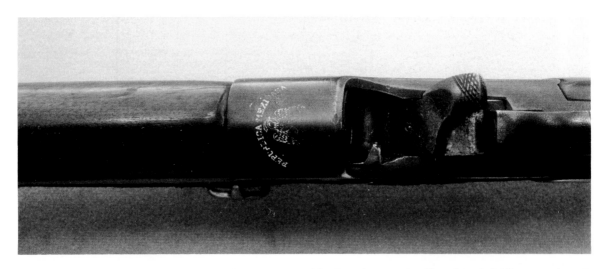

Top view of the markings on the Mexican Model 1897 Remington Rolling Block Rifle, showing the faded Mexican eagle with snake surmounted by "REPUBLICA MEXICANA." Note that the action is open. *(Author's collection)*

From top to bottom: (next page)

Remington 7mm Army Rolling Block Rifle. This export model rifle with bayonet lug and original bayonet is in very fine condition, with the barrel retaining most of the original bright blue finish, with some brown patina beginning to show. The barrel is marked "7mm S.M." ahead of the 9.25" upper handguard and is secured to the forend by two barrel bands, the upper with sling swivel, with the buttstock inletted for a similar sling swivel; the upper tang is marked with the usual "REMINGTON ARMS COMPANY ILION N.Y., with patent dates through MARCH 16th, 1874." Equipped with what appears to be an early Krag sling, the rifle is shown with the original short bayonet, 12.94" overall, with a blade measuring 8.19" in length. Missing the original cleaning rod.

Remington 7mm Army Rolling Block Rifle. An export model rifle similar to, but different from the preceding rifle. The rifle measures 45.25" overall, with a 30.0" round barrel and a 10.25" upper handguard; full stocked, the barrel is secured by two barrel bands, the upper with a sling swivel, with another sling swivel inletted into the buttstock. This gun is in absolutely mint condition, with all of the original bright blue and case-hardened finish.

Remington 7mm Uruguayan Military Carbine. Fitted with a 20.50" barrel and measuring 35.50" overall, the carbine is equipped with a 3/4-length forestock with wooden upper handguard. The single front barrel band with side mounted sling swivel, while the rear sling swivel is inletted into the stock. Markings include a large circular stamp in the lower right side of the buttstock, "EJERCITO URUGUAY 1112A;" the left side of the frame has a saddle ring bar and ring, while the upper tang is marked "REMINGTON ARMS CO./ILION, N.Y. U.S.A./PATENTED OCTR. 22nd 1902." The barrel is also stamped "Cal. 7mm." The entire weapon is in excellent shape, with at least 98 percent of the original blue finish on the barrel, the case-hardened action, having lost all of its color, has turned a silver-gray. The wood is in excellent condition, with a slightly oversize correct replacement upper handguard; the overhang can be seen in the picture.

Remington Model No. 4 S "Military Model" Rolling Block Sporting Rifle. In excellent original condition, retaining at least 90-95 percent of the original blue and case-hardened finish, this fine specimen is marked on the barrel, "MODEL 4-S REMINGTON ARMS-UNION METALLIC CARTRIDGE CO/REMINGTON WORKS, ILION, N.Y. U.S.A.-PATENTED JULY 22 1902," with the Remington logo, and "22 SHORT OR LONG"; the left side of the frame stamped "MILITARY MODEL."

Remington Model No. 4 Rolling Block Rifle. This is the take-down model fitted with a 24" full octagonal barrel in .32 caliber rimfire. This particular specimen is in really excellent condition, with at least 95+ percent of the original bright blue finish on the barrel and 95+ percent of the original case-hardened finish on the action. The varnished stock shows little usage, with only a small bruise on the left side of the forend.

Remington New Model No. 4 Rolling Block Rifle, serial #J284773. This is the take-down model with 22.50" full octagonal barrel in .32 caliber rimfire. As can be seen, the rifle is in excellent condition, with at least 90 percent of the original blue finish on the barrel, and virtually all of the original case-hardened finish on the action. The varnished stock is in exceptionally fine condition.

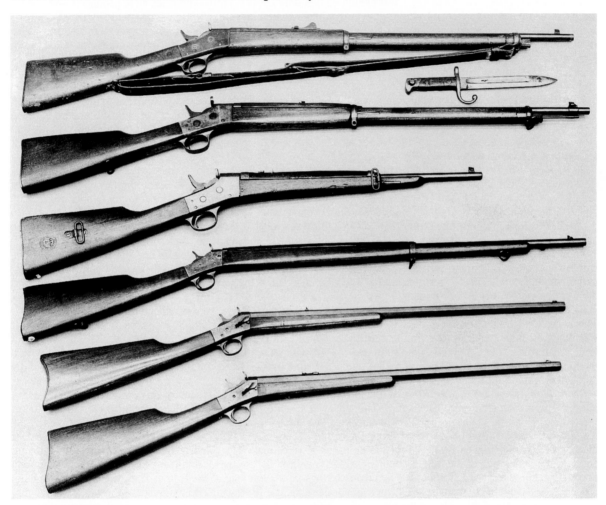

This picture illustrates several styles of longarms produced by Remington.

REMINGTON ROLLING BLOCK SPORTING RIFLES, VARIOUS TYPES.

During the period from 1868 to 1902, an almost infinite variety of Rolling Block Sporters were offered to the public with a great variety of features, i.e., calibers, barrel lengths, weight, stocks, finishes, butt plate styles, as well as sights, giving the collector an absolute field day in building a collection. It is my understanding that no guide exists today that would detail all of the myriad of different variations and styles that exist and will possibly be encountered. What is detailed here are the basic, standard models as offered to the public. Bear in mind that all of these models could be, and were, embellished by the substitution of the features previously listed, as well as others.

Standard to all guns are a barrel with a blued finish, and a case-hardened action. Remington markings are found on the tang with varying patent dates, while barrels were marked "E. REMINGTON & SONS, ILION N.Y." The calibers in which these guns were available are too many to list by every model, but an attempt will be made to highlight those calibers most often encountered.

Sporting Rifle No. 1. While the exact quantity manufactured is not known, the figure is estimated in the many thousands. Some of the calibers available include .40-50, .40-70, .44-70, .45-70, .50-45, .50-70, and many other centerfire cartridges, as well as rimfire cartridges, including .44 and .46 calibers. Octagon barrels in 28.0" and 30.0" lengths are standard, while round barrels are sometimes encountered. Standard sights are a dovetailed blade front sight and a folding leaf type rear sight. All of these basics were subject to special order change.

Long Range "Creedmore" Rifle. These rifles are rated as some of the finest rifles ever produced by Remington; manufactured between 1873 and 1890, it is estimated that only a few (?) thousand rifles were produced, some standardized, while many were custom-built. Standard calibers available were .44-90, .44-100, and .44-105. Other calibers could be special ordered. Standard barrels are half round/half octagon 34.0" in length, fitted with a globe front sight and a long range Vernier tang sight. Buttstocks were available in all different grades of wood, from plain grain to fancy grain, with a checkered pistol grip considered standard; forends were available checkered or uncheckered, with or without an iron cap (usually standard). Special sights, butt plates, levels, etc., were all optional equipment for the well-heeled purchaser.

Mid-Range Target Rifle. The Mid-Range Target Rifle was produced in five basic stock configurations between 1875 and 1890, from straight sporting to the pistol grip Creedmore with a wide variety of sights. Standard calibers were .40-70, .44-77, .45-70, .50-70; the half round/half octagon barrels were available in two lengths, 28.0" and 30.0". Probably the most desirable rifle would be one with a Vernier tang peep sight, matched with a globe front sight and a checkered pistol grip stock.

Short Range Rifle. This model rifle, made from 1875 through 1890, came in many styles, lengths, and variations; centerfire calibers that are standard are .38 extra long, .40-50, .44 S&W, .44 extra long, as well as .38 extra long RF, .44 extra long RF, and .46 caliber RF. The full round or full octagonal barrels come in two lengths, 26.0" and 30.0", with a variety of sights available. Stocks were available with or without a checkered pistol grip.

Black Hills Rifle. Manufactured from 1877 to 1882, this was a reliable, moderately priced sportsmen and hunters' rifle available in caliber .45-60 centerfire, with a 28.0 barrel fitted with plain open sights on a simple buttstock and forend.

Light Baby Carbine. Manufactured from 1892 to 1902, the total produced is estimated in excess of 2,000. The carbine was produced only in caliber .44-40 with a 20.0" lightweight barrel, fastened by a single barrel band to the carbine-style forend. There is a sling ring bar and ring attached to the left frame, the standard finish is blued, and the weapon weighed in at 5.75 pounds.

Remington Model 11/2 Sporting Rifle. Several thousand of these rifles were produced between 1888 and 1897. This is the lightweight version of the No. 1 Sporting Rifle, except that the frame is the same as the No. 1 frame. It was made for both centerfire and rimfire cartridges, with RF in .22, .25 Stevens, .25 long, .32, .38 long and extra long. Centerfire calibers are .32-20, .38-40, and .44-40. The straight, plain walnut stock could be ordered with a medium weight octagon barrel between 24.0" and 28.0" in length. Barrels are fitted with a blade front sight and a notched elevator adjustment sporting-type rear sight.

Remington Model 2 Sporting Rifle. While the exact number of rifles produced of this model are unknown, the numbers are considered quite substantial. The rifle was produced in a great variety of calibers, from .22 RF to .38RF, as well as .22 centerfire to .38-40 centerfire. The standard octagon barrel was available in 24.0 and 26.0" lengths, and came with a bead front sight and sporting-style notched ramp elevator type rear sight. The finish is blue, with a case-hardened frame; all of the mountings are of iron. The oiled walnut stock has a slight rounded curve to the under-side of the butt, recognized as the "perch-belly" style. Markings on earlier models were on the upper tang, but later production models had the markings on the left side of the frame. This rifle had many special order options available to the purchaser, such as Vernier tang and wind gauge rear sights, checkering, etc. Two distinguishing features of this rifle are the size of the action, which is smaller than the No. 1, and the apparent curved configuration of the stock at the join to the frame.

Remington New Model No. 4 Rolling Block Rifle. The smallest and lightest rolling block rifle ever made by Remington, this rifle was manufactured from 1890 to 1933, with the total quantity produced estimated at over 50,000. This rifle was manufactured in rimfire calibers only, being available in .22 caliber RF short, long, and long rifle, .25 Stevens, and .32 short and long. The standard production barrel is a 22.50" octagon barrel, although a 24.0" barrel was available in .32 caliber; round barrels were introduced during the latter years of production. Standard are bead front sights and V-notch rear sights. All mountings are iron, and the standard finish is blue with a case-hardened frame. Apparently, a take-down model of this rifle became available to the public after the turn of the century. Markings included various renditions of the company name, address, and patent dates.

Remington Model No. 4 S "Military Model" Rolling Block Sporting Rifle. This rifle was also well known as the "Boy Scout Rifle," and was manufactured from 1913 to 1923, with quantities estimated from a low of 10,000 to a high of 25,000. The stock is a full military-style stock, the upper handguard and 28.0" round barrel held to the stock by a single barrel band with sling swivel. There is another sling swivel inletted into the bottom of the buttstock. Often these rifles will be found with a stud on the underside of the barrel for bayonet attachment; the bayonet itself is extremely rare and is seldom found on the market. Earliest specimens produced are marked "BOY SCOUT," on the frame, while later production models are marked "MILITARY MODEL" on the frame. It would appear that military academies were the prime target for sales of these weapons.

Remington No. 5 Rolling Block Rifles and Carbines. The No. 5 model was produced in three basic types based on the No. 1 action, but with an action made for smokeless cartridges: the sporting and target rifle; the Model 1897 Military rifle; the Model 1897 carbine. These models were manufactured from 1897 to 1905, with the total quantity produced estimated at more than 100,000. Finishes are blue with case-hardened frames and butt plates; patent dates are on the upper tang, while the Remington name, address, and caliber is stamped on top of the barrel.

Sporting and Target Rolling Block Rifles. Produced from 1898 until 1905, with the quantity made unknown. The available calibers were .30-30, .303 British, 7mm, .30 U.S., .32-40 HP, .32 U.S., and .38-55. Barrels were available in two lengths, 28.0" and 30.0" (the 30.0" barrel was standard for .30 U.S.). Sights are open type rear sights and blade front sights. The stocks are plain and straight, fitted with a half-length forend with a slight curve to the tip. The only extras available were set triggers.

Model 1897 Military Rolling Block Rifle. Produced between 1897 and 1902, these rifles were mainly made for export to Central and South America. Fitted with a 28.25" barrel in either .30 U.S. or 7mm Mauser, the stock is full musket style, with a wooden handguard from the front of the receiver to the lower band; the stock and the barrel are held together by two barrel bands, the upper band with a sling swivel, and a second swivel inletted into the buttstock. A bayonet stud for a knife-type bayonet is located at the end of the forestock.

Model 1897 Military Rolling Block Carbine. With the exception of a 20.0" barrel available in the same calibers as the rifle, a short carbine forend with wooden handguard fastened by a single barrel band, and a side mounted sling ring bar and sling on the left frame, the rifle and carbine are identical. Again, these weapons were intended for the export market.

Remington No. 6 Rolling Block Type Rifle. Produced for the youth market, these rifles are of the take-down type, with a large knurled knob for the barrel release underneath the frame of the rifle. The action is a much modified and slimmer version of the rolling block action, having a small knob on the block to open the breech. These rifles were manufactured between 1902 and 1933, with the quantity produced estimated at well in excess of 250,000. Fitted with a 20.0" barrel, the calibers available were .22 short, long and long rifle, as well as .32 short and long. The rifle was also available in smoothbore for shot cartridges. The standard finish is blue overall with a case-hardened frame on the earliest production types.

Remington No. 7 Rifle, Rolling Block Action. This rifle was the last rolling block introduced to the market, and is considered by collectors to be one of the most unusual Remington rifles ever made. Produced between 1903 and 1911, it is estimated by expert Remington collectors that less than 1,000 specimens were manufactured. The No. 7 has a markedly distinctive profile, with an extremely defined checkered pistol-grip style stock and a checkered forend. The butt plate is of hard rubber with the Remington logo in shield design. Behind the hammer is a beautifully designed bracket upon which is mounted a Lyman-type folding, tang peep sight. The rifle is made on the Model 1871 pistol action, with half round/half octagon barrels available in 24.0", 26.0", and 28.0" lengths; calibers available were .22 short and long rifle, as well as .25-10 Stevens. Finishes are blued throughout, with the action and triggerguard case-hardened. Marked on the barrel "REMINGTON ARMS CO. ILION, N.Y. U.S.A." with standard two-line Remington address and patent dates, as well as "P" and "S" identical to the Model 1871 pistol, on the left side of the frame.

REMINGTON MODEL 1867 NAVY CADET ROLLING BLOCK RIFLE

Manufactured during the year 1868 at Springfield Armory using only Remington Navy Carbine actions. The total quantity made was 498 pieces. Fitted with a 32.50" round barrel in caliber .50-45 centerfire cadet cartridge, with the overall rifle length 47.37". The rear sight is the same as the one used on the Model 1864 Civil War Musket. The action is identical to the Navy carbine action, bearing anchor markings on the left side of the frame and the "P/F.C.W." initials on the right side of the frame. Tang markings are the same as on the Navy carbine, and the heel of the butt plate is marked "U.S." Two different finishes were available: a case-hardened action with bright barrel and hardware, or the entire rifle is completely blued. The stock is not fitted for sling swivels; however, the Cadet Rifle takes the same bayonet, front sight, upper and lower barrel bands, nose cap, butt plate and ramrod as the Model 1867 Springfield trap-door cadet rifle.

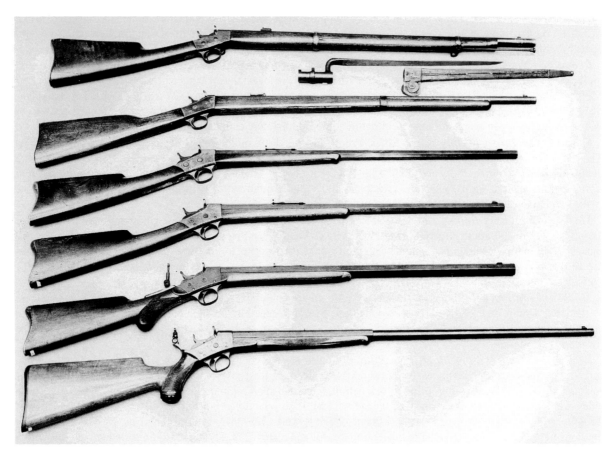

Remington model rolling block type rifles.

From top to bottom:

Remington Model 1867 Navy Cadet Rolling Block Rifle. This Cadet rifle is in very fine overall condition, with all of the metal retaining traces of the original bright blue finish. This stock was originally inletted at the bottom for a sling swivel, with the inletting professionally filled in at sometime in the past; the inletting for the tang of the triggerguard was also oversized and filled in at the same time to accommodate the narrower tang as found on the Cadet Rifle. The rifle is equipped with the original angular socket bayonet and scabbard, with both in excellent condition.

Remington Model No. 4 S Military Model Rolling Block Sporting Rifle. This rifle is a variant from others of this model, for, while the usual Remington address and patent dates are present, the model number has been omitted. The left side of the frame is marked "AMERICAN BOY SCOUT," while most other production models are marked "BOY SCOUT" or the later "MILITARY MODEL." While generally in very good condition, this rifle is missing the bayonet lug screw, front and rear sling swivels, the upper wooden handguard, and the steel barrel band.

Remington Rolling Block No. 2 Sporting Rifle, serial #20237. Fitted with a 26.25" full octagon barrel in caliber .32 RF. Retaining at least 98 percent of the original bright blue finish on the barrel, the case-hardened action has all of the original finish with approximately 85 percent of the original bright coloring. The semi-deluxe stock is in excellent condition.

Remington Rolling Block No. 2 Sporting Rifle, serial #22691. This rifle is in excellent condition, retaining at least 95+ percent of the original bright blue finish, with the action retaining almost all of the original case-hardened finish; fitted with a 24.0" full octagon barrel in .22 caliber. The oil-finished stock is in excellent condition.

Second from bottom: (previous page)

Remington No. 2 Sporting Rifle, serial #797. Fitted with a 24.0" full octagon barrel in .32 caliber RF, with Lyman-style rear sight, the rifle is equipped with a rare pistol grip. The condition of the rifle would rate as fine, with some traces of the original bright blue finish on the barrel mixed with a brown age patina. The walnut stock and forend in very fine condition.

Remington No. 7 Rifle, Rolling Block Action, serial #300317. Fitted with a 28.50" half round/half octagon barrel in .22 caliber RF, this rare weapon is in very good overall condition, the finish having turned brown with age. The checkered forend with its distinctive downward curved end piece is in excellent shape, as is the buttstock with its attractive lightly-striped grained wood.

From top to bottom: (top next page)

Factory Engraved Remington No. 1 Rolling Block Sporting Rifle. With the action elaborately and heavily scroll engraved, the steel butt plate unengraved, but artistically worked, and beautifully oil-finished flame-grained walnut buttstock and forend, this rifle is a gem! Fitted with a 30.0" full round barrel in caliber .46 RF, the barrel also has a Beech's combination front sight and superior quality folding leaf, adjustable rear sight, while the tang is fitted for a Lyman-style tang peep sight. In excellent condition, with the barrel retaining at least 95 percent of the original bright blue finish and the action with virtually all of the original case-hardened finish, the colors only slightly age-dulled.

Remington Mid-Range Rolling Block Target Rifle, serial #7690. This rifle really comes equipped! Fitted with a 28.0 half round/half octagon barrel in .40 caliber, there is a spirit level wind gauge front sight; the tang is mounted with a 320-yard Vernier tang sight. The oil-finished buttstock with hard rubber butt plate, and forend are in excellent condition, the portion of the stock at the wrist checkered with scalloped edges, while the checkered forend with horn cap also shows scalloping. This piece retains approximately 75+ percent of the original blue finish, which has mixed with an age-brown patina, while the case-hardened frame retains most all of the original finish, the colors having dulled with age. The globe section of the front sight was filed off and the original front sight replaced with an inletted knife blade front sight with the spirit level a modern reproduction.

Remington Rolling Block Long Range "Creedmore" Rifle, serial #6696. Although completely professionally refinished at some time in the past, this rifle is still a beauty! Fitted with a 34.0" half round/half octagon barrel in .44-100 caliber, the barrel is equipped with an adjustable wind gauge front sight with a provision for a spirit level, which is presently mounted with the sight insert retainer instead of the spirit level. The tang is mounted with a correct 500-yard Vernier tang sight, with no provision for mounting the sight at the rear upper position on the buttstock.

Remington No. 1½ Rolling Block Sporting Rifle, serial #1124. This rifle is in excellent condition, fitted with a 26.25" full octagon barrel in .22 caliber; the most unusual aspect of this rifle is that, with the exception of the blued front and rear sights, the entire rifle is nickel plated overall. Approximately 98 percent of the nickel finish is remaining, while the plain wood stock and forend are in very fine shape.

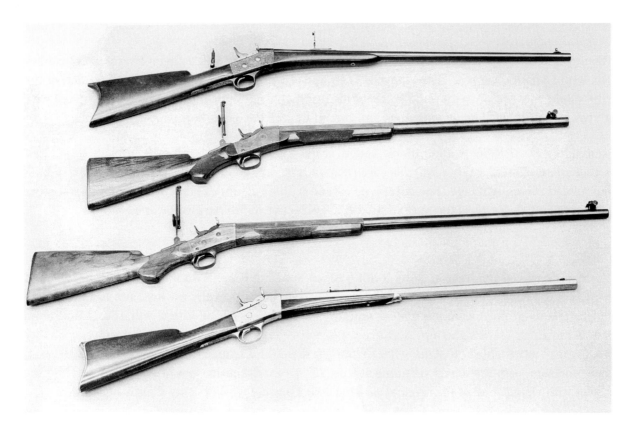

Remington model rolling block type rifles.

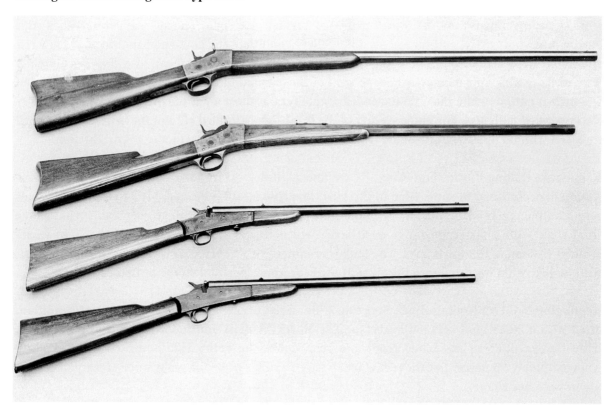

Remington model rolling block type rifles.

From top to bottom: (bottom previous page)

Remington Rolling Block Shotgun, with 32.0" round barrel in 20 gauge. This shotgun is in mint condition, with little, if any loss of the original bright blue finish on the barrel or of the case-hardened colors on the action and butt plate. The oil-finished stocks are absolutely excellent.

Remington Model No. 11/2 Sporting Rifle, serial #1499. The 28.0" full octagon barrel in .32 caliber RF, with the barrel retaining 95+ percent of the original blue finish, while the action and the butt plate have at least 95 percent of the original case-hardened finish. The entire condition of the rifle is excellent, especially the varnished walnut stocks.

Remington No. 6 Rolling Block Type Rifle, serial #S1060803. This "Boy's" rifle is fitted with a 20.0" barrel in .32 caliber RF, the left side of the frame stamped "PATENTED JULY 22, 1902." The rifle is in virtually mint condition, retaining at least 99+ percent of the original bright blue finish on the barrel, while the case-hardened frame is bright, and the varnished walnut stocks are also mint.

Remington No. 6 Rolling Block Type Rifle, serial #370712. This "Boy's" rifle is fitted with a 21.0" smooth bore barrel in .32 caliber; the left side of the action is unmarked, however the word "SMOOTHBORE" is stamped in addition to the usual markings on the barrel. This rifle is also in virtually mint condition, with 99+ percent of the original bright blue finish on the barrel, with the action retaining at least 99+ percent of the case-hardened colors. This earlier production model also has excellent to mint varnished walnut stocks.

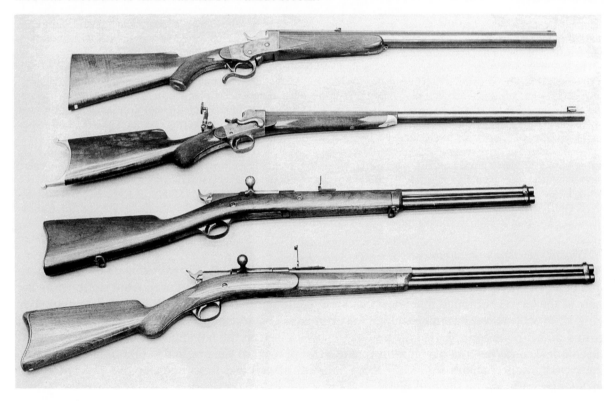

From top to bottom:

A scarce Pieper Liege 7-Shot Goose Volley Rifle, serial #459. Fitted with a barrel approximately 26.0" in length with seven separate bores (see detail picture) in .32 caliber RF, it is considered unusual to find a scarce rifle such as this in a caliber other than .22 caliber RF, or .22 WRF. The top of the barrel rib is marked "H PIEPER LIEGE," while the borders of the action are engraved. In excellent to mint condition, this interesting and desirable variant of the rolling block rifle retains at least 98 percent of the barrel finish and the bright case-hardened finish on the action; the checkered forend and stock also in excellent condition.

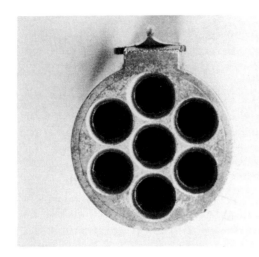

Detail of the Pieper Liege 7-Shot Goose Volley Rifle bores.

THE NO. 3 REMINGTON-HEPBURN RIFLE

The Remington-Hepburn No. 3 Rifle was patented in 1879 and introduced first in 1880, with a wide number of variations listed in the Remington catalog until 1907. Designed by Lewis L. Hepburn, superintendent of the Mechanical Department at the Remington plant (a member of the American Creedmore International Shooting Team). It is difficult to categorize Hepburns, as it appears that factory nomenclature for certain of the models changed over the years and the names given did not always remain the same; standard models and variations thereof would be dropped, while others were introduced. Anyone really interested in this subject will find much further information in the book *Single Shot Rifles* by James Grant.

The Remington-Hepburn is a simple, strong action, easily operated by the side mounted lever on the frame, which operates the breech, dropping it downwards for loading and extraction. There are features common to all Hepburns, such as case-hardened actions with blue barrels. With the exception of the full stock "Creedmore Military" model and the under-lever "Walker" type rifle, all Hepburns will be found with checkered pistol grip buttstocks; on finer grade models, it is standard for forends to be checkered to match the stock checkering; on plain grades, the forends are plain, however they could be checkered by special order. Forend tips are another area with many differentiations: hardened metal tips on early production models were later changed to horn or hard rubber, inset along the underside of the lip; fancy match grades usually had nickel-plated, or case-hardened tips, or on special order, full horn or hard rubber to match the pistol grip caps. Many different styles of double set triggers were available on special order.

Markings are the same throughout, with barrels marked "E. REMINGTON & SONS, ILION, N.Y." or "REMINGTON ARMS CO." The right side of the action was marked "HEPBURN'S PAT. OCT. 7th, 1879." Caliber markings are usually stamped on the underside of the barrel, just forward of the tip of the forend.

Second from top: (previous page)
Remington-Hepburn No. 3 Sporting and Target Rifle, serial #8741. Fitted with a 28.0" half round/ half octagon barrel in .38-55 caliber, the rifle is equipped with a Lyman peep front sight, while the rear of the barrel is capped for mounting a telescopic sight. The tang is fitted with a Lyman-style tang sight with elevation and windage adjustments. The stocks are a deluxe checkered walnut, with a nickel-plate Swiss-style butt plate and cheek piece on the left side of the stock. In excellent mechanical condition, the barrel retains at least 90 percent of the original bright blue finish, while the case-hardened action shows the same amount of original finish. Ninety-five percent of the nickel plate remains on the butt plate.

REMINGTON-KEENE MAGAZINE BOLT ACTION RIFLE AND CARBINE

Manufactured between 1880 and 1888, the total quantity of weapons produced is estimated at approximately 5,000. This was Remington's first bolt action firearm, with the Keene having an outside manually cocked hammer; the magazine was tubular and attached under the barrel. A magazine cut-off is incorporated allowing the weapon to be used as a single shot. Barrels are 24.50", with the round barrel standard for sporting rifles; half round/half octagon barrels were available on special order. Calibers available were .45-70 (the greatest quantity produced, most widely used, and most popular), .40 caliber, and .43 caliber. The standard finish is overall blue, with a case-hardened hammer and iron mountings. A straight walnut stock is standard, while pistol grip stocks and finer grained woods were optional.

Markings are on the left side of the breech ,"E. REMINGTON & SONS, ILION, N.Y./PATENT FEB. 24, MARCH 17, 1874 JAN. 18. SEPT. 26, 1876. MAR. 20. JUL. 31 77."

The Frontier Model. This rifle was made for the U.S. Department of the Interior for arming the Indian Police, and will be found marked "U.S.I.D." with serial number and inspector's marks on the left side of the frame. The rifle is fitted with a 24.0" barrel with a carbine-style barrel band at the muzzle, and is equipped with sling swivels. The butt plate is carbine-style without the flanged top.

Carbine Model. This is the scarce one! With a full stock running almost to the muzzle and a tubular magazine holding seven cartridges, the carbine is fitted with a 22.0" barrel fastened by two barrel bands, and equipped with an iron forend tip. The rear sight is a short folding leaf military-style; the butt plate is also military.

Army Rifle. This rifle is also scarce. Fitted with a 32.50" barrel with a stock running almost to the muzzle, the barrel is secured by two barrel bands and a narrow iron forend cap; there is a sling swivel on the upper barrel band, and another sling swivel inletted into the underside of the butt.

Navy Rifle. Other than a barrel measuring 29.25" in length, the Navy rifle is identical to the Army rifle described below.

Bottom Pistols: (page 181)

Remington-Keene Magazine Bolt Action Carbine. The 20.0" (2.0" shorter than described above) barrel, in .45-70 caliber, is marked at the breech with a "T", while the left side of the receiver is marked "45-70," and "U.S.N.", struck twice, the first time lightly so that only the bottom portions of the letters are visible; the comb of the stock is also marked "U.S.N." There is a difference of opinion as to whether or not these markings are genuine, as they are quite old. Mr. Moldenhauer was of the opinion that they were false, as there was no known contract for government purchase other than those carbines purchased by the Department of the Interior for use by Indian Police. The carbine itself is really an outstanding specimen, with at least 95 percent of the original bright blue finish on the barrel and action, while the magazine tube shows at least 75 percent finish. The only thing detracting from the quality of the carbine is the old, crude, re-blued replacement rear sight.

Remington-Keene Sporting Rifle. This sporting rifle is in basically fine condition, with at least 80 percent of the original bright blue finish, with only some age thinning to be seen. The checkered semi-pistol grip walnut stock is in fine refinished condition. Fitted with a 24.50" half round/half octagon barrel in .45-70 caliber.

REMINGTON-LEE MAGAZINE BOLT ACTION RIFLE

The Remington-Lee Magazine Bolt Action Rifle was manufactured between 1880 and 1907, with the total produced somewhat in excess of 100,000 weapons, the majority of which were made for the export market. The basic weapon as produced was a military musket with full stocks fastened by two barrel bands; the carbine version was fitted with a short stock and the barrel was fastened by a single barrel band; the sporting rifle had the barrel attached by means of a screw from the underside of the stock. The main means of identifying these weapons was by the detachable box magazine set into the stock just ahead of the triggerguard.

The manufacturing history of this weapon is typical of the twists and turns that have taken place within the firearms industry over the years (continuing to this day!). The rifle was patented by James Paris Lee of Bridgeport, Connecticut, in 1879; in 1880, Lee received a contract from the U.S. Navy for the manufacture of 300 full stock rifles in .45-70 caliber. Lee formed the Lee Arms Company to produce this contract, and then let the contract to the Sharps Rifle Company to do the actual manufacture; Sharps ceased all operations in 1881, with Lee then turning over all the parts and tooling to Remington Arms Company for completion of the contract. Remington was also licensed at this time to produce the Lee rifles for export sales. After making some modifications to the Lee system, Remington secured contracts with foreign governments, as well as with the U.S. Army and Navy, making further refinements and modifications. This resulted in several variations that are recognized by collectors, if not by the manufacturer. All models were made in three basic categories: Military Rifle, Military Carbine, and Sporting Rifle.

Model 1879: Made by Sharps. This original contract produced a total of approximately 300 rifles, with the majority military models; one carbine was produced, and a few sporting rifles. The military model is fitted with a 28.0" barrel, fastened to the full stock by two barrel bands, and was made in .45-70 caliber; the magazine is flat sided. The barrel is marked "SHARPS RIFLE CO. BRIDGEPORT, CONN. U.S.A." and "OLD RELIABLE" in a rectangular cartouche.

Model 1879: Made by Remington. As made by Remington, the right side of the magazine is flat, while the left side has a raised rib for engagement of the cut-off device. The markings on the receiver are: "LEE ARMS CO. BRIDGEPORT, CONN. U.S.A." and "PATENTED NOV. 4, 1879."

The U.S. Navy Model, of which approximately 1,300 were made, is fitted with a 28.0" round barrel in .45-70 caliber, fastened to the full stock by two barrel bands. The breech of the barrel bears inspector, naval anchor, and proof marks.

Military Rifle; this rifle is identical to the Navy model without U.S. military markings, as the majority (approximately 1,000) were made for the export market in either .45-70 or .43 Spanish calibers. Different barrel markings will be encountered, including Chinese.

Sporting Rifle. This rifle was available with a choice of barrel length of either 28.0" or 30.0", the barrel half round/half octagon, in calibers .45-70, or 45-90. The rifle is stocked with a pistol grip sporting-style half stock. This is considered a rare rifle, as only 400 to 500 pieces were manufactured.

Models 1882 and 1885. At this time, the magazine was redesigned providing two grooves down each side as a guide for the magazine follower. The basic difference between the two models is the extractor and cocking knob on the bolt, both being larger in the Model 1885. Markings differ for the two models, with the Model 1882 marked "LEE ARMS CO. BRIDGEPORT, CONN., U.S.A." and "PATENTED NOV. 4, 1879"; or "E. REMINGTON & SONS, ILION, N.Y. U.S.A. SOLE MANUFACTURERS & AGENTS." The Model 1885 may be found with either of the above markings, or "REMINGTON ARMS CO./ILION, N.Y. U.S.A." and "LEE PATENT NOV. 4. 1879."

Model 1882 U.S. Army Contract. This rifle, production of which is estimated at 770 pieces, is fitted with a 32.0" round barrel in .45-70 caliber, fastened to the full stock with two barrel bands. Markings are "U.S." and inspector's initials at the breech, and inspector's markings on the right side of the stock.

Model 1885 U.S. Navy Contract. The navy contract rifle is the same as the above, with the inspector markings on the right side of the stock, and naval inspector initials and anchor on the receiver ring. Approximately 1,500 rifles are estimated to have been produced.

Foreign Military Models. It is estimated that approximately 10,000 of the Model 1882 rifles and 60,000 of the Model 1885 rifles were produced for shipment overseas, both military and civilian models. Many of these were made on contract for foreign governments, such as China, Spain, Egypt, and Russia, with calibers available in .45-70, .43 Spanish, .45 Gardner, and .42 Russian; the most popular caliber was the old reliable .45-70. All rifles are equipped for the same socket bayonet as the Model 1873 Springfield.   A small quantity of 1882/1885 carbines were made in a half-stocked version, fitted with a 24.0 round barrel; these are considered scarce.

Model 1882/1885 Sporting Rifles. It is estimated that only 200 Sporting Rifles were made of these two models; available in barrel lengths of 26.0" and 30.0" octagon barrels, with available calibers of .45-70 and .45-90. These sporting rifles are extremely scarce.

Model 1889. Manufactured between 1899 and 1907, these rifles were made mainly for smokeless powder, and incorporated many changes to the extractor to handle rimless cartridges. The magazine was now designed with three grooves to each side to facilitate the action of the magazine follower. Markings for all weapons were "REMINGTON ARMS CO./ILION, N.Y. PATENTED AUG. 26th 1884. SEP'T 9th 1884. MARCH 17th 1885. JAN. 18th 1887."

Full Stock Military Rifles. The Model 1889 was quite similar to the Models 1882/1885 with the main difference found at the tip of the forend, which had been redesigned to accept a knife-style bayonet; the rifle also incorporated an upper handguard from the receiver to the lower barrel band. There were also slightly different contours to the bolt and cocking piece. Fitted with 29.0" barrels, rifles were available in calibers 6mm Lee, .30-40, .303 British, 7mm, and 7.65mm.

Military Carbine. The military carbine is a scaled-down version of the military rifle, fitted with a 20.0" barrel available in the same calibers as the rifle. The carbine is fitted with a 3/4-length stock with upper handguard from the receiver to the single barrel band.

Sporting Rifle. The sporting rifle was available in barrel lengths as follows: 26.0" or 28.0" octagonal; 24.0", 26.0" and 28.0" round barrels. Calibers are the same as for the military rifle, with the addition of .30-30, .303, .32 Special, .32-40, .35 Special, .38-55, .38-72, .405, .45-70, and .45-90. Walnut half stocks with checkered pistol grips and grasping grooves on both sides of the forestock are standard. Standard also are open type front and rear sporting sights, with a large number of optional sights available on custom order. Special orders were also available for the finer grained wood stocks.

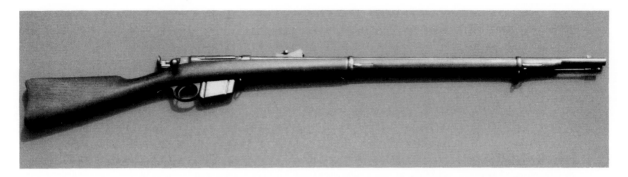

Model 1882 Remington-Lee Magazine Bolt Action Rifle, serial #53865. This rifle is in caliber .45-70, and was not made under U.S. contract; it bears the marking "REMINGTON ARMS COMPANY, ILION, N.Y. U.S.A./SOLE MANUFACTURERS AND AGENTS," on the top side of the left side rail. This rifle is in exceptional condition, showing little active use, the metal retaining at least 95+ percent of the original blue finish, while the walnut stock shows only minor storage and rack dings. *(Museum of Connecticut History)*

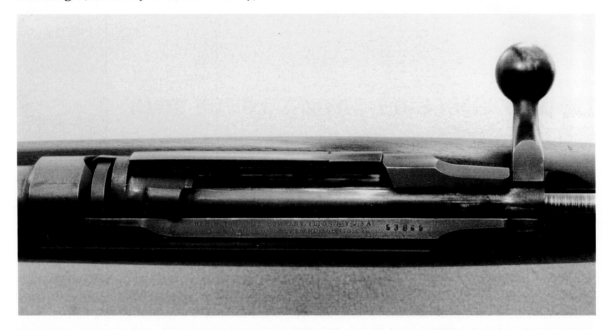

Top view of the action of the Remington-Lee Magazine Bolt Action Rifle, showing the markings on the top left side rail. *(Museum of Connecticut History)*

From top to bottom: (next page)

Remington-Lee Magazine Sporting Rifle, serial #75813. Fitted with a 24.0" barrel in .405 caliber, this sporting rifle has a special order windage adjustable front sight and a folding peep sight mounted on the end of the bolt. The checkered semi-pistol grip walnut stock is other than standard grade, and is fitted with a monogrammed checkered hard rubber butt plate. With 99 percent of the original blue on the barrel and action, this is truly an outstanding example of this model. Other than slight handling marks, the varnished stock is in excellent condition.

Semi-sporterized Military Model Remington-Lee Magazine Bolt Action Rifle. Fitted with a 29.0" barrel in caliber 7mm, this rifle is in complete, excellent condition, but for the forestock having been cut off several inches forward of the barrel band.

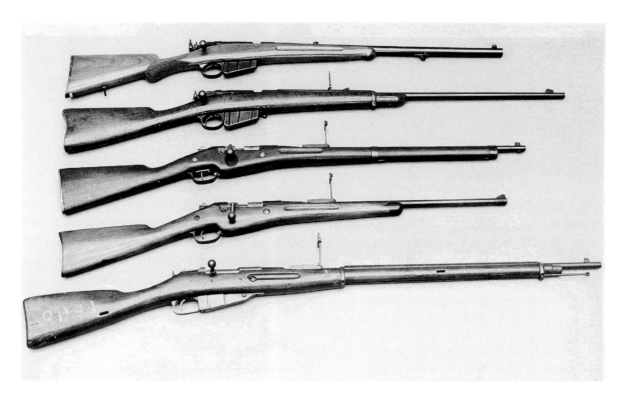

REMINGTON-LEBEL MODEL 1907/15 BOLT ACTION RIFLE

Due to battle attrition, contracts by the French government were let to commercial firms in the United States for the production of French Army Lebel Model 1907/15 bolt action rifles. It is estimated that the Remington plant manufactured only a few thousand of this model. The rifle is fitted with a 31.50" barrel in caliber 8mm Lebel, with a full military stock and blued finish. The rifle is marked on the right side of the barrel at the breech "RAC 1907/15" and on the left side of the action in script: "REMINGTON/M'LE 1907-15."

Middle rifle: (above)
Remington-Lebel Model 1907/15 Bolt Action Military Rifle. Fitted with a 25.50" barrel in caliber 8mm Lebel, this rifle has been shortened at some time in its career, while this is further confirmed by the removal of the upper and lower sling swivels. With the noted exceptions, this rifle is virtually in mint condition, with at least 99 percent of the original blue finish, and showing extremely little usage to the wood.

Sporterized Remington-Lebel Model 1907/15 Bolt Action Military Rifle. In very fine condition, this rifle has been professionally sporterized by the removal of the barrel bands and sporterizing the military stock.

REMINGTON MOSIN-NAGANT BOLT ACTION RIFLE

The Russian Military Commission in the United States during the first World War contracted with Remington and Westinghouse during the period 1916-1917 to produce the Model 1891 Mosin Nagant Rifle. Prior to 1900, Russia had produced this rifle at its own arsenals at Tula, Ishevsk, and Sestroryetsk, and also contracted for the rifles to be manufactured at Steyr, Austria, and Chatellerault, France. Due to inadequate production facilities in Russia, and the staggering losses of men and material suffered during the early stages of the war, it was necessary to have rifles made on contract at SIG (Switzerland), Valmet, and Tikkakoski (Finland), as well as Remington and

Westinghouse in the United States. Remington's contract was for a total of 1,000,000 rifles, however, this contract was terminated by the Russian Revolution and it is not known exactly how many rifles Remington actually produced. Interestingly enough, the U.S. government contracted, from Remington and Westinghouse, for a further 280,000 rifles for training purposes by U.S. troops in the States.

During the Allied Intervention in Russia after the close of the first World War, Allied troops were sent to northern Russia, as well as Siberia, to protect Allied interests during the revolution; this inevitably involved armed conflict with the Russian communist armies. Much to their disgust, men of the 339th Infantry Regiment (Detroit's Own!) and the 310th Engineers, quartered in England and slated for duty in Russia, were forced to turn in their Model 1917 Enfield rifles in exchange for the M1891 Mosin-Nagant. It was this rifle, along with a small supply of French Lebel M1907/15 rifles equipped for grenade launching, that our troops were equipped with during their long stay in Russian territory.

Fitted with a 30.50" barrel in caliber 7.62 x 54R Russian, the overall length of the rifle is 51.30", with a full military style straight stock; the full upper handguard held to the forestock by two barrel bands (prior to 1908, there was no upper handguard). The finish is blue overall. Sling swivels are mounted through slots in the stock. The rear sight is a folding leaf over tooth-like elevation notches, with a blade front sight. The rifle is marked on the top of the barrel at the breech in an arched manner, "REMINGTON/ARMORY/(DATE)," while the top of the receiver is marked with the crest of Czar Nicholas II.

Bottom: (previous page)
Remington Mosin-Nagant Bolt Action Rifle, serial #626852. This rifle is in fine condition, with not a lot of evident use. The markings on the breech of the barrel are as follows: "REMINGTON/ ARMORY/1917 NO 626852." This rifle has obviously been issued to, and used by Chinese forces, as the right side of the stock is heavily marked with Chinese characters, the left side with three large Chinese painted characters.

REMINGTON-WHITMORE MODEL 1874 DOUBLE BARREL HAMMER SHOTGUN & RIFLE

This was one of the first mass produced, reasonably priced double barrel shotguns made in the United States; produced c. 1874 to 1882, with the total quantity made estimated at approximately 2,000. The action is rather unusual and interesting in that the top lever is pushed forward and upward at the same time, allowing the barrels to open for loading and extracting. Available were the standard hammer double shotgun, the combination shotgun/ rifle, which is quite scarce, and the double rifle, which is identical to the others described, but with original rifle barrels. As only a few were made, the double rifle is extremely rare. The standard steel barrels (damascus as an option) were available in lengths of either 28.0" or 30.0", while the walnut stock was available straight or half pistol grip style. The finish is blue, with damacus barrels having a twist finish. Both the locks and the breech are case-hardened. Markings are on the top of the breech; "A. E. WHITMORE'S PATENT AUG. 8. 1871, APRIL 16, 1872," and on the rib "E. REMINGTON & SONS, ILION, N.Y."

From top to bottom: (next page)
Remington-Whitmore Model 1874 Double Barrel Hammer Combination Rifle/Shotgun, serial #1905. This scarce combination rifle/shotgun is in generally excellent condition, the finish having turned an even age-brown, with only traces of the original blue in protected areas; the case-hardened finish has turned a dull silver color with age, while the walnut stocks are in fine condition. Fitted with steel barrels 28.0" in length, the right barrel in caliber .45-70, the left barrel in 12 gauge shotgun. The barrel rib is marked "E. REMINGTON & SONS, ILION, N.Y."

Remington-Whitmore Model 1874 Double Barrel Hammer Shotgun, serial #148. Interestingly enough, the shotgun is fitted with 32.0" barrels (special order?) in 10 gauge, with the customary marking on the barrel rib. The shotgun is in excellent condition, with the barrels retaining at least 95 percent of the original twist damascus finish, the case-hardened action retaining all of the slightly dulled original finish. The walnut forend and deluxe checkered walnut buttstock in excellent condition.

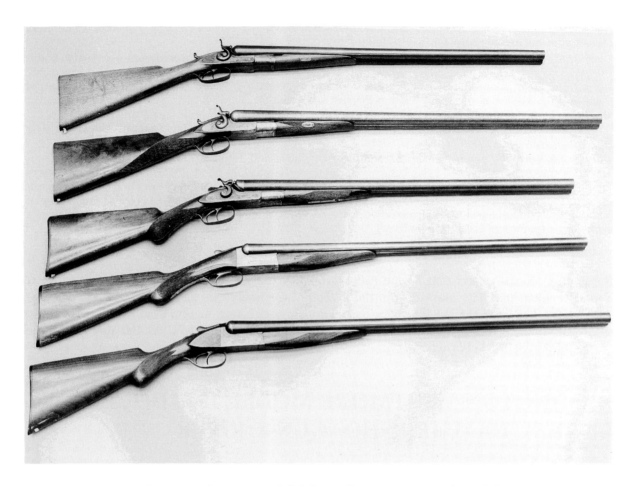

REMINGTON MODEL 1882 DOUBLE BARREL HAMMER SHOTGUN

   Approximately 7,500 Remington Model 1882 Double Barrel Hammer Shotguns were made between 1882 and 1889. Available in either 10 gauge or 12 gauge, barrel lengths were 28.0" or 30.0", in either steel or damascus. The stock was available either straight or half pistol grip style with a hard rubber butt plate, while the finish is blued, with damascus barrels having a twist finish; locks and actions were case-hardened. Barrels are marked "E. REMINGTON & SONS, ILION, N.Y." with "U.S.A." added on later models; the action was marked "REMINGTON ARMS COMPANY." The action is typical top lever release. The company advertised six different grades available in their original catalogs, with select grains of wood, finer grades of checkering, as well as engraving options.

Middle rifle: (above)
Remington Model 1882 Double Barrel Hammer Shotgun, serial #14291. The 28.0" barrels are in 12 gauge, signed on the rib "E. REMINGTON & SONS, ILION, N.Y." The shotgun is in excellent condition, retaining at least 95 percent of the original blue twist damascus finish, while the action retains all of the age-dulled case-hardened finish. The walnut stocks are in excellent condition.

REMINGTON MODEL 1883, MODEL 1885, MODEL 1887,

MODEL 1889 DOUBLE BARREL HAMMER SHOTGUNS

Made between 1883 and 1909, it is estimated that appproximately 30,000 plus of all models were produced. Barrels, available in steel or damascus in lengths of 28.0" to 32.0", were in 10 gauge, 12 gauge, or 16 gauge. Details for these shotguns are the same as for the models previously discussed, the appearances being quite similar over the years, with only contour and hammer shape changes by which to tell the difference. Many grades and options were available to the buyer.

REMINGTON HAMMERLESS SHOTGUNS MODEL 1894 AND MODEL 1900

Made between 1894 and 1910, it is estimated that over 2,000 pieces of the combined models were manufactured. Barrels were available in lengths from 28.0" to 32.0" in either 10 gauge, 12 gauge, or 16 gauge (model 1900 in 12 and 16 gauge only) with either steel barrels or damascus twist. As was customary, there were many grades and options available to the customer.

Second from bottom: (previous page)
Remington Model 1894 Hammerless Double Barrel Shotgun, serial #307448. Fitted with 28.0" barrels in 16 gauge, the action is marked on both sides of the frame "REMINGTON ARMS COMPANY." The action is fitted with a single trigger, and is in excellent shape overall, retaining approximately 65 percent of the original blue finish, the case-hardened action having turned an age-silver color. The checkered walnut stocks are in fine coondition, with the addition of a two-inch wooden spacer added to the butt, which is equipped with a hard rubber butt plate with Remington-UMC logo.

Remington Model 1884 Hammerless Double Barrel Shotgun, serial #Q367425. Fitted with 30.0" barrels in 12 gauge with auto-ejectors. The frame is marked on both sides "REMINGTON ARMS COMPANY." The shotgun is in really excellent condition, with at least 98+ percent of the original blue twist damascus finish on the barrels, and the action retains all of the original dull case-hardened finish. The checkered walnut stocks are also in excellent condition.

From left to right, top to bottom: (next page)
Shown in this picture are a group of eight pamphlets and catalogs relating to Remington products;
A pamphlet on the *Description and Rules for the Management of the Remington Navy Rifle Model 1871*. The National Armory. Springfield, Massachusetts, 1870. 6.0" x 8.75", with a blue paper cover.

An original catalog for the Remington-Lee Magazine Rifle; printed in black ink on light yellow pages, the tan cover illustrates the rifle and bayonet, 16 pages, 8.0" x 6.0".

A catalog titled *Reduced Price List. Illustrated Remingtons' Breech-Loading Rifles, Shot Guns, Revolvers, Repeaters, and Ammunition, Gun Mounting*, c. 1877, 42 pages, with many engraved illustrations of the various models of weapons offered at this time, 5.50" x 7.63".

The *Illustrated Catalog of the 'Remington' Breech-Loading Fire Arms and Ammunition*, 1878. Together with a Treatise on Rifle Shooting; History of Gun Making; Records of International Rifle Matches; Rules and Regulations for Shooting at Long Range, etc., etc..." 91 pages of text and illustrations, including 12 pages of advertisements for various shooting paraphenalia. 7.50" x 5.375".

Examples of several Remington product pamphlets and catalogs.

Original copy of the *Illustrated Catalog of the 'Remington' Breech-Loading Fire Arms and Ammunition*, 1879, 85 pages of text and illustration; 7.50" x 5.375".

Original catalog, *Breech-Loading Fire-Arms*, 1881. Rifles and Shot-Guns. Illustrated. E. Remington & Sons. Price-List. Revolvers and Repeaters. Ammunition, Gun-Mounting, Armory, Ilion, N.Y., 52 pages of text, illustrations and price lists, 6.0" x 9.25".

Pamphlet form catalog titled *Price-List*, E. Remington & Sons, Manufacturers of Arms and Ammunition. Armory, Ilion, N.Y. Salesrooms, 281 & 283 Broadway, New York, 48 pages of price lists, illustrations, etc., 6.0" x 9.25"

An original catalog, *1889 Price List*, Remington Arms Company, Ilion, N.Y. Manufacturers of Double Barrel Shot Guns, Rifles, Derringers, Etc. Established 1816, Agents: Hartley & Graham, New York. Winchester Repeating Arms Co., New York, New Haven and 418 & 420 Market Street, San Francisco. Government Contractors," 16 pages of text and illustration, 10.0" x 6.25".

The New Remington, Small Calibre Model 1897, with an illustration of the rifle and its bayonet on the cover. Printed in English and Spanish, there are nine pages of text. 5.375" x 7.0".

Remington Arms Company, Ilion. New York. 1898, 40 pages of text, price lists, and illustrations. 9.25" x 6.0".

The 1901 edition of the *Remington Arms Company* catalog, with 48 pages of text, price lists, and illustrations. 9.25" x 6.0".

An original catalog, *Remington Firearms*, 1903, Remington Arms Company, Ilion, New York, 64 pages of text, price lists, and illustrations, 7.0" x 8.0".

A leather-bound, deluxe catalog for 1911-1912 for all of the diverse products and services offered by Remington-UMC. The cover is embossed in gold letters on red morocco leather *Remington-UMC*. Remington Arms-Union Metallic Cartridge Company, 191 pages of text, illustrations, etc., with an insert of "Restricted Selling Prices in effect February 1st, 1912. 9.0" x 6.0".

A deluxe edition of the *Remington UMC, Modern Firearms and Ammunition*, 1917-18. The Remington Arms Union Metallic Cartridge Co. Inc., the name "G.W. Harvey" embossed in the lower right hand corner, 208 pages of text, illustrations, and price lists. 9.0" x 6.0".

A deluxe copy of the 1923 Catalog No. 107 of *Remington Modern Firearms and Ammunition*. Imitation morocco leather covers, with gold lettering, 192 pages of text, price lists, and illustrations. 9.0" x 6.0".

Examples of the original Remington firearms and supply catalogs.

Bibliography

ARMED FORCES OF LATIN AMERICA, Adrian J. English. Jane's Publishing Co., Ltd., London, England. 1984.

THE BOOK OF PISTOLS, W.H.B.Smith/Joseph E. Smith. Stackpole Books, Harrisburg, Pa. 4th Edition. 1972.

THE BOOK OF RIFLES, W.H.B.Smith/Joseph E. Smith. Stackpole Books, Harrisburg, Pa. 4th Edition. 1972.

CATALOG - THE KARL MOLDENHAUER COLLECTION OF REMINGTON FIRE-ARMS, Richard A. Bourne Co., Inc., Hyannis, Mass. 1980.

FLAYDERMAN'S GUIDE TO ANTIQUE AMERICAN FIREARMS ... AND THEIR VAL-UES, 3rd. Edition. Norm Flayderman, DBI Books, Northfield, Ill. 1983.

GUNS OF THE WORLD, Hans Tanner, Editor, Petersen Publishing Co., Los Angeles, Ca. 1972.

MEXICAN MILITARY ARMS, THE CARTRIDGE PERIOD, James B. Hughes, Jr., Deep River Armory, Inc., Houston, Texas. 1968.

MILITARY BOLT ACTION RIFLES, 1841 - 1918, Donald B. Webster. Museum Restoration Service, Alexandria Bay, N.Y. 1993.

QUARTERED IN HELL; The Story of The American North Russian Expeditionary Force, 1918-1919. Dennis Gordon/Hayes Otoupalik, Gateway Printing, 1982.

REMINGTON ARMS IN AMERICAN HISTORY, Alden Hatch. Rinehart & Co., Inc., New York and Toronto. 1956.

RIFLES OF THE WORLD, John Walter, DBI Books, Northfield, Ill. 1993.

STANDARD CATALOG OF FIREARMS, 3rd. Edition, Ned Schwing/Herbert Houze, Krause Publications Inc., Iola, Wis. 1993.

WORLD'S GUNS and OTHER WEAPONS, Philip McFarland/Burton Brenner, Golden State Arms, Inc. Pasadena, Ca. 1958.

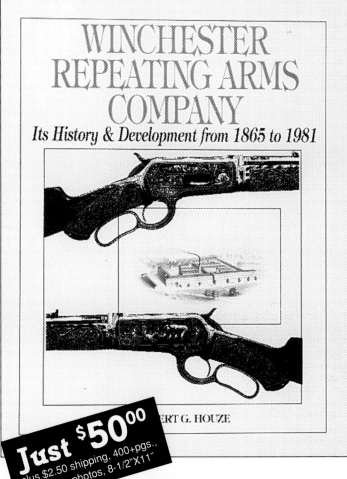

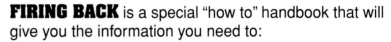

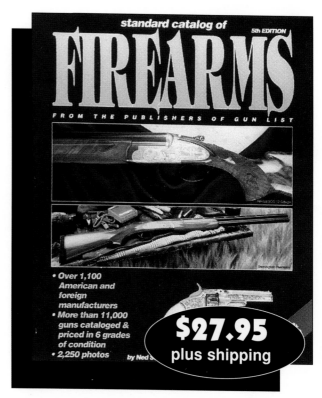